D1105996

HANS TOCH

Michigan State University

The social psychology

# of social movements

The Bobbs-Merrill Company, Inc.

A Subsidiary of Howard W. Sams & Co., Inc.

PUBLISHERS   Indianapolis   New York   Kansas City

HM
131
.T57

On *page ii*: Käthe Kollwitz, STURM, *Ferdinand Roten Galleries, Baltimore, Maryland*

Hans Toch: THE SOCIAL PSYCHOLOGY OF
SOCIAL MOVEMENTS

Copyright © 1965 by The Bobbs-Merrill Company, Inc.
Printed in the United States of America
LIBRARY OF CONGRESS CATALOG CARD NUMBER: 64-66077

First Printing

Preface

MORE than fifteen years ago, at a time when my academic involvements were limited to evening college courses, I developed an interest in social movements. I am no longer sure how it all started. I suspect that I found myself personally attracted to some movements and that I was somewhat alarmed by others. I infer that early experiences had left me with the feeling that society could be importantly affected—for better or worse—by particular kinds of groups. And I assume that I must have gained pleasure and excitement from the opportunity of exploring beliefs and practices at variance with my own.

In any event, I remember myself as a regular reader of sectarian publications. I remember attending all manner of meetings, rallies, convocations, and seances, and I recall browsing through dusty tomes dealing with religious and political movements of the past and searching out newspaper reports on the activity of contemporary groups.

In one of my undergraduate courses I read Cantril's *Psychology of Social Movements* and began to suspect that it was possible to combine business with pleasure. In 1952, when I entered Princeton as a graduate student, I was delighted to verify my assumption. With Cantril's support, I began to transform curiosity into questions and to change my concern into a framework for inquiry. The result of the transformation is recorded in these pages.

v

It is perhaps not surprising that the strategy of this book recapitulates the ontogeny of my own evolution. I have tried to present illustrations of sufficient diversity to convey a sense of the universality and import of social movements. I have tried to communicate some of the latent tragedy in membership and some of the finality of its impact. I have tried to capture some of the humor and pathos, some of the despair and urgency, and some of the inexorable logic of collective action. I have tried to spell out some human implications which make social movements important to all of us.

It is my hope that the student or lay reader will find this material of sufficient personal interest to join me in posing questions and considering answers. I further hope that some will advance beyond this book toward more intensive investigations of their own. My method of presentation assumes that good research starts with interest in the substance of one's concern. The opposite sequence—which begins with research indoctrination—appears to me to introduce the cart before the horse.

But then, I might as well confess that this book is deviant in a number of respects. For one, it is a relatively informal essay, and it is as free of technical terms as I have been able to make it.

Second, the exposition relies heavily on "folksy" illustrations—a method of documentation that has been in disrepute since the carefree days in which psychologists described, in touching detail, the funeral services of the black ant.

In justification, I shall not retreat into my role as a teacher. I shall also not claim that I seriously object to conventional forms of presentation and documentation. True, it is sometimes hard for me to distinguish instances in which the use of nomenclature increases understanding, from occasions in which it meets the demands of fashion. And in considering laboratory data, I have often felt that the transition from synthetic arrangements to fullblooded life was not convincingly bridged.

But such considerations were not paramount in determining the way I wrote this book. I feel that there are two legitimate ways to gain respectability for a new area of concern. One is to link it to an established body of knowledge; thus the new becomes a proving ground for available tools and familiar hypotheses.

An alternative method is to try to make a case for the new in its own right. This involves an accent on unique features, and the development of tailor-made concepts and tools. In this book, I have tried to make an informal start at demonstrating the potentiality of social movements as psychological subject matter, in a somewhat more systematic fashion than has been done before. The premise of my efforts is that the strategy of defining a field on its own merits facilitates, rather than impedes, its assimilation into the ongoing stream of inquiry.

Thus my use of real-life illustrations represents an attempt to remain within one universe of data—to show that it is available for use. And I have tried to avoid directing the interpretation of these data, by keeping my own speculations on a first-order level. In other words, this book reflects a *point of view* but does not present a self-sufficient logical edifice. Its intellectual architecture is more analogous to a compound of huts that invites subsequent redevelopment.

None of us can lay claim to the exclusive legitimacy of our views. A cow has a right not to lay eggs, but cannot deduce from its limitations the intrinsic superiority of dairy products over the derivatives of the barnyard. This book represents one way of looking at its subject matter. I hope that it will not be taken to task because it fails to reflect other viewpoints.

My title contains the term "social psychology." To the extent to which there are *social* psychologists and social *psychologists*, I probably fall among the latter. But I trust that this book is *neither* psychology *nor* sociology, and that at the same time it qualifies as *both*. I have presented a frame of reference, without worrying about its classification. *Some* psychologists and *some* sociologists may feel affinity for my viewpoint; others will not. Disciplinary affiliation should be irrelevant to this judgment.

Although I cannot blame anyone for my own failings, there are many persons whom I must credit with contributing to this book. My chief debt is to Hadley Cantril, whose influence on these pages will be obvious to anyone familiar with his writings. A more personal contribution has been his encouragement throughout these years, which has made me face up to my task. Another source of faith has been Albert Hastorf, who twice convinced publishers to lend credibility to my promises.

There are innumerable students and colleagues to whom I am indebted for stimulation and ideas. Among student term papers I have read, many have provided food for thought and a few have left a tangible impression on this book. I should like to express my appreciation to Walter DeVries, Ann Dixon, Henry Horwitt, James A. Ralston, Joyce Randall, George Royce, and Bruce Scorsome among those who have drawn my attention to particular movements, or provided me with source material which I have added to my collection. Many students have helped somewhat less directly. One to whom I owe a special vote of thanks is Steven Deutsch, who has frequently served me as sociological consultant.

I am indebted to Gabriel Almond, who kindly permitted me to excerpt and quote interview transcripts from his monumental study of Communist defectors. Stanley Hoffmann supplied bibliographical suggestions related to the Poujade movement; Theodora Abell translated French newspapers and Assembly debates. Jack Block, Hadley Cantril, Gilbert Geis, Egil Fivelsdal, Sverre Lysgaard, Thomas Mathiesen, Milton Rokeach, Harold Walsh, and Dagfinn As were among Norwegian and American colleagues who read individual chapters of this book, and who helped me with criticism and suggestions.

The manuscript is a product of a sabbatical year that I spent as a Fulbright Research Fellow in Oslo, Norway. I am grateful to Michigan State University for allowing me the time, to the U. S. Educational Foundation for financial support, and to the Institute for Social Research (and Eric Rinde) for physical facilities. It is these commodities which have ultimately made this book possible.

Final votes of thanks must go to Ann Toch, who typed the entire manuscript and tried to tolerate me during the various stages of its inception.

H.T.

Oslo, Norway
June 26, 1964

To The Memory of Maxim

CONTENTS

xi

The career of members

Contents

Determinants and motives

one

The nature of
social movements

1 ▷ THE SOLUTION OF COLLECTIVE PROBLEMS

ONE summer afternoon in 1959, Elijah Muhammad stood before ten thousand followers in Washington's Uline Arena and said to them:

> You have cried, wept, prayed, shouted, come to the back door, down the chimney, through the window. . . .
>
> The church has failed you; Christianity has failed you; the government of America has failed you. You have not received justice from any quarter.[1]

Mr. Muhammad was telling his listeners that they had exhausted the more common resources of the social order.

When people feel themselves abandoned or frustrated by conventional society, they can sometimes by-pass established institutions and create informal social organizations "on the side." Such grass-roots movements serve to provide otherwise unavailable services, to protest indignities, to escape suffering, to release tension, to explain confusing events, or in some other way to create a more tolerable way of life than is afforded by existing formal organizations.

It is these byways of social change that constitute the subject of this book. In Chapter 1 we shall show how groups can arise to satisfy needs

[1] E. Muhammad, "Justice for My People," *The Islamic News* (July 6, 1959).

3

neglected by society. We shall try to apply this psychological perspective in the remaining chapters of Part One.

Part Two of the book explores the fate of individual members. Here, the typical recruit into a social movement will be traced through the stages of joining (Chapter 6), belonging (Chapter 7), and defecting (Chapter 8).

More general issues are dealt with in Part Three, where we shall be concerned with questions of motivation, social change, and negative or positive evaluation.

The early view

Collective efforts to deal with deficiencies in the Establishment have throughout history amused, astonished, puzzled, irritated, challenged, and at times horrified unaffiliated spectators. When they were small-scale, they have been viewed as ridiculous amateur performances; when they turned the tides of history, they were perceived as illegitimate interferences with otherwise lawful change.

Until the advent of the field of "collective behavior" in sociology a few decades ago, spontaneous social phenomena have not been generally classed as deserving serious attention, but rather as curiosities or monstrosities in an otherwise rational world. And in the beginning, the formal study of collective behavior continued prescientific traditions. The attention focused on groups which could be viewed as social aberrations—as extensions of parallels of individual mental disease.[2] Even today, when social scientists speak of "collective behavior," they often refer to negatively valued group phenomena such as panics, mobs, riots, hysterias, and fads. Our field of inquiry, however, is no longer restricted to transitory events of an exotic or spectacular nature of which we disapprove.[3]

[2] G. LeBon, *The Crowd: A Study of the Popular Mind* (London: T. F. Unwin, 1879); C. Mackay, *Memoirs of Extraordinary Popular Delusions* (Boston: L. C. Page, 1932); E. D. Martin, *The Behavior of Crowds* (New York: W. W. Norton, 1920); E. A. Strecker, *Beyond the Clinical Frontiers*, (New York: W. W. Norton, 1940). For a position that contrasts with these "irrationalistic" approaches to collective behavior, see the belief-centered analysis of N. J. Smelser, *Theory of Collective Behavior* (New York: Free Press, 1963).

[3] To qualify as exhibiting collective behavior—as the term is usually defined—a group must (1) be large; (2) act spontaneously; (3) be relatively unorganized; (4) try to promote change; and (5) develop unpredictably. Among the kinds of groups which this definition excludes are small groups, although it is sometimes hard to decide if a group is "large" or "small." Also excluded are most of the *organizations* or *institutions* of conventional society—that is, groups in which people occupy defined positions, and in which the main object is to perpetuate or promote the existence of the group,

Social movements

Social movements are usually comprised under the general heading of collective behavior. They are distinguished from other forms of collective behavior as being groups which are relatively *long-lasting* and which have a clear *program* or *purpose*. They are viewed as forms of collective behavior nevertheless, because they are *large* groups and because they *arise spontaneously*.

The key element in most definitions of social movements is the requirement that they must be *aimed at promoting or resisting change* in society at large. A social movement, in other words, is defined as a large-scale, informal effort designed to correct, supplement, overthrow, or in some fashion influence the social order.[4]

For the psychologist, these kinds of efforts must be motivated. They must stem from specific discontents of specific people with specific situations in which they find themselves. They must also represent the kinds of difficulties that people feel can be resolved through collective action, rather than privately. In accord with these premises, a psychological definition of social movements could read: *A social movement represents an effort by a large number of people to solve collectively a problem that they feel they have in common.*

This statement is not as simple as it sounds. In particular, the concept of a "problem" implies problems of its own. When can a group of people be said to have a problem? How is a "collective problem" to be described? What kinds of problems can be solved by resorting to social movements, and what constitutes a solution? The remainder of this discussion will address itself to these questions.

Problem situations

For an outside observer of any sort—whether he is a social scientist, journalist, welfare worker, tourist, or other kind of spectator—the indexes to the possible existence of a problem are usually a set of concrete, observable,

---

and of the social order that contains it. For definitions of collective behavior, see H. Blumer, "Collective Behavior" in A. M. Lee, ed., *Principles of Sociology* (New York: Barnes & Noble, 1951); R. H. Turner and L. M. Killian, *Collective Behavior* (Englewood Cliffs, N. J.: Prentice-Hall, 1957), pp. 3 ff.; K. Lang and Gladys E. Lang, *Collective Dynamics* (New York: Thomas Y. Crowell, 1961), pp. 11 ff.

4 Blumer, "Collective Behavior"; Turner and Killian, *Collective Behavior*, p. 308; Lang and Lang, *Collective Dynamics, pp.* 489–496. See also R. Heberle, *Social Movements: An Introduction to Political Sociology* (New York: Appleton-Century-Crofts, 1951).

"objective" conditions that comprise a personal handicap and/or an unfavorable environment. Old age, disease, low income, unemployment, physical suffering, and starvation are among such problem situations.[5]

Often, relevant information for the diagnosis of problem situations can be obtained in shorthand form in the shape of financial statistics, ecological tables, and other summaries of demographic data. Here the principle of *ex pede Herculem* (we infer Hercules from his foot) applies: a few dry items of statistic permit us to reconstruct the occasions for manifold human suffering. When we are told, for example, that three quarters of all land in Latin America is owned by two per cent of the population, and that despite abundant resources more than half of all Latin Americans eat below subsistence level, we begin to think in terms of social inequities and resulting hardships. Similarly, we may come to regard American farm wage workers as underprivileged when we discover that the average migratory agricultural worker earns $5.00 a week and can usually find only 150 to 160 days of work a year. And we sense physical misery behind the data that one out of every three black South Africans never survives birth and that, if he does, his chances of reaching sixteen are little more than fifty-fifty and his estimated life span is about half that of his typical white compatriot.[6]

But statistics do little more than point up deficits in the social ledger. They cannot describe and define the world that actually faces various types of underprivileged people. The farm workers we have mentioned are a case in point. Volumes of statistics would not begin to convey the picture of patched hovels and stinking outhouses, overnight rides in crowded trucks, and heavy work under the midsummer sun. In order accurately to define an "objective" problem situation, more or less systematic observations must supplement demographic data. The following, for example, is an excerpt of an account by Dale Wright of the working conditions of migrant farm workers:

> In the first hours of that miserable day, my hands became grimy and encrusted with the green insecticide they spray on tomatoes. It covered my

[5] Although the components of a problem situation are objectively specifiable, the outside observer must exercise judgment in deciding what constitutes a personal or social deficit. The line between a "problem" and a "no problem" situation must be subjectively drawn.

[6] For migrant labor statistics, see U. S. Dept. of Labor, *Farm Labor Market Developments* (January 1959), p. 8, covering 1951–58. South African mortality statistics are quoted from S. Abdul, *The Truth about South Africa* (Austria: International Society of Socialist Youth, 1963), p. 6; Latin American statistics are available in any standard source book, such as note 8 following.

khaki pants and ate its way into my legs. It collected under my finger nails, covered my shoes and socks and festered in the scratches I received from the tomato vines.

But picking the tomatoes was the easy part of the job. The hard part was lugging the heavy baskets to the end of the rows—often as far as 150 feet—to be loaded onto the trucks.

All around me were men and women—all ages—dragging themselves along the rows on their hands and knees in the near-90-degree heat.

Toilet facilities? There were none. . . .[7]

Similarly, Latin American statistics could be elaborated with descriptive data such as the following description of a Peruvian slum that stretches for several miles atop an old garbage dump:

El Monton is one of a dozen *barriadas* in and around Lima, and in them subsist 400,000 souls. Children, with festering sores on their bare legs, play in the exposed garbage, adults forage through it, picking out bits of cardboard or strips of metal to patch their shanties. . . . Occasional breezes carry with them the odor of decayed garbage, which comes to the surface and mixes with the dry earth spilling from the unpaved alleys and the excrement of the open sewage. . . . The walls help you shut your eyes to the haphazard jungle of paper shacks and the scrawny bodies of babies left untended by working mothers; it is difficult to close your ears to the moans of older folk dying of malnutrition . . . you can never get rid of the fetor, the stink that clings to your clothing and makes you want to retch and rush to your shower and send everything quickly, immediately to the cleaners or to the fire.[8]

The impact of problem situations

Even relatively vivid and detailed descriptions of conditions, however, no matter how pathetic and dramatic, only *provide clues to human problems*. The focus of a problem is not in the problem situation, but in its *impact* on individual people. The diagnosis of problems must therefore carry us to the *experiencing* person. In the case of South Africa, for instance, we must deal with the experiences of Bantus imprisoned for not carrying their 96-page pass, the impressions of laborers severely beaten by their masters, the feeling of wives living alone while their husbands serve as in-

[7] D. Wright, *The Forgotten People* (reprinted by Consumers' League of New Jersey, Maplewood, N. J., 1961), pp. 3–4.

[8] G. Clark, *The Coming Explosion in Latin America* (New York: McKay, 1963), pp. 7–8.

dentured farm workers, and the reactions of bright young natives who discover that education is reserved for whites.[9] Among migrant farm workers, we must concern ourselves with individuals like Alonzo, described by Dale Wright as "an emaciated man of about 40 [who] coughed [blood] and spat incessantly as he bent over his task":

> Yeah, they say it's consumption. It don't make no difference. I gotta keep working. The doctor, he can't do nothing for me. I got no money for medicine, I gotta woman and a lotta kids. I gotta keep picking tomatoes. . . . Don't know nothing else. . . . This job is just like the last one. Next be just like this one. Never no different. Never will be.[10]

Even from this brief excerpt, it is obvious that Alonzo's problem is far more complex than low income and underemployment. It involves his health, the health of his family, his educational level, and feelings such as despair and resignation.

The impact of a problem situation can only be understood and predicted when data are available about the attitudes, feelings, expectations, and needs of affected persons. The following excerpt of a statement drafted in 1961 by a group of Alaska Eskimos may serve to illustrate this point:

> We always thought our Inupiat Paitot was safe to be passed down to our future generations as our fathers passed it down to us. Our Inupiat Paitot is our land around the Arctic world where we the Inupiat live, our right to hunt our food any place and time of year as we always have, our right to be great hunters and brave independent people, like our grandfathers, our right to the minerals that belong to us in the land we claim. Today our Inupiat Paitot is called by the white man our aboriginal rights.
>
> We were quiet and happy and always thought we had these aboriginal rights until last year when agents of the Fish and Wildlife Service arrested two Inupiat hunters of Point Barrow. They arrested these natives because they shot Eider ducks for food. They told these natives they could not hunt Eider ducks in 1960 because of a Migratory Bird Treaty with Canada and Mexico. The other men of Barrow, 138 hunters, all walked up to Fish and Wildlife agents to be arrested also; each man had an Eider duck in his hand. Each man said "we are all hunters, it is our right to hunt food, and if you arrest two you must arrest all."[11]

The problem in this case is no more a duck-hunting issue than the Boston Tea Party could be defined as a tea lovers' conclave. A piece of

[9] P. Van Rensberg, *Guilty Land, the History of Apartheid* (New York: Praeger, 1962); N. C. Phillips, *Tragedy of Apartheid,* (New York: McKay, 1960).

[10] Wright, *Forgotten People*, p. 3.

[11] "Inupiat Paitot," *Indian Affairs*, No. 44 (December 1961), p. 1.

legislation that to outside observers—including officials of the Fish and Wildlife Service—might have appeared relatively trivial, to the Eskimo hunters represented a breach of faith without understandable justification, and meant not only a serious limitation of food supply, but also a curtailment of freedom of action, and an interference with one's basic right to live according to one's customs and traditions.

A second illustration of the subjective character of problems may be drawn from the 1960 teachers' strike in the city of New York. Issues like salary increases and collective bargaining rights were in the forefront of the reasons for the strike. The undercurrent, however, was provided by feelings such as those exemplified in the following interview excerpt:

> "From the time we go to take the examinations for our license we are made to feel like dirt," he said. "The clerks at the examining board are surly to us, as are many of our superiors when we get the job. We are smothered in red tape and regulations and made to feel that we—the teachers—don't really count.
>
> "[The Superintendent] treats us like children. He acts condescendingly and paternalistically towards us. He refers to us constantly as 'my' teachers. We are not his teachers, as he found out on Monday. Maybe this sounds like a quibble over semantics, but when it comes on top of so many other things, it is enough to set off the fuse."[12]

Here, obviously, it would have been difficult to extrapolate the problem from objectively specifiable conditions. "Surly" officials and "red tape" give the appearance of relatively mild inconveniences. However, when they impinge on strong needs, such as the desire to experience a modicum of personal dignity and self-respect, they may constitute the occasion for a serious problem.

Problems as predispositions

Social movements draw their members from the ranks of persons who have encountered problems. The Cuban revolutionary leader Fidel Castro, in his 1953 courtroom speech "History Will Absolve Me," referred to his prospective following in these terms:

> The people we counted on in our struggle were these:
> Seven hundred thousand Cubans without work, who desire to earn their daily bread honestly, without having to emigrate in search of livelihood.

[12] *The New York Times* (November 9, 1960).

Five hundred thousand farm laborers inhabiting miserable shacks, who work four months of the year and starve for the rest of the year, sharing their misery with their children, who have not an inch of land to cultivate, and whose existence inspires compassion in any heart not made of stone.

Four hundred thousand industrial laborers and stevedorers whose retirement funds have been embezzled, whose benefits are being taken away, whose homes are wretched quarters, whose salaries pass from the hands of the boss to those of the usurers, whose future is a pay reduction and dismissal, whose life is eternal work and whose only rest is the tomb.

One hundred thousand small farmers who live and die working on land that is not theirs, looking at it with sadness as Moses did the promised land, to die without possessing it; who, like feudal serfs, have to pay for the use of their parcel of land by giving up a portion of their products; who cannot love it, improve it, beautify it or plant a lemon or an orange tree in it, because they never know when a sheriff will come with the rural guard to evict them from it. . . .

Ten thousand young professionals: doctors, engineers, lawyers, veterinarians, school teachers, dentists, pharmacists, newspapermen, painters, sculptors, etc., who come forth from school with their degrees, anxious to work and full of hope, only to find themselves at a dead end with all doors closed, and where no ear hears their clamor of supplications.

These are the people, the ones who know misfortune and, therefore, are capable of fighting with limitless courage.[13]

Castro's listing is a long one, covering almost every segment of the Cuban population. Despite the heterogeneity of the list, however, there is a common denominator: Every one of the catalogued classes of persons was faced (in 1953) with an objectively specifiable problem situation. The speech implies that each of these groups also *experienced* its hardships. This being the case, Castro could justifiably view the people involved as *predisposed to join a social movement* (such as his own) *designed to remedy their difficulties.*

Even this type of "objective" predisposition, however, is not a sufficient condition for membership in a social movement. Although many of the persons referred to by Castro *did* become actively involved in his revolutionary enterprise, many others did not. There are also groups of persons, such as the migrant farm workers we have discussed, whose reactions to their problems ("ain't nuthin' you can do about it," "never escape," etc.) are clearly not conducive to involvement in remedial efforts. It may be

---

[13] F. Castro, *History Will Absolve Me* (New York: Fair Play for Cuba Committee, 1961), pp. 34–35.

recalled, as an extreme case in point, that peasants in the Middle Ages saw their families die of starvation within earshot of orgies in the manor on the hill, or directly under the walls of feudal granaries, without even momentarily permitting themselves to question the assumption that such inequity had been ordained by God. Studies of concentration-camp inmates and of other persons subjected to extreme privation paint a similar picture. They show that people under very adverse circumstances can become preoccupied with their physical survival and with other short-term concerns, and may even fail to resist in the face of imminent and certain death.[14]

From predisposition to susceptibility

For a person to be led to join a social movement, he must not only sense a problem, but must also (1) feel that something can be done about it and (2) want to do something about it himself. At the very least, he must feel that the status quo is not inevitable, and that *change is conceivable*. This frame of mind is illustrated, for instance, in Martin Luther King's speech to participants in the 1963 civil rights March on Washington:

> I have a dream that one day on the red hills of Georgia the sons of former slaves and the sons of former slaveowners will be able to sit down at the table of brotherhood. I have a dream that one day even the state of Mississippi, a state sweltering with the heat of oppression, will be transformed into an oasis of freedom and justice. I have a dream that my four little children will one day live in a nation where they will not be judged by the color of their skin, but by the content of their character. This is our hope. This is the faith that I go back to the South with—with this faith we will be able to hew out of the mountain of despair a stone of hope.[15]

A second stage in the process would be the feeling that a better world is *concretely attainable*. This is the realization that has recently evolved in underdeveloped regions, and that has been labeled the "Revolution of Rising Expectations." Halvard Lange, Foreign Minister of Norway, in a 1961 speech concerned with underprivileged people, put the matter in these terms:

> Poverty, misery, illiteracy, chronic ill health are an integral part of their daily life. Until recently, they have endured these evils in passive despair because they had no vision of anything better.
> But today they know and understand that hunger, disease, fruitless

[14] B. Bettelheim, *The Informed Heart: Autonomy in a Mass Age* (Glencoe, Ill.: Free Press, 1960).

[15] *The New York Times* (August 29, 1963).

toil and early death are not inevitable, *that it is possible to create conditions in which they and their children can have a better life.* What has aptly been termed "the revolution of rising expectations" is under way.[16]

James C. Davies, a sociologist, has pointed out that people must expect an improvement in conditions before they embark on revolutions. Ultimately, he writes, "it is the dissatisfied state of mind rather than the tangible provision of 'adequate' or 'inadequate' supplies of food, equality or liberty which produces revolution."[17]

But even the "dissatisfied state of mind" is not enough. As a last step, there must be *a desire to become involved in the accomplishment of change.* The person must feel the need to seek clarification or "do something." He must embark on what has been called a "search for meaning" or for "symbols" that offer to resolve his problem.[18] And he must look around for other people with whom he can join in attempts at a solution.

Susceptibility

When a person searches for meaning, he can be defined as "susceptible" to social movements, although susceptibility here is a matter of degree. A *mild* increase in susceptibility would involve a slight lowering of sales resistance to available solutions. The person would tend to listen with increasing care to proposals which he could view as relating to his problem. He would be less likely to reject them out of hand or to try to find flies in the ointment that promised him a cure.

A *strong* increase in susceptibility creates "gullibility" or suggestibility. It involves a tendency to jump at promising propositions, and a readiness to adopt them. A person in this condition may seem to go out of his way to make himself available as a prospective member. He may habituate street corners listening to speakers, or he may avidly read and discuss every available item of sectarian literature. Adolf Hitler, in his days as a disillusioned young man living in Vienna, provides a good illustration of susceptibility in this extreme form:

> He buried himself in anti-Semitic literature, which had a large sale in Vienna at that time. Then he took to the streets to observe the "phenomenon" more closely. "Wherever I went," he says, "I began to see Jews. . . .

[16] *The New York Times* (January 10, 1961, italics added).

[17] J. C. Davies, "Toward a Theory of Revolution," *Amer. Sociol. Rev.* (February 1962), p. 6.

[18] H. Cantril, *The Psychology of Social Movements* (New York: Wiley, 1941), pp. 53 ff.; H. Lasswell, *The Psychopathology of Politics* (Chicago: Univ. of Chicago Press, 1930), p. 188.

Later I often grew sick to the stomach from the smell of these caftan-wearers."[19]

On a behavioral dimension, susceptibility may range from *passive* to *active*. Many susceptible persons simply wait with an air of quiet expectancy for the Answer to present itself. Susceptibility, in these cases, is no more than a readiness to accept, or—in the words of William James—a "will to believe."[20] This condition can be inferred, for instance, in the following autobiographical statement:

> I had prayed that if there was a true church, God would lead us to it.
> Within a few weeks after that prayer a series of articles appeared in the daily paper, taken from a national magazine, giving the beliefs of the great religions of America. We read them all. The one on Adventists was the last to appear and we could see right away that this church was truly according to the Bible.[21]

The other extreme is the type of active search exemplified by Flying Saucer Contact Weekend, in which interested persons try to establish communication with extraterrestrial friends. During this annual affair, Flying Saucer Club members all over the globe concentrate on telepathic messages, scan the skies, watch unassigned TV channels, and listen to unused radio bands in an effort to reach saucer pilots. Not surprisingly, Flying Saucer Contact Weekend does yield numerous "contacts" with Unidentified Flying Objects and their crews.[22]

This type of result occurs because susceptibility, unlike virtue, is usually rewarded. The Winter of Discontent evokes the Summer of Faith—presupposing, of course, an intermediate season, in which new meanings become available for adoption.

Susceptibility and appeal

Although there undoubtedly exist some people whose personalities are so constituted that they become equally susceptible to almost every proposition they encounter, most people would feel responsive only to certain types

---

[19] W. L. Shirer, *The Rise and Fall of the Third Reich* (Greenwich, Conn.: Fawcett, 1962), p. 47.

[20] W. James, *The Will to Believe and Other Essays in Popular Philosophy* (New York: Longmans Green, 1902).

[21] "Why I Became an Adventist," *Review and Herald*, 138, No. 1 (June 8, 1961), p. 22.

[22] *U-Forum* (publication of the Grand Rapids Flying Saucer Club, Michigan, September–October 1956), p. 18; East Lansing *Michigan State News* (May 19, 1959).

of solutions at particular stages of their lives and in particular situations. This selectivity is partly related to the problems that create the state of susceptibility in the first place. A woman concerned with her failing health, for instance, would no more tend to throw herself into an agrarian reform movement than a Chinese peasant is likely to find himself involved in a health fad or in the Christian Science church. A Midwestern farm boy may be attracted to a 4H Club, but is less likely to become interested in urban renewal.

A person's educational level, the social influences that operate on him, the kinds of past experiences he has had, and other factors that determine his outlook on life are also likely to enter into his selective susceptibility. An individual with a college education, for example, would be much less prone to adopt an oversimplified economic scheme than would a person who has not graduated from grammar school. An intensely religious upbringing can lead one to prefer religious to secular solutions (when these are otherwise equivalent). And younger men may be more likely to become involved in radical activities than are men of middle age.

Factors such as these restrict the range of social movements to which a person is attracted. Within this range, other influences may determine which movement he joins. For instance, a person may have the type of background that would increase his susceptibility to either left-wing politics or fundamentalist religion, but not to fascism, middle-of-the-road solutions, or liberal protestantism. For example,

> In Holland and Sweden, recent studies show that the Communists are strongest in regions which were once centers of fundamentalist religious revivalism. In Finland, Communism and revivalist Christianity often are strong in the same areas. In the poor eastern parts of Finland, the Communists have been very careful not to offend people's religious feelings. It is reported that many Communist meetings actually begin with religious hymns.[23]

With respect to the people in these areas, the Communist party and the Pentecostal Church may have been in a competitive position.

How are such competitions resolved? In some instances, simple personal preference or social pressure exercised by friends and relatives could easily turn the tide. In other cases, the decisive factor might be a trivial historical accident, such as attending a revival meeting *before* encountering a visiting Communist official, or vice versa.

The same relationship holds between social movements and institu-

[23] S. M. Lipset, *Political Man* (London: Mercury, 1963), p. 108.

tions that compete with them for the candidacy of susceptible persons. Many people, for instance, might shrink from participation in a communal venture, and instead opt for a course of action more within the accepted institutional framework. Social movements may in this fashion unsuccessfully compete against commercial offers to solve the same problems. The following advertisement, for instance, might lead a potential member of a lonely hearts club to take an extended vacation:

> *What's the matter with you, Everett Haygood?* When you were 16 you had it all figured out. You were going to make a lot of money at something (you weren't sure what, but *something*) and you were going to marry Veronica O'Hare, go around the world in a sloop and then live on Park Avenue. But Veronica (who never went out with you anyhow) married Jack Dillon, the closest you got to a sloop was an afternoon on a friend's 12 footer, and you're still living with your mother, who's sure your boss is afraid of you. You're now 34 years old. You make 8,300 dollars a year and every summer you take your vacation in days so you can fix the screens, get rid of the crab grass, take your mother on one of these group picnics at the lake, and sunbathe in the back yard. Mr. Haygood, next year you'll be 35. In 5 years you'll be 40 and in 15 years you'll be 50. Aren't you going anywhere? Tickets by Astrojet to California are only $145.10 one way, plus tax. . . . Mr. Haygood, we all get older, but you're being positively grim about it. Why don't you call . . . your travel agent?[24]

A prospective member of a mystic group may instead respond to the following:

> Just fiddle with your Fidget Stone and feel euphoria set in. Prettier than pills—more fun than a massage—soothing as a lullaby. Hand carved of genuine Jade ("Good Luck" stone of the Orient). You'll love to handle it. Carry it—rub it—[25]

Commercial and public institutions of various kinds can duplicate the functions of social movements to a greater or lesser extent. Medical treatment and psychotherapy are alternatives to Alcoholics Anonymous; a revival meeting may have its attendance reduced by the Saturday night dance, and prospective revolutionaries may vent their spleen at the corner tavern. Social movements thus must compete with enterprises that can reduce or sidetrack the susceptibilities of prospective members. They must also combat habits that may favor individual rather than group action and must try to

---

[24] American Airlines advertisement, *The New York Times* (April 30, 1963).
[25] Advertisement for Marchal Jewelers, *The New York Times* (June 8, 1963).

counter the tendency of people to remain unaffiliated or inactive. In order to lure susceptible persons from alternative outlets, a social movement must advertise or promote itself.

Social movements—like other advertisers—must show that they can respond to the needs of their clients. They must demonstrate their ability to furnish solutions which make it worth expending time, energy, and dedication. They must publicize offerings which people can find useful and desirable.

Any aspect of a social movement that succeeds in "selling" the movement by attracting members to it becomes an *appeal*. Appeals are *psychologically relevant* commodities. They are features of the movement that tie into the susceptibilities of people. In other words, "susceptibility" and "appeal" can be understood only in relation to each other. A person must be susceptible *to* something, or he is not susceptible at all. In turn, appeals derive their appealing quality from the fact that someone is attracted to them.

As an illustration, consider the fact that many people harbor vague resentments against the telephone company. At times, these resentments may even be intense and specific. This may occur, for instance, after a telephone subscriber receives an announcement informing him that his telephone number has been replaced by a set of seven digits. If the subscriber becomes indignant, this fact could make him susceptible to a social movement, *provided there exists a social movement which is a vehicle for such resentment*. Consider the converse situation: A new group proposes to fight against the telephone company's digit dialing system. Would the program of this group contain appeals? This depends, of course, on *whether there exist persons who are interested in entering the fray*. In sum, both susceptibilities and appeals would be defined by their encounter. In the case of our illustration, they are created as follows:

> The Anti-Digit Dialing League started over a cup of coffee in San Francisco when the conversation, quite by accident, drifted to the new Digit Dialing system. Both coffee drinkers had found the new system extremely confusing and difficult to use. They also wondered whether the change was really necessary. As a consequence they inserted a tiny notice in the classified section of a newspaper inquiring whether other people had experienced the same thoughts. They signed the ad, Anti-Digit Dialing League.
> *The response was incredible. Over thirty-five hundred people responded within ten days in the San Francisco Bay Area alone. As word about ADDL spread throughout the country, people wrote in wanting to start chapters of*

ADDL *in other cities across the country. It quickly became obvious that* ADDL *was expressing a deep but previously unorganized concern of telephone users that the telephone company had somehow forgotten about them.* This is the reason that ADDL started; it was an expression of widespread concern.[26]

We are dealing here with the type of situation that the philosophers Dewey and Bentley have called a "transaction."[27] This means that two things may be shaped when they encounter each other to such an extent that one may view each as a product of the other.

Appeals acquire meaning because they address themselves to susceptibilities. Since susceptibilities arise out of human problems, appeals must contain offers to solve problems. Elijah Muhammad made such an offer to his Washington audience in 1959:

> As to you, indeed so great an assembly of witness has not met here for foolishness. You are seeking something. You are seeking an answer to your four hundred year old problem of slavery, servitude and fifth-class citizenship. I am here with the solution to this problem.[28]

It is this transaction that constitutes the crux of the social psychology of social movements. The task of the student is to isolate the psychological bond that ties appeals and susceptibilities to each other.

The appeals of social movements

Social movements in search of a mass following frequently follow a *saturation* method, and try to present a "cafeteria" of appeals, catering to a diversity of needs. Hitler's Nazi movement, in the days immediately prior to its advent to power, directed appeals at practically every segment of the German population. Industrial leaders, for instance, were promised a strong anti-Communist stand, and the guarantee that all revolutionary activities among workers would be crushed. Prussian land owners and officers were attracted through the prospect of remilitarization, and the assurance that land reform programs would be nominal. Middle-class Germans were appealed to through strongly worded attacks against large corporations, department stores, war profits, "international capitalism," Jews, and Communists. Youth was reached with promises of a bright future, with refer-

---

[26] *Phones Are for People* (San Francisco: Anti-Digit Dialing League, 1962, italics added).

[27] J. Dewey and A. F. Bentley, *Knowing and the Known* (Boston: Beacon, 1949).

[28] Muhammad, "*Justice.*"

ences to the "inertia and indifference of your fathers," as well as with the glamour of the Hitler Youth and the "strength through joy" movement.[29]

Finally, the bulk of the voting population, the workers, farmers, and small-business men, were each presented with promises of economic improvement, as illustrated in the following excerpt of Hitler's first speech as German chancellor:

> The National Government will, with iron determination and unshakable steadfastness of purpose, put through the following plan:
>
> Within four years the German peasant must be rescued from the quagmire into which he has fallen.
>
> Within four years unemployment must be finally overcome. At the same time the conditions necessary for a revival in trade and commerce are provided. . . .
>
> In economic administration, the promotion of employment, the preservation of the farmer, as well as in the exploitation of private initiative, the Government sees the best guarantee for the avoidance of any experiments. . . .[30]

The tenor of this program stands in sharp contrast to the platform encountered in the early stages of the Nazi movement. The following excerpt from one of Hitler's earliest speeches (September 18, 1922) typifies this approach:

> We in Germany have come to this: that a sixty-million people sees its destiny lie at the will of a few dozen Jewish bankers. This was possible only because our civilization had first been Judaized. The undermining of the German conception of personality by catchwords had begun long before. Ideas such as "democracy," "majority," "conscience of the world," "world solidarity," "world peace," "internationality of art," etc. disintegrate our race-consciousness, breed cowardice, and so today we are bound to say that the simple Turk is no more man than we.
>
> No salvation is possible until the bearer of disunion, the Jew, has been rendered powerless to harm.
>
> 1. We must call to account the November criminals of 1918. It cannot be that two million Germans should have fallen in vain and that afterwards one should sit down as friends at the same table with traitors. No, we cannot pardon, we demand—Vengeance.
>
> 2. The dishonoring of the nation must cease. For betrayers of their fatherland and informers the gallows is the proper place. Our streets and squares shall once more bear the names of heroes; they shall not be named after Jews. In the question of guilt we must proclaim the truth. . . .[31]

[29] Cantril, *Social Movements*, pp. 233 ff.
[30] A. Hitler, *My New Order* (New York: Reynal & Hitchcock, 1941), p. 145.
[31] *Ibid.*, p. 45.

This early version of the Nazi appeal, proclaiming "the Glorious Father-land has been stabbed in the back by Jews" and demanding retribution, was aimed at the shame, confusion, and pride *present to some degree in most Germans* at this historic juncture. The movement offered a coherent expla-nation for the problem situation, and a scapegoat for feelings of frustration and resentment.[32] Whereas later the attempt was made to provide many ap-peals designed to cater to diverse susceptibilities, the early platform relied on a *catch-all appeal* aimed at *relatively general* predispositions.

A third type of appeal ties into specific susceptibilities of a particular type of person. Each of the following paragraphs, for instance, makes a *specialized* case for a social movement:

Been waiting years for happiness? Share the inner power of Mayanry for rich, new, vital living.[33]

Have you outgrown gods, saviors and supernaturalism? Is all your concern for people? Then you're a Humanist. Welcome to the American Humanist Society.[34]

The Proletarians have nothing to lose but their chains. They have the world to win.

Workingmen of all countries, unite![35]

Chinese have now suffered under a foreign government more than two hundred and sixty years. The Manchus have done us enough cruelty. Now is the time to raise an army and overthrow the Manchu government and regain the sovereignty of our country.[36]

In each case, the group specifies the state of mind it feels it can respond to, and outlines its brand of solution for the person's problem. When some-one of the kind described comes to feel that the prescription could serve his needs, the movement's message becomes certified as an appeal.

[32] The fact that the explanation forming the core of this appeal is incorrect has no more bearing on its appealing character than has the fact that in the subsequent cafeteria program many of the promised actions could not be carried out, and were probably not seriously intended.

[33] "The Mayans" advertisement, *Life Today* (April–May 1956), inside back cover.

[34] American Humanist Association advertisement, *New Republic* (April 6, 1963), p. 31.

[35] K. Marx and F. Engels, *The Communist Manifesto*, The Bobbs-Merrill Reprint Series in the Social Sciences (Indianapolis, New York: Bobbs-Merrill) S-455, p. 44.

[36] Sun Yat-sen, "Revolutionary Manifesto" (1905), in N. Gangulee, ed., *The Teach-ings of Sun Yat-sen* (London: Sylvan Press, 1945), p. 31.

The enhancement of susceptibility

Although appeals themselves cannot create problems, they can call attention to problem situations, or reinterpret potential problem situations so as to create susceptibility. An excellent illustration of this type of appeal is the recruiting speech delivered by Pope Urban II to promote volunteers for the First Crusade, in which he said:

> The invaders befoul the altars with the filth out of their bodies. They circumcize Christians and pour the blood of the circumcision upon the altars or into the baptismal fonts. They stable their horses in these churches, which are now withdrawn from the service of God. Yea, the churches are served, but not by holy men—for only the Turks use them. And who else now serves the church of the Blessed Mary, where she herself was buried in body in the Valley of Jehoshaphat?
>
> Even now the Turks are torturing Christians, binding them and filling them with arrows, or making them kneel bending their heads, to try if their swordsmen can cut through their necks with a single blow of the naked sword. What shall I say of the ravishing of the women? . . . The time may come when you will see your wives violated and your children driven before you as slaves, out of the land.[37]

After resentment has been evoked by means of descriptive passages of this kind, a call for vengeance becomes more plausible. Joining the movement can then be made further attractive by appeals to feelings of pride ("you have the courage and fitness of body to humble the hairy heads"), justice ("ye who have been thieves, become soldiers. Fight a just war"), worthwhileness ("whosoever shall offer himself . . . shall wear the sign of the cross"), security ("your possessions here will be safeguarded"), guilt ("if any shall lose their lives . . . their sins will be requited them"), ambition ("wrest that land . . . and keep it for yourself"), and other prevalent values and aims, including that of relief from boredom (through the pursuit of adventure), which was a prospect highly prized in the Middle Ages.

Disguised or latent appeals

Appeals may relate to susceptibilities different from those at which they are ostensibly aimed. For example, a group may ostensibly engage in political action, while serving as a social outlet or as a means of expressing

[37] H. Lamb, *The Crusades: Iron Men and Saints* (New York: Doubleday, 1931), pp. 39–40.

protest; scapegoats may be provided under the guise of assigning responsibility for a social problem, and conservatively stated invitations may implicitly hold out extravagant promises. Such latent appeals are especially common among social movements whose offerings might otherwise appear too controversial or lacking in respectability.

Ideology

On rare occasions, the main appeals of a movement may consist of things like physical facilities and opportunities for social life. Pay and employment opportunities have attracted some persons to some movements. By and large, however, the most important appeals of a social movement are contained in its *ideology*.

The term "ideology" denotes a set of related beliefs held by a group of persons. The ideology of a social movement is a statement of what the members of the movement are trying to achieve together, and what they wish to affirm jointly. Such a statement points down the road along which the social movement is moving, and specifies the principles and objectives that guide its journey.

Ideologies may be formalized in some sort of platform, they may be scattered in speeches and in literature, or they may have to be inferred. However recorded, the ideology of a social movement *defines* the movement, and contrasts it with other movements and institutions. It also furnishes an objective description of solutions offered by the movement for the problems of its members.

Many social movements are *specialized*, with ideologies consisting basically of a single belief and its corollaries. This type of ideology is illustrated by the following list of convictions contained in a publication of the American Sunbathing Society:

> *We believe* in the essential wholesomeness of the human body, and all its functions.
>
> *We endeavor* to foster the desire to improve and perfect the body by natural living in the out-of-doors.
>
> *We believe* that sunshine and fresh air in immediate contact with the entire body are basic factors in maintaining healthy bodies.
>
> *We believe* presentation of the male and female figures in their entirety and completeness needs no apology or defense and that only in such an attitude of mind can we find true modesty.
>
> *We accord* to every part of the body an equally normal naturalness

wholly devoid of any vulgarity or obscenity. In this view an elbow, a pubic arch, or a nose, are equally respectable.

We *believe* that children raised in the nudist philosophy will be healthier in mind and body. They will learn to look on life as being essentially pure, *Nudism* will teach them moral and physical cleanliness; never to degrade but keep their thoughts and actions clean.

Our Goal? A healthy mind in a healthy body.[38]

To become a nudist, a person would simply have to favor unclothed outdoor activities. He would promote such practices on the assumption that they are conducive to physical and mental health. These beliefs comprise a very coherent scheme, in which the relationship among component beliefs is clear and obvious.

This condition is not always apparent at first glance. The following platform is a case in point:

WE, THE PEOPLE OF THE UNITED STATES OF AMERICA, must return to "Good Old Fashioned" Americanism IF we are to save our Great Republic from becoming a small pawn in the hands of fuzzy-brained, anti-Christ, world government planners.

1. The Reds must be kicked out of the U.N. or the U.N. out of the U.S.A.

2. The "Pink-to-Red" professors must be kicked out of the schools.

3. The Pink-to-Red writers must be gagged.

4. The "trashy" literature, "sexy" movies, and "crime" T-V must be cleaned.

5. The Mongrelization of the White Race must be stopped.

6. The flooding of our Country with Anti-Christ Aliens must be stopped.

7. Only Congress has the power to coin and regulate the value of our money. . . .[39]

The first three items of this seven-point program seem to be premised on the assumption that Communists are prevalent in international and intellectual circles. The last four recommendations, relating to the treatment of sex and crime in the mass media, to integration, to immigration, and to the method of coining money, cannot be subsumed under this heading. To include them, one must expand the premise to read "Communist immigrants and other foreigners have taken over our universities, our economy, and

[38] *Information about Nudism and the A. S. A.* (Mays Landing, N.J.: The American Sunbathing Association, undated).

[39] 1958 and 1960 *Platform* of H. W. Roberson, candidate for Democratic Primary, 23rd District of Illinois (printed leaflet).

our mass media, and are promoting the destruction of the U.S. by backing integration, by lowering the intellectual level of our population, etc." Underlying this statement, in turn, must be a deep suspicion of "aliens," comprising non-Americans, non-Christians, nonwhites, intellectuals, and other nonkindred spirits.

This same type of ideological theme underlies the apparently heterogeneous platform of the Daughters of the American Revolution. In their 1963 convention, the D.A.R. voiced strong opposition to a nuclear test ban treaty, to foreign aid, to urban renewal, to immigration, and to the United Nations, among other institutions. In other resolutions, the same group opposed cultural exchange and reciprocal trade programs, teen-age voting, the flying of the Panamanian flag in the Panama Canal Zone, the United Nations Children's Emergency Fund (UNICEF), the Atlantic Alliance, and the use of pictures of foreign personalities, places, and events on commemorative stamps.[40] Resolutions have also condemned the U.N. Genocide Convention and the Universal Declaration of Human Rights because these would "endanger the rights of U.S. citizens and destroy free speech, free press, free religion, and the right to own private property."[41] Implicit in most of these items, again, is a strong distrust of persons who are "different"—and therefore "alien."[42]

The analysis of ideologies

To analyze ideologies it is sometimes necessary to isolate underlying themes and to dissect out of catalogued beliefs the generalizations and assumptions that lend them unity and coherence, because frequently it is these underlying premises that are appealing. Clearly, for instance, any matron who takes solace in the fact that she belongs to a "pure" and "superior" ethnic group (surrounded by an ocean of "the wrong kind" of people) would endorse propositions limiting the sphere of influence of "aliens" in her affairs.

Even where there are no latent premises, however, ideologies require analysis, because in almost every case certain beliefs are central to the basic premises of the movement, whereas others are peripheral or incidental. The

40 *The New York Times* (April 20, 1960; April 20, 1961; and April 20, 1963).

41 M. Strayer, *Daughters of the American Revolution* (Washington, D.C.: Public Affairs Press, 1957), p. 103.

42 A study by A. L. Green, "The Ideology of Antifluoridation Leaders," has similarly shown that opposition to fluoridation can be based on resentment against authority and fear of government (*J. Social Issues*, 17, [1961], pp. 13–25).

platform of Gabriel Green, 1960 Presidential candidate of the Amalgamated Flying Saucer Clubs of America, is an example in point. This document contains planks dealing with a variety of issues, such as Puerto Rican statehood, technical aid to underdeveloped areas, and unionized labor. Of most import to Saucer Club members, however, would probably be the following provision:

> *Flying saucers:* We affirm that flying saucers are real, that in reality they are true spacecraft manned by people from other planets, who are visiting and making contact with various persons of our planet for the purpose of imparting information which can be used for the benefit of all men of earth. We deplore the actions of our government in withholding information on this subject which is so vital to the welfare of our nation and its people.[43]

Similarly, the American Program of the World Union of Free Enterprise Socialists (American Nazi Party) contains proposals ranging from the abolition of the Federal Reserve system to the restoration of the family. Closest to the central concern of the movement, however, is the section on "The Jewish Problem," which reads in part:

> We shall investigate, try and execute all Jews proved to have taken part in Marxist or Zionist plots of treason against their Nation or humanity. . . .
>
>   We shall establish an International Jewish Control Authority to carry out the above measures on a world-wide basis, to protect the rare honest Jews from the wrath of the people newly awakened to the truth about the Jews, and to make a long-term, scientific study to determine if the Jewish virus is a matter of environment, and can be eliminated by education and training, or if some other method must be developed to render Jews harmless to society.[44]

There is nothing about the ideology itself that testifies to the centrality of this belief. *The ultimate test of how central a belief is, is not its position in the logical structure or its objective importance, but the way it is perceived by the believer.*

The connotations of beliefs

From the viewpoint of the believer, the overtones and undercurrents of a belief may be as important as its message. A particular belief may come to carry connotations which considerably transcend its literal wording—and

---

[43] *AFSCA World Report* (Amalgamated Flying Saucer Clubs of America, July–August 1960), p. 4.

[44] *Program of the World Union of Free Enterprise Socialists* (undated leaflet published by the American Nazi Party, Arlington, Va.).

a psychological characterization of the belief must include these connotations. Without them, a statement that carries the burden of an entire world view may be dismissed as trivial; violently charged debates may appear to revolve around innocent details, and people may seem to die over the niceties of a dictionary definition.

Reading a list of doctrines of the Seventh Day Adventist Church, for instance, we might assign a relatively low priority to the statement designating Saturday rather than Sunday as the "sabbath" referred to in the Fourth Commandment. Actually, as Seventh Day Adventists see it,

> . . . the matter of selecting the right day for the Sabbath involves a great deal more than simply choosing between the seventh day and the first. When we choose the seventh day instead of the first, or vice versa, we are showing what we believe about God and Creation. We are showing what we believe about His Word. We are showing what we believe about His Law. And we are giving our answer to the greatest of all questions, "What think ye of Christ?" The Sabbath-versus-Sunday question is not a small matter: it is not merely quibbling over days. In choosing a day, one is choosing one's Master, and this affects his eternal destiny.[45]

What is involved for the Adventist, in other words, is the conception of God and his role in the universe. The rejection of Saturday as the day of rest, in this view, implies a denial of the assumption that Genesis refers to six 24-hour days. Keeping the Sabbath is an act which symbolically affirms the literal interpretation of biblical text.

An example of an ideologically centered debate requiring an understanding of subjective connotations is the bitter conflict between the Raskolnik and Orthodox factions of the Russian Orthodox Church. This dispute was so acrimonious that it became a common occurrence for a group of persons to lock themselves into a barn and set it on fire. The subject of this battle was a decision to have congregations cross themselves with three fingers instead of two, and to sing "Alleluia" three times in the course of the service. It had also been decided to transcribe the word "God" slightly differently, and to carry out other innovations in procedural details. These would appear to be trivial matters *unless* one took into consideration that, to the persons involved,

> . . . rites reflect different interpretations of the cardinal Christian dogmas dealing with the blessed Trinity, the nature of our Lord, and the doctrine of the Church. The Raskolniks therefore accused the Orthodox of adopting such heresies as Arianism, Macedonianism, Nestorianism, and papism.[46]

[45] K. H. Wood, "Remember the Sabbath Day," *Review and Herald*, 138 (1961), p. 16.

[46] S. Bolshakoff, *Russian Nonconformity* (Philadelphia: Westminster, 1950), p. 55.

Our final illustration is the *landsmaal* movement in Norway, which promoted a compounded folk language that is now one of two official languages in the country. Far from being expert in linguistics, the advocates of *landsmaal* were intense nationalists, reacting against Danish ascendancy in Norway. The *landsmaal* movement was also partly an antiurban peasant movement, in that

> . . . it was carried by a desire to improve the prestige and social status of the peasant as a participant member of an integrated bourgeois society by asserting the cultural values of the peasant as an integral part of Norwegian culture.[47]

Just as advocating a peasant language can thus help to glorify the honest, simple outdoor way of life, and resting on Saturday can come to embody a personalized conception of God, so other beliefs can acquire various connotations in line with the purposes they serve. Ideologies are human instruments, and their meanings always depend on their use.

Ideologies may be systematic in the hands of systematic persons; they may be consistent, if they are held by persons who prize consistency. On the other hand, in many ideologies logic and other formal systems may take a back seat. A social movement can defend the underdog while being blatantly anti-Semitic—or it can assume that big business is Communist-dominated. Such ideologies have their internal logic, of course (both may assume a conspiracy which has undermined our ostensible power structure), but in any event they must be accepted on their own terms. Any other approach not only sets up caricatures of the beliefs people hold, but also precludes insights into the reasons why people hold their beliefs.

The four-step road to appeals

How do beliefs become appeals? What type of sequence culminates in the adoption of beliefs?

Our analysis has suggested a four-step scheme, graphically represented in the figure following. The first step is the posing of a problem situation for a group of persons. Typically, this would occur when society fails to provide adequately for their needs or aspirations.

Such problem situations give rise to problems (Step 2) if they register psychological impact—that is, if they create some degree of unhappiness.

[47] P. E. Munch, "The Peasant Movement in Norway: A Study in Class and Culture," *Brit. J. Soc.*, 5 (March 1954), p. 73.

Schematic representation of the four-step sequence to
membership

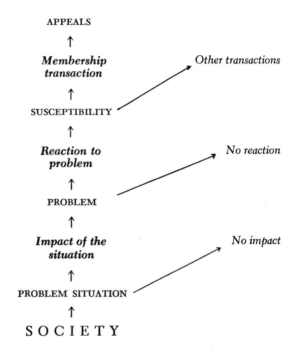

SOCIAL MOVEMENT

APPEALS

↑

Membership   Other transactions
transaction

↑

SUSCEPTIBILITY

↑

Reaction to   No reaction
problem

↑

PROBLEM

↑

Impact of the   No impact
situation

↑

PROBLEM SITUATION

↑

S O C I E T Y

Although many persons who feel they have a problem will lapse into apathy, resignation, and despair, others will begin to search for plausible solutions. They will view available diagnoses and prescriptions with increasing sympathy. The advent of this susceptibility is Step 3 in our sequence.

Susceptibility is selective, but not deterministic. It increases the probability that certain beliefs will be found appealing. Should the person (in this condition) encounter a social movement advocating such beliefs, the final step in our sequence occurs. This final step—the intersection of beliefs and susceptibilities—marks the point at which nonaffiliates become members.

Our next three chapters will furnish illustrations of several types of such junctures. In these examples, we shall trace the concrete steps from problem situations to their solutions. We shall try to show how the specific needs of special groups of people can be uniquely satisfied by particular movements.

2 ▷ ILLUSIONS AS SOLUTIONS

"**B**ELIEF" has been defined as "an attitude of welcome which we assume toward what we take to be the truth."[1] Some propositions are clearly more "welcome" than others, insofar as one can gauge relative appeal. A child asking what happens to him after death, for instance, will not be equally satisfied with the reply "you become a corpse, and you ultimately serve as fertilizer" and the assurance that "good children go to paradise." He will prefer the latter answer (other things being constant) *because it promises a more desirable fate.*

This tendency to prefer—and to adopt—beliefs that imply a favorable prospect will be the subject of the present chapter. We shall concern ourselves here with social movements that assure their members an imminent improvement in their conditions.

Promises of improvement are implicit, to some degree, in most social movements, but movements do vary in the extent to which they assess the problems on the way to Utopia, and in the realism of the means they prescribe for arriving there. Here we shall be concerned with *eager and optimistic* assessments of probabilities—with the tendency to offer blind hope, quick relief, or easy escape. We shall deal with social movements that "solve" problems by *predicting rapid transitions to a better world.*

---

[1] F. C. S. Schiller, *Problems of Belief* (London: Hodder and Stoughton, 1925), p. 14.

Illusions

Sigmund Freud called beliefs that are "derived from man's wishes" *illusions*. He pointed out that an illusion is not necessarily a false belief. An underprivileged girl, for instance, may predict that a prince on a white charger will come to fetch her, and "it is possible; some such cases have occurred." What matters, however, is that the belief *attempts to create a more satisfying reality*. "Thus we call a belief an illusion when wish-fulfillment is a prominent factor in its motivation, while disregarding its relations to reality."[2]

For Freud, religious beliefs fell into this category. He pointed out that life in general, and nature in particular, presents man with impersonal threats from which there is no escape. Death, for instance, is a disaster which cannot be averted. And although culture stands between every individual and his helplessness, there are innumerable reminders. Thus we can all recall catastrophes such as those experienced by Kansu, China, in 1920, when 180,000 of its inhabitants were wiped out by an earthquake, and in 1932, when 70,000 more perished under similar circumstances. On a smaller scale, one may consider sample headlines in our daily newspapers, such as "Crash Kills Four Deaf Mutes" and "Tragedy Ends 'Dream'; Piano Topples, Kills Child." Such incidents are obviously inequitable and equally obviously unreasonable.

Primitive man, more or less alone and completely exposed to the capriciousness of fate, formulated—according to Freud—a set of wish-fulfilling constructs to deal with his condition. Freud assumed that these beliefs survive in modern religion. Thus, for instance, our religious view holds that life serves a "higher" purpose, that benevolent fate watches over man, that death is not inorganic lifelessness, that human laws apply to the universe, that justice ultimately prevails, and that all of nature is somehow prearranged by someone supremely good, wise, and just. Freud did not regard these beliefs as necessarily false, but their usefulness impressed him more than their probable validity:

> We say to ourselves: it would indeed be very nice if there were a God, who was both creator of the world and a benevolent providence, if there were a moral world order and a future life, but at the same time it is very odd that this is all just as we should wish it ourselves. And it would be still odder if our poor ignorant enslaved ancestors had succeeded in solving all these difficult riddles of the universe.[3]

[2] S. Freud, *The Future of an Illusion* (New York: Doubleday, 1957), pp. 53–54.
[3] *Ibid.*, pp. 57–58.

In other words, the "it would-be-nice-if" character of these propositions was for Freud their essential feature. An illusion must create a better world. And it must do so, not because such a development is *probable* in the future, but because it is *needed* in the now. The originator of an illusion must be a person who has gone out of his way to accept an improbable, desirable solution, at the expense of more obvious alternatives. This tells us, in turn, that his problem did not call for probability-defined truth, but demanded hope. In extreme cases, it suggests that *the person, faced with an intolerable situation, searches for and finds a miracle.*

There are social movements composed of persons of this kind, and these movements offer promises of miraculous solutions. Such are the movements to be dealt with in this chapter. We shall examine three instances of wholesale suppression of human needs which evoked expectations of unlikely escape. We have selected three movements which differ in the nature of the situations that produced them. All three, however, involve the effects of ethnic discrimination, which has proved to be one of the most common sources of human despair.

Dead end situations

Few slums can approximate the squalor of "Back o'Wall," "Foreshore Road," "Davis Lane," and other settlements in western Kingston and eastern St. Andrew in Jamaica. The word "shacks"—which is customarily used to refer to the dwellings located here—carries excessively favorable connotations. A typical home might consist of two old automobile tires and some cardboard. Sanitary facilities are nonexistent, and human waste is deposited in the open—as is garbage. The inhabitants are squatters, and therefore not entitled to water, sewage disposal, trash collection, light, and other amenities. The resulting conditions breed not only discomfort, but epidemic disease.

Western Kingston is inhabited by Negroes, who constitute the bottom of the Jamaican color-shaded social hierarchy. Negroes in Jamaica make up the ranks of unskilled labor. In western Kingston, however, most heads of family are unemployed. Yet, despite the chronic unavailability of jobs, rural migrants arrive daily in search of work which is not there. It becomes increasingly hard to find odd jobs needed for physical survival, and life becomes a hopeless effort to stay alive in a hostile world. There is no objectively foreseeable improvement.

In this context, if a social movement arises, it must be one offering a "miraculous" solution. Such a movement is that of the Ras Tafari Brethren, whose ideology may be summarized in four basic points:

1. Ras Tafari (Emperor Haile Selassie of Ethiopia) is the Living God.
2. Ethiopia is the black man's home.
3. Repatriation is the way of redemption for black men. It has been foretold, and will occur shortly.
4. The ways of the white man are evil, especially for the black.[4]

The beginnings of the Ras Tafari movement can be precisely dated to November 1930. On the tenth of that month, the Ethiopian nobleman Ras Tafari was crowned Emperor Haile Selassie, King of Kings, Lord of Lords, and the Conquering Lion of the Tribe of Judah. When this news was published in Kingston (on the front page of *The Daily Gleaner*) several persons decided independently that the coronation was Redemption as prophesied in the Bible, and particularly in Revelation 5:2, 5:

> And I saw a strong angel proclaiming with a loud voice, Who is worthy to open the Book, and to loose the seals thereof? . . . And one of the elders saith unto me, Weep not: behold, the Lion of Judah, the Root of David, hath prevailed to open the Book and to loose the seven seals thereof.

Several founders of the Ras Tafari movement had been followers of Marcus Garvey, the Jamaican prophet whose Back to Africa movement we shall have further occasion to discuss (p. 237). Unlike Garveyites, however, the Ras Tafari Brethren had no hope of subsidizing their transportation, or of earning their keep after relocation. Despite such obvious impediments, as early as 1933 five thousand persons purchased photographs of Haile Selassie (for one shilling each) to serve as their "passport to Ethiopia." In 1955, groups appeared at three piers in Kingston claiming that the ghost of Garvey had announced the availability of shipping. In preparation for a 1958 Ras Tafari convention, brethren "as far away as Montego Bay sold their belongings and giving away their proceeds came to Kingston in the firm belief that at the end of the Convention they would embark for Africa.[5]

When the 1958 Meeting ended, many remained in the slums of Kingston because they were too ashamed to return to their communities. And in the summer of 1959 another migration to the capitol took place. More than 15,000 persons invested their shillings in a card marked "Free" to serve as a ticket for scheduled October "sailings." They had been assured that no passport would be necessary "for those returning home to Africa."[6]

---

[4] M. G. Smith, R. Augier, and R. Nettleford, *The Ras Tafari Movement in Kingston, Jamaica* (Kingston: Inst. Social & Econ. Research, University College of the West Indies, 1960), p. 53.
[5] *Ibid.*, pp. 18–19.
[6] *Ibid.*, p. 20.

The degree to which a person accepts unrealistic and improbable promises of escape reflects the extent to which life has become intolerable for him. Ras Tafaris grasped at any straw leading out of Jamaica, because they had become completely alienated, in the sense that they felt surrounded *only* by threats and impediments. *There was not a single redeeming feature in the world that surrounded them.* There was nothing which could command loyalty, or which could be viewed as a source of satisfactions. The sociologist George Simpson cites as one of the most frequent conversational themes among Ras Tafaris "The Hopelessness of the Jamaican Situation for Black Men." Ras Tafaris argue, according to Simpson, that

> The Jamaican Government, the worst government in the world, is corrupt and nothing can be expected from it. The politicians are out only for themselves; they want your vote and nothing else. . . . Black men are slaves today, and their slavery is worse than during the days of slavery because they are mentally enslaved. The white man keeps black men in poverty. "It is like being in prison, and there is no freedom until we go back home."[7]

The same theme is reflected in a favorite Ras Tafari song quoted by Simpson, one of whose stanzas goes:

> Here we are on this land.
> No one think how we stand
> The hands that are on us all day.
> So we cry and we sigh,
> For we know not our God.
> So we always be crying in vain.[8]

The need to "cry in vain" is obviated, for the Ras Tafari, by the prospects of returning to Ethiopia;

> The white man tells us to wait until Jesus comes, but we're not going to wait. In the near future, we are going back to our Homeland. The only future for the black man is with Ras Tafari. Our God and Our King is here to deliver us, and when we go back to that land no one will ever get us again.[9]

The reference to Jesus is of interest, because the Ras Tafari movement draws its membership from the same underprivileged groups that supply recruits to the revivalist cults in Jamaica. The Ras Tafaris and the revivalists are bitter enemies, with the Ras Tafaris maintaining that conventional

[7] G. E. Simpson, "The Ras Tafari Movement in Jamaica: A Study of Race and Class Conflict," *Social Forces*, 34 (December 1955), p. 169.
[8] *Ibid.*, p. 168.
[9] *Ibid.*, p. 169.

Christianity is an oppressive instrument of the white man. It is probable that the members of revivalist sects are indeed somewhat less alienated from the world, in the sense that they can share its religion. However, they clearly also resort to miraculous solutions, comprising not only a strong emphasis on Life Hereafter, but also elements of magic, healing, and witchcraft for more immediate use.

In a later chapter, we shall discuss the fact that beliefs initiate processes designed to secure evidence to reinforce them. Beliefs in miracles are no exception to this rule. In the case of the Ras Tafaris, for instance, their belief in the divinity of the Ethiopian emperor was supported by a 1936 photograph showing Haile Selassie standing with one foot on an unexploded Italian bomb. Similarly, the feasibility of emigration to Ethiopia was confirmed for them by a 1955 Ethiopian edict whereby five hundred acres of "fertile and rich land" were set aside for "the Black People of the West, who aided Ethiopia during her period of distress." Despite their strongly motivated belief in the improbable, Ras Tafari Brethren have been described as "surprisingly well informed about events, in Jamaica and elsewhere."[10] They view these events, however, as invariably tending to demonstrate the plausibility of the Ras Tafari dream.

Frustrated expectations

The Ras Tafari movement illustrates that illusory beliefs originate in an intolerable situation. But how does a situation become intolerable in the first place? In the Kingston slums, this question seems to answer itself, because of the extremity of the Jamaican Negro's dilemma: There is objectively no place for him to turn; his perceptions *correctly* reveal a maze of blind alleys, and show him that there is *in fact* no prospect of satisfying life in Jamaica. The desire to escape is the logical last resort.

But this need not necessarily be the case. A situation can become intolerable not because it has no solution, but because the preferred solutions are not available, or because attempted solutions seem to fail. What matters is that the person *feels walled in, irrespective of objectively specifiable alternatives.* He perceives the workaday world to be closed, and he therefore looks for a way out. He is motivated by a feeling of futility and despair.

To illustrate this sequence, it may be of interest to review the social movement of Alfred Charles Sam, which culminated in August 1914 when

[10] Smith *et al., The Ras Tafari Movement*, p. 31.

. . . the British merchant vessel *Liberia* cleared the port of Galveston and steamed off into the Gulf of Mexico, en route to the Gold Coast Colony, British West Africa. On board were sixty American Negroes, their jubilance somewhat restrained by their apprehensions, but intent, nonetheless, upon resettling in a location where life might be easier for them and where political and social equality might be their right. They were returning, they believed, to their own people and to a better existence than they had found in the New World.[11]

Left behind were many other would-be emigrants, five hundred of them in a tent city on the outskirts of Galveston and an equally large number in a temporary settlement at Weleetka, Oklahoma. These persons, despite their misery and impending disappointment, were relatively fortunate: of those who sailed on the *Liberia*, only a small handful were slated to survive. The rest would succumb to the adversities of the jungle and to the hostility of colonialists and natives.

The tragic outcome of the movement of Alfred Charles Sam could have been easily anticipated. Any realistic assessment would have discouraged even the most hardy individual from migrating to the Gold Coast. But realistic assessment was impossible for Sam's followers. To understand why, it is necessary to review a sequence of events beginning with the settlement of eastern Oklahoma in 1898:

Before the official opening of the Oklahoma territory to settlement, many whites and Negroes were already scattered among the Indian residents. Some of the Negroes were former slaves of the Indians, and others were Southern slaves who had moved West after the Civil War. With the opening of the territory, large numbers of Negro laborers arrived to work on the Fort Smith and Western Railroad, which extended westward from the Arkansas border. Many of these Negro workers expected to escape oppression through settlement along the frontier.

They were not disappointed. Although segregation was maintained in the newly settled areas, it took the form of separate Negro and white communities, which were economically and socially equivalent.

The Negroes chose not to interpret the segregated town sites as the transfer of the ghetto from southern towns. Instead, they viewed this segregation as indicative of a promising future for themselves and other members of

[11] W. E. Bittle and G. L. Geis, "Alfred Charles Sam and an African Return: A Case Study in Negro Despair," *Phylon* (2nd Quarter, 1962), p. 178. By permission of Atlanta University.

their race. . . . Negro enclaves [were] begun with fantastically high hopes of political and social freedom and of self-direction and wish-fulfillment.[12]

One of the communities established in this fashion along the tracks of the railroad was the town of Boley, which was founded in 1904. Booker T. Washington wrote of Boley that it offered the Negro an opportunity for "the propagation, culture and consummation of his refined ideas" as well as "the means whereby he can transmit to his children the fit of man and womanhood, in a sense of equal fitness for the multitudinous avocations of life."[13]

These aspirations were not held lightly by the inhabitants of Boley, but were systematized into an ideology that became their dominant concern. New settlers were recruited with appeals such as

> Come and help us prove to the Caucasian race and not only to the Caucasian race but to the world that the Negro is a law-making and law-abiding citizen, and help us solve the great racial problem that is now before us.
>
> .   .   .   .
>
> What are you waiting for? If we do not look out for our own welfare, who is going to do so for us? Are you always going to depend on the white race to control your affairs for you? Some of our people have had their affairs looked after by the white man for the past 30 years, and where are they today? They are on the farms and plantations of the white men . . . with everything mortgaged so that they cannot get away and forever will be so long as they are working upon their farms and trading in their stores.[14]

The growing population of Boley was not only economically prosperous, but looking forward to participation in the political control of their county:

> If we fail in this effort, we will never have the opportunity again; there is not another spot so desirable in the country, where the Negro has a chance to settle down in a little community of his own and sleep under his own vine and fig tree.[15]

In 1906, the aspirations of the citizens of Boley became fleeting reality. Through its almost unanimously Republican vote, the Negro community was able to outvote a Democratic majority among whites. The 1907 county

---

[12] W. E. Bittle and G. L. Geis, "Racial Self-fulfillment and the Rise of an All-Negro Community in Oklahoma," *Phylon* (3rd Quarter, 1957), p. 251.

[13] *Ibid.*, p. 252.

[14] *Ibid.*, pp. 253–254.

[15] *Ibid.*, p. 254.

convention of the Republican Party named two Negroes as candidates for County Commissioner, and their election seemed assured. The whites rallied at once, and ruthlessly disenfranchised the Negro community. The election board simply refused to certify Negro returns, and declared the Democrats to be officially elected. The State Supreme Court upheld this illegal action, and a discriminatory amendment was added to the Oklahoma constitution to preclude future political activity by Negroes.

> For the Negroes, something horrible had occurred. They had done nothing untoward, and they now found themselves slapped hard for doing it. . . . The Negro was forced to face the fact that once again, though now in what had been defined as a new milieu, he was cut off from the major institutions which provided a functional guarantee of civil liberties. . . . The political activity of the Boley Negro had been brought to an abrupt end. But what was clearly of more importance, the elimination of his fundamental franchise prerogative belied and foreshadowed the relegation of the Okfuskee Negro to his traditional Southern caste status. Not only would all avenues of political expression be cut off, but all avenues of social and economic expression as well.[16]

This closing of "avenues of social and economic expression" occurred promptly and openly. White Farmers' Commercial Clubs were set up with the express purpose of driving Negro farmers out of the area. The boycott organized by these groups was especially effective when a depression in cotton prices brought ruin to small farms. Discrimination also took other forms. In 1913, a mother and child were lynched.

> The economic and political setbacks added up to almost complete disillusionment on the part of Okfuskee County Negroes. "All Men Up—Not Some Down," the motto of the Boley *Progress*, was not only meaningless but mocking. The appeal "on to Boley" had been reduced to a hollow dream, pushed mercilessly back into the fantasy world from which it had sprung. There would be no Negro autonomy in Oklahoma, no Negro dignity, no Negro peacefulness. There would be no growing respect and admiration from white neighbors and no industrial and agricultural prosperity. Nothing had been changed, nothing had been bettered.[17]

In fact, things *had* changed. Second-class citizenship had—prior to Boley—been accepted as a fact of life. The Boley experiment had raised the possibility of change, and had thereby converted the formerly *inevitable* into a *solvable problem*. When the solution failed, the problem remained.

[16] *Ibid.*, p. 257.
[17] *Ibid.*, p. 258.

Moreover, since hope had been fanned to a very high level during the Boley settlement campaign, a return to the assumption of inevitable second-class citizenship was inconceivable. Further, Boley had been regarded as an *exclusive* solution, and this meant that its failure seemed to invalidate *all* available remedy.

The combination of need and perceived futility defines intolerability. In the case of Boley, it meant that there *had to be* a way out. But where? Where was there an environment in which Negroes could be free and self-determining, and in which the Boley Dream could be revived?

> They could go North, but there they would encounter more white Americans as well as an industrialized atmosphere with which they were not familiar. Besides, the best the North could offer was an opportunity to be left alone, and these were not the kind of men who had envisioned condescending tolerance, but the kind who wanted an active role in the shaping of their own and their children's destiny.[18]

Even prior to the appearance of Alfred Charles Sam, there were some who talked of escaping to Africa. Letters of inquiry had been written, and one group had left with full intention of emigrating. At this juncture, on May 11, 1913, Sam arrived, at the invitation of prominent local citizens, to describe his proposals for the settlement of the Gold Coast.

The plan was simple: Those desiring to go to Africa could buy shares in Sam's Akim Trading Company, founded to promote commerce with the Gold Coast:

> Since the ships to be used (and yet to be acquired) would be large, it would be possible to transport a limited number of colonists to the Gold Coast on each voyage. These people would be established on lands for which Sam had previously arranged and would promote colonies, designed both as havens for American Negroes and as centers of instruction for Africans. Since the company would soon be engaged in a highly lucrative trade, the cost of transportation for the colonists would be small. Sam decided that the purchaser of any one share of stock would be entitled to a trip to Africa for himself and his dependents. Food for the voyage would be provided on board for a slight additional fee.[19]

The resources of the Gold Coast were painted, for the benefit of potential shareholders, in the most vividly glowing colors. Crops were said to grow without being tended, bread could be picked from trees, tall bushes yielded incredible amounts of cotton, and diamonds could be found after

[18] *Ibid.*
[19] Bittle and Geis "Alfred Charles Sam," p. 184.

every hard rain. The settlers were also assured status: American know-how would make it possible for them to provide technical assistance to underdeveloped Africans. This prospect was especially attractive to the Oklahoma Negroes:

> To them, Sam represented an escape which they believed was a solution, but he also represented removal to a land where they could continue their conceived roles as leaders, pioneers and persons of prestige and importance. They were not skulking off to Africa as beaten men and women, but they were instead returning proudly to their homeland, full of the ideas that residence in America had taught them and equipped with the skills which had made their nation famous. The Americans believed they were on their way to save the Africans, to "uplift" them, as the pioneers preached on their landing at Saltpond.[20]

By early September, four hundred families in Boley alone were ready to sail. A few weeks later, five thousand stockholders awaited instructions in Oklahoma, and many of these moved to tent-cities at Weleetka. The faith of Sam's followers was unshaken by sobering critiques of his prospectus, by attempts to prosecute Sam, and by almost universal laughter and harassment. The combined attempts of American and British authorities to nip the hopeless venture in the bud met with complete failure. After various delaying tactics, the old steamship purchased and outfitted by Sam steamed out of Galveston as a personification of unassailable hope and indestructible faith.

The probabilities of Sam's venture, to be sure, were not as low as those of the shilling passports and ambiguous biblical passages underlying the Ras Tafari dream, but the odds had to be supplemented to a similar degree. The Kingston Negro, after all, had nothing to lose by emigrating, whereas the Oklahoma migrants left means of subsistence and a culture with which they still identified. Their willingness to withdraw roots and to face the unknown under these circumstances is not only a tribute to the powers of persuasion of Alfred Charles Sam, but (more fundamentally) evidence of the potency and perseverance of aspirations born during Reconstruction days.

Nativism and millenarianism

Among social movements of interest to anthropologists, the cargo cults of Melanesia occupy a position of distinction. These cults have been traditionally classified under the heading of *nativistic movements*. A nativistic movement has been defined as "any conscious and organized attempt on the

[20] *Ibid.*, pp. 193–194.

part of a society's members to revive or perpetuate selected aspects of its culture.[21]

Cargo cults have been more recently classified as *millenarian movements*, which are "movements in which the imminence of a radical and supernatural change in the social order is prophesied or expected, so as to lead to organization and activity, carried out in preparation for this event."[22] The "radical and supernatural change expected" is in the nature of a *desirable* development:

> In some cases, the millenium is expected to occur soon, on this earth: in others, the people are expected to enter an abode of heavenly bliss in the future; in yet others, there is only an expectation of relatively minor improvements of life on earth, though these usually develop quickly into one of the more radical forms.[23]

This listing implies that the psychological mechanism underlying millenarian movements is *wish-fulfillment*, and that millenia may constitute creations designed to deal with unsatisfying reality. The implication of nativism is similar. Since nativistic movements occur when a culture is destroyed, they may be viewed as efforts to preserve the unpreservable, and as attempts to escape into an already unreal past. The bridge between millenarianism and nativism is provided by the fact that most of these movements built their dream world with material which is suffused with nostalgia. For example, although cargo cults exist that rely on the U. S. Air Force or the French Communist Party as a source of aid,[24] the spirits of dead ancestors are the most popular agents of liberation for cargo-cult members. These figures out of the past not only are congenial, but also have proved useful in achieving happiness on prior occasions.

Cargo cults

New Guinea was first sighted by Europeans in 1512. This ominous event culminated in an era of rapid colonization in the nineteenth century. Germany raised her flag over the northeast part of the island in 1884, and other European powers soon followed suit.

---

[21] R. Linton, "Nativistic Movements," *Amer. Anthropologist*, 45 (1943), p. 230.

[22] P. M. Worsley, "Millenarian Movements in Melanesia," *Rhodes-Livingstone Inst.*, 21 (March 1957), p. 19.

[23] *Ibid.*

[24] *Ibid.* A typical contemporary cargo cult episode occurred in Port Moresby, Papua: "The natives . . . charged that a strange plane which flew over the island one night carried cargo which President Johnson was going to distribute among them, but the plane had been stolen by Australia, which administers the island under United Nations mandate." (New York *Herald Tribune* [March 24, 1964].)

Life in Melanesia prior to the arrival of the colonists had been exceedingly simple. The natives engaged in farming. Food was plentiful and no strenuous efforts were required to obtain it. Status was earned through the number and quality of feasts one could sponsor, and the "host with the most" was likely to find himself village chief. No other formal organization was necessary. Interpersonal disputes were settled privately, and villages had little interest in each other. Religion served material ends. It mainly consisted of prayers and sacrifices designed to convince the spirits of ancestors to help enhance one's personal or agricultural fertility.

The European colonist of Melanesia viewed the natives as a source of cheap labor for rubber plantations and for copra and gold mines. Recruitment methods were initially very direct, with "blackbirding" (kidnapping) prevalent among the Germans. Labor was indentured—usually for three years—and working and living conditions were indescribably bad. Rumors of crowded barracks and long working hours soon filtered back to the villages, and made recruitment more difficult. This problem was counteracted by assessing a "head tax" that natives could not afford, with exemptions for indentured laborers.

Native life was dramatically disrupted. Most tangibly, the absence of men prevented family formation and undermined the economy. As late as 1937, 22 per cent of the adult male population of New Guinea were indentured laborers. Traditional social organization was weakened: the young men returning from white plantations rejected the authority of their parochial elders; village authorities also could not compete with administrators appointed by the colonists.[25]

Psychologically, the advent of the white invaders had introduced with extreme suddenness a variety of new experiences not provided for in native frames of reference. The possessions of the settlers—their clothing, weapons, furnishings and means of transportation—were obviously desirable. But where did these commodities originate, and how could they be obtained?

Three observations by the natives seemed to help them to answer this question: (1) The possessions of European colonists arrived as cargo in ships (later, in planes), and these ships (and planes) seemed to appear out of nowhere. (2) Europeans did not work for their material benefits, but obtained them in return for mysterious pieces of paper. (3) Europeans obviously attached great importance to religion, if one considered their strenuous

---

[25] For a description of the impact of colonists in Melanesia, see P. Worsley, *The Trumpet Shall Sound* (London: McGibbon and Kee, 1957).

missionary efforts. The sum of these data, viewed from the vantage point of traditional native religion, led to the premises of the cargo cults:

> The official dogma of the movement asserted that Europeans were not the all-powerful beings they appeared to be, but that their power really derived from their secret knowledge of a hidden portion of Christian doctrine which they kept from the islanders. *It was, in fact, the spirits who made the goods the Europeans imported;* confirmatory evidence was that the Europeans were unable to repair mechanical contrivances when these broke down, but had to send them away.[26]

The passage refers to the Pako Cult (started in 1932), but hundreds of cargo cults have held similar views with minor variations. Basic assumptions have remained more or less unchanged from the Tuka Movement (1885) and the Milne Bay Movement (1893) to contemporary vigils at makeshift airstrips and control towers.

Typical of the more elaborate cargo cults is the Papuan movement, called by Europeans the "Vailala Madness," which began after the end of World War I and lasted for twelve years. Like most cargo cults, the Vailala movement started among formerly indentured laborers. As in the case of other cults, it was sparked by a prophet who had been strongly subjected to European influences. The cult's premises, as usual, were an admixture of transmuted Western influences and strongly anti-European sentiments. "Some day, very soon," the prediction ran, "a large ship filled with cargo will arrive. This cargo will be distributed among us by the spirits of our ancestors. The spirits will help us defeat and kill the Europeans. They will then turn our own skins white, and no one will have inferior black skin. Our old 'things,' like huts and tools (which cannot compare with the cargo we shall receive) can of course be destroyed." These prophecies were revealed in dreams, and were partly deduced from the doctrine of resurrection preached by missionaries.

Contemporary descriptions of Vailala rituals frequently emphasized presumably irrational and exotic conduct. One European observer, for instance, notes:

> The natives were taking a few quick steps in front of them and would then stand, jabber and gesticulate, at the same time swaying the head from side to side; also bending the body from the hips, the legs appearing to be held firm. Others would take quick steps forward and stop, placing the hands on the hips, jabbering continuously, swaying the head from side to

---

[26] Worsley, "Millenarian Movements," p. 20 (italics added).

side and moving the trunk of the body backwards and forwards, remaining in this position for approximately one minute.[27]

Such observations made it difficult to see that there is in fact a close analogy between Vailala ceremonials and conventional Western evangelism. The meetings conducted by Vailala evangelists were quite similar to revivalist camp meetings in that they featured healings, trances, and conversion experiences. What most strikingly differentiates Melanesian revivalism from the Christian variety is not ritual, but the this-worldly nature of its objectives. Cargo cults were aimed at alleviating the adversities of existence, and supernatural means were purely incidental to this end:

> . . . while the actions taken in the magical type of movement are ineffective as a means of effecting changes in the environment, nevertheless they represent attempts to solve real problems of everyday life, even if the means adopted to secure these ends be incorrect. The people set themselves real tasks. . . . They make a logical interpretation of an irrational social order, given the facts at their disposal.[28]

Cargo cults customarily resorted to fantasy and illusion because no other means of attaining improvement were available to the Melanesians. They used magic because magic had "worked" in relation to past problems. And they believed in supernatural intervention because they saw that others (the Europeans) could secure privileges from "extraterrestrial" sources. Eventually, other native movements sprang up which experimented with more sophisticated forms of problem solution, such as strikes and demands for higher wages, improved social services, more self-rule, etc. At this point, the mystery and urgency of the problem situation appear to have diminished sufficiently to permit a more "down to earth" approach to a solution.

The occasion for miracles

Every one of the movements we have discussed features low probability solutions to the problems of its members: in every case, the chances of bringing about improvements in the fashion which is prescribed are objectively very small. But from the vantage point of the persons involved, the required transmutation of reality appears probable. The Ras Tafari member sees no pressing reason why he should *not* migrate to Ethiopia (other than the perversity of the Jamaican authorities); Sam's "back to Africa" following fore-

<hr>

[27] F. E. Williams, "The Vailala Madness and the Destruction of Native Ceremonies in the Gulf Division," *Papuan Anthropological Reports*, Port Moresby (1923), p. 10.
[28] Worsley, "Millenarian Movements," pp. 26–27.

saw no major acculturation problem in the jungles; and the cargo cultists viewed the intervention of supernatural agents as routine. To the believer, a miracle is a natural occurrence.

There are several mechanisms which can create discrepancies between actual and perceived probabilities. One of these, illustrated by the cargo cults, is experience with cataclysmic change. The Melanesian native had been subjected to innovation through the sudden and inexplicable advent of the white man. Why could not this fate be reversed? It is a plausible assumption that ills which come about miraculously should be miraculously curable: every disaster can carry the implication of a miracle. This is one reason why movements such as the Townsend Plan and Father Divine arose out of the depression of the 1930's.[29]

Another mechanism is illustrated by the Ras Tafaris. Here, conditions had progressively deteriorated to the point where all reasonable avenues of personal development had been closed. Given a realistic frame of mind and a clear sense of proportion, the average Kingston slum dweller would be forced to conclude that "there is nothing to aim for, except death through starvation in a country which has no place for me." He would be forced to recognize the pointlessness of his existence, and to become aware of his exclusion from any social pattern or sequence of advancement. This is a psychological option that cannot be exercised, because of the obvious discomforts it would bring. Like the psychotic patient who is driven into a fantasy world by the increasing intolerability of his real existence, the member of society who finds himself in a corner *must* adopt low probability solutions to avoid facing the hopelessness of his fate. *Miracles provide prospects of change in situations that are objectively hopeless, and offer comfort and a basis for enduring situations that are objectively intolerable.*

A related mechanism, illustrated by the movement of Alfred Charles Sam, is that of *delaying the recognition of defeat.* Sam's followers had induced themselves (through the Boley Experiment) to hope for improvement of their lot. When strong expectations of this kind are raised, the removal of means for their realization initiates a search for alternative means. The stronger the expectations, the more likely it is that this search will continue after obvious possibilities are exhausted. The miracle functions to retain psychologically essential prospects; it not only brightens the future, but validates the present and sanctifies the past. Without it, purposefulness would frequently be devoid of meaning.

Miracles, then, are means of self-preservation. The extremity of

[29] Cantril, *Social Movements*, Chs. 5, 7.

miraculous solutions is a reflection of the extremity of the problems they solve. Extreme situations differ in the way they come about. They may be produced through the gradual closing of avenues of development; they may occur through the sudden destruction of familiar forms of existence; they may range from the denial of means of physical survival through the dashing of people's hopes. They may consist of the cumulative display of evidences of failure, or of a dramatic confrontation with defeat.

Whatever the genesis or shape of the extreme situation, the belief in a miracle can provide a psychological solution for it. It can do so in several ways. One way is to "make sense" of disasters by countering unlikely misfortunes with equally improbable resolutions; another is to create a make-believe reality, within which meaningful existence is possible; lastly, by delaying the recognition of extremity, hope for a miracle can provide a framework for continued goal-oriented behavior, which might otherwise seem like a farce.

In these ways, belief in miracles can preserve vestiges of humanity when the essentials of human life are completely suppressed. Although belief in miracles does not (as a rule) improve conditions, it ameliorates the travails of adjustment. With luck, it permits survival until higher probability solutions become available.

3 ▷ THE BENEFIT OF PERCEIVING CONSPIRACIES

IN the foregoing chapter, we illustrated the fact that some social movements deal with the problems of their members by depicting the future in optimistic, overly favorable terms. The present chapter will be concerned with the reverse of this solution. We'll try to show that an exaggeratedly jaundiced view of society can also "solve" problems. We shall deal with social movements which are premised on the assumption that humanity is being conquered by a powerful, pervasive conspiracy. We shall try to examine the mechanisms whereby such an apparently repulsive belief can come to constitute an appeal.

For purposes of illustration, we shall focus on ultra-right-wing movements in the United States. The salience of the conspiracy premise is obvious here, and emerges even in a cursory review of the ideology of these movements. One distributing agency of "patriotic" publications, for instance, lists among the titles in its catalogue such items as the following:

The Iron Curtain over America
The Age of Treason
America's Betrayal
Plot Against Christianity
Coming Red Dictatorship

    The Architects Behind the World Communist Conspiracy
    Federal Reserve Conspiracy
    Beasts of the Apocalypse
    The Hidden Hand
    The Invisible Government
    Know Your Enemy
    Roosevelt's Road to Russia
    An American Patriot Gives Count-down on Communist
      Take-over of the U. S. (a recording).[1]

Although these titles provide a cumulative impression of the conspiracy theme, we must review some publications in detail to determine the nature of the perceived danger:

The "menace"

Know Your Enemy is an illustrated pamphlet of some sixty pages published in California, and issued through various right-wing distribution channels.[2] It is subtitled "Counter-Intelligence Information." The cover carries small photographs of Stalin, Senator Lehman, Justice Frankfurter, and Henry Morgenthau, Jr., with the caption "Stalin and the secret government of the United States." The inside cover contains pictures of 18 American Communist Party officials, with a preface which identifies some of them as Jews.

The body of *Know Your Enemy* begins by pointing out that the chief source of Communism lies within the United States. (This follows from premises such as "the State Department and certain other agencies have been used to strengthen the Soviets.") The remainder of the first chapter deals largely with evidence suggesting that most American Communists are Jewish.[3] The point of the analysis is that "the Communist Party is itself only a front for a deeper, all-Jewish conspiracy."[4]

Chapter 2 is entitled "Bolshevism was Jewish." It contains material purporting to show that the Communist revolution in Russia was organized and financed by Jews. The third chapter elaborates the same theme. In this

---

[1] *Patriotic Educational Materials* (Union, N. J.: Christian Educational Association, undated catalogue.).

[2] R. H. Williams, *Know Your Enemy* (Santa Ana, Calif.: Williams Publications, 1950).

[3] There are exceptions, of course. For instance, "I have been unable to verify the racial identity of Owen Lattimore." Eugene Dennis, general secretary of the American Communist Party, was born Francis Xavier Waldron, Jr.: "He may be gentile."

[4] Williams, *Enemy*, p. 8.

chapter, it is argued that the absence of extreme anti-Semitism in the U.S.S.R. confirms the assumption that the Soviet government is still Jewish-dominated. Even the firing of Russian Jews in powerful positions is viewed as designed to help the Jewish cause: it prevents anti-Semitic outbreaks among the masses, thereby insuring continued Jewish domination.[5]

The fourth and major chapter of *Know Your Enemy* is called "Zionism and the Anti-Defamation League."[6] The first section deals with three persons who are presumed to be the most powerful men in Washington. One of these figures is Henry Morgenthau, Jr., who allegedly attempted to starve Germany to promote the interests of the Soviet Union. Another is Senator Herbert Lehman, who presumably financed the Red Army through "the Communist inspired UNRRA," and who "master-minded" Radio Free Europe, which aids in "the final triumph of the world revolution."

Justice Frankfurter (the third member of the triad) is discussed in a separate section, beginning: "The son of an Austrian revolutionary, brought to America at the age of 12, Felix Frankfurter proved to be the leading master mind behind the revolution in this innocent, naive republic." This theme is elaborated with accusations ranging from "he indoctrinated hundreds of young Americans . . . with Marxism" to "is acknowledged . . . to be the master of the U. S. State Department." Marxism and the State Department are then related to each other, under the heading "Frankfurter Agents Sabotage U. S." Among the persons discussed in this section are Secretary Acheson ("no man since President Roosevelt has so elaborately sabotaged this republic"), Alger Hiss (a Frankfurter "protégé"), and General Lyman L. Lemnitzer ("another high Jewish official"). The General is accused of having withheld military equipment from anti-Communist governments; General Mark Clark (whose mother is identified as Jewish) is mentioned as having turned iron curtain refugees back to the MVD.

The next section, "The Anti-Defamation League," deals with the hypothesis that "The ramifications of this invisible machine are almost beyond the comprehension of the gentile mind." First we are shown how American civilization is destroyed through Jewish-backed civil rights programs. Attacks on restrictive housing covenants, for instance, threaten the destruction of "those islands of peace and culture in which some Anglo-Saxons have tried to preserve race and freedom"; Fair Employment Practices laws bring Negroes into large industrial cities, and subject them to Communist propaganda.

Another ADL activity is the "character assassination" of anti-Com-

[5] *Ibid.*, p. 33.
[6] *Ibid*, pp. 34–51.

munist candidates, and the backing of political stooges. Third, there is the "Jewish secret police," comprising thousands of special agents: "This gigantic GPU or gestapo is the heart of the terrorist revolution in America." The Anti-Defamation League also engages in censorship "to protect the Frankfurter program." The net result of this effort is that

> It may be too late to stop the avalanche of Marxism. Even if we are able to destroy the Anti-Defamation League and deport or restrain its leaders, we now face the fact that the big Jewish communities are organized like nothing ever before in history, and they have been trained by the Anti-Defamation League."[7]

The most discouraging aspect of the total situation is dealt with next: From the Jewish vantage point, it is *immaterial* who wins the Third World War. *No matter how the war ends, the Zionists will be the real victors:* "The Zionists aim to dominate the West; the communists the East, both producing the same revolution, both promoting the same world government, police backed—a world dictatorship."

One possible contingency, for instance, is an American victory, followed by forced immigration of Asiatics into the United States. Wartime controls are anticipated, followed by strict regimentation in all areas of life. Popular protests will lead to the establishment of slave labor camps. Obviously, "the only way to stop the avalanche is to break up the Zionist secret government." But how is this to be accomplished?

The last few pages of the pamphlet deal with "strategy and tactics" for last-ditch preventive action. The measures advocated here include the mobilization of Civil Defense forces and civilian armies under the control of governors and mayors, internment of Jews in areas the Russians would otherwise attack, deportation of internal enemies, restoration of segregation and restrictive immigration, and support of reliable anti-Communists such as Ukrainian nationalists, Spanish fascists, and German military leaders. Ultimately, however,

> We must organize locally for defense of our communities and families. Then use our organized strength to give moral support to state and national leaders, and insist that they take suitable steps for a full and permanent solution of the race problem.

The text ends with the injunction: "Start with your trusted neighbors; organize your group, and presently we will have courageous leaders aplenty. It is you who must take the initiative."[8]

In this fashion the pamphlet returns to its original theme, that of pro-

[7] *Ibid.*, p. 48.
[8] *Ibid.*, p. 56.

viding "counter-intelligence" information for persons wishing to take informed defensive measures. To help in this task, the author—a recognized expert on the machinations of covert, dangerous forces—claims to have "spotted" the enemy. He claims to have documented the premise that specific threats, such as manifestations of Communism, are mere symptomatic manifestations of a more serious and pervasive menace. He has "identified" the sources of this inclusive threat (the Jews), and has "named" individuals in powerful positions whose manipulations are speedily sealing the fate of civilized humanity. Against this overwhelming danger, the reader is invited to make a courageous and intelligent last stand.

Variations on the theme

A few brief references to other representative publications follow. Detailed summaries are not essential, because the Great Conspiracy literature is relatively uniform in its approach to its problem.

The Architects Behind the World Communist Conspiracy is a Canadian publication, issued by an organization that calls itself the "Canadian Intelligence Service." The group also distributes American, British, and Canadian literature. Sample items include Red Fog Over America, Hidden Government, No Wonder We Are Losing, The Yalta Betrayal, and Zion's Fifth Column. The link with other patriotic organizations is exemplified by the overlap in catalogues. It is also noteworthy that The Architects . . . displays a laudatory quotation on its cover from the author of Know Your Enemy.

The Architects . . . is a closely documented volume. It begins with the revelation that Karl Marx was Jewish, and continues with a long list of particulars intended to show that Communism is a Jewish product. Among the incriminating items are: (1) Jewish bankers provided financial support to Japan during the Russo-Japanese War (thus weakening Czarist Russia); (2) of the 388 members of the revolutionary government in Russia, 371 were Jews; and (3) the Russian Imperial family was assassinated by a Jew. The pamphlet also contains the usual dossier of Jewish Communist spies, but includes Canadians as well as Americans. The exposé ends with a plea for knowledge, and the recommendation:

> After you have read this revelation of treason and subversion, send copies to friends, public officials and influential citizens throughout your community and province. Don't break the chain—keep the revelation growing.[9]

[9] R. Gestick, The Architects Behind the World Communist Conspiracy (Flesherton, Ontario: Canadian Intelligence Publications, undated), p. 16.

The Coming Red Dictatorship is a large sheet, closely printed on both sides and profusely illustrated. It is subtitled "Asiatic Marxist Jews Control Entire World as Last World War Commences. Thousands of Plotters Placed in Key Positions by Invisible Government. Few Were Ever Elected." Fifty photographs depict Jewish public figures, each with an identifying caption. Included are Albert Einstein ("30 Communist Citations"), Bernard M. Baruch ("Most Powerful Man in the World"), Felix Frankfurter ("Placed Many Reds in Government"), Anna M. Rosenberg ("Loaded Defense Department with Reds"), Harry Dexter White ("Treasury Department Spy"), Sidney M. Hillman ("Man Behind F. D. R."), and Rabbi Hillel Silver ("Top Zionist Powerful in Washington"). The text of the leaflet begins: "The information printed here is not available from any of the regular channels of information which are controlled by our enemy." The reader is informed:

> UNLESS YOU ACT AT ONCE to stop this plot which has been steadily progressing for many years, and especially the last twenty years, and now has its key men in the desired positions of power, ready to pull the strings which will submerge Gentile humanity forever.[10]

The remainder of the text consists of excerpts from *The Protocols of the Elders of Zion* (the forged minutes of a Jewish plot to enslave humanity, which were publicized by Henry Ford) and evidence linking Jews to the Russian revolution, as well as items of information intended to show that "[President] Eisenhower has moved the Jews into top positions in our government in readiness for the day when they will 'snap the trap.' "[11]

The final plea ("you have only one chance left . . . there is no time to delay") is addressed to federal and state legislators. They are enjoined to organize, to outlaw Communism, and to banish the Anti-Defamation League.

The appeal of conspiracy

Later in this chapter we shall consider how the conspiracy premise is related to social movements of the far right. We shall also have occasion to explore the psychological forces behind conspiracy beliefs. At this point we return to the question: what can make conspiracies appealing? Do most people *reluctantly* adopt conspiratorial beliefs, because they find the evidence overwhelming? Is there necessarily a special kind of person who finds

---

[10] *The Coming Red Dictatorship* (Union, N. J.: Christian Educational Association, undated), p. 1. (The passage is quoted in its entirety.)
[11] *Ibid.*, p. 2.

conspiracies attractive? Or are there aspects of the conspiracy theme which are intrinsically congenial, in the sense that they might attract anyone to this type of explanation?

Although we shall continue considering the Jewish Communist conspiracy, it is clear that conspiratorial conceptions are far from limited to the political right. An editorial in the Moscow *Red Star*, for instance, provides the following interpretation of a series of army revolts in Eastern Africa:

> The similarity of the army mutinies in Kenya, Uganda, and Tanganyika and their coincidence in time *suggest the existence of one master plan and of one center from which the whole thing was directed.*
> Equally suspicious was the instant readiness of the British forces to intervene.[12]

A letter to the editor of a liberal pacifist magazine contains the observation:

> Bomb tests continue to spray their poisonous radioactive particles across the earth. It seems clear that the administration's belittling the advice of many scientists and the many appeals from America and abroad to stop the tests, *indicates that irresponsible militarists are at the helm.* . . . At least, we can speak out against the *money-empire-mad terrorists* whose pretext for their destructive policy is fear of Russia.[13]

In its official platform, the Socialist Workers Party contends that all social evils in the United States

> . . . stem directly from the capitalist system under which the country is ruled by big banks and giant corporations. The few who control the monopolies put their private interests ahead of the needs of the many who do the work. These privileged few enjoy lavish and growing prosperity, but their greed remains insatiable. Not content with today's peak profits, they clamor and scheme to get more.[14]

The man in the street on occasion shows a distinct predilection for theories entailing plots. After the assassination of President Kennedy, for example, the majority of Americans refused to believe that the suspected assassin had acted on his own. Most felt that "some group or element" could be held responsible, although only a handful could specify the identity of the "conspirators."[15]

[12] New York *Herald Tribune* (February 12, 1964, italics added).
[13] "Letters," *Fellowship* (November 1957), p. 30 (italics added).
[14] *Socialist Workers Party Election Platform* (New York: Socialist Workers Party, 1964), p. 3.
[15] *Public Opinion News Service* (December 6, 1963).

What are the attractive features of such an explanation? One, obviously, is the opportunity to focus accumulated resentments against a tangible enemy. For example, when the bubonic plague swept Europe in the fourteenth century (costing twenty-five million lives), popular indignation exploded against the Jews, who were accused of poisoning wells to spread the disease. Although nothing constructive was done to curb the epidemic, the persecution of Jews furnished an illusion of remedy, as well as some emotional relief.[16]

In addition to providing a concrete target for tensions, conspiracies can simplify the believer's system of reasoning and his conception of social causation. The first of these advantages is shared with many other types of ideologies; the second is relatively specific to conspiracy beliefs. In a conspiracy, causation becomes centralized (in that all events can be blamed on one group of plotters), and it is also integrated (because the plotters presumably *know* what they are doing and *intend* the consequences of their actions). The Jews, for instance, are seen as responsible for both sides of the cold war, for the complexities of government, for the civil rights movement, for the course of history, and for the fluoridation of water supply. These and other worrying, disconcerting, and confusing developments become part of a coherent pattern, the key to which is the evil, scheming mind of the "ubiquitous" Jew.

This integrating function of the Conspiracy is illustrated by the following excerpt from a tract circulated by the right-wing magazine *American Mercury:*

Four planned sinister events took place in 1913:
1. The graduated income tax law was passed (16th Amendment).
2. The Federal Reserve Banking Act was passed.
3. The Anti-Defamation League was organized by B'nai B'rith.
4. The Rockefeller Foundation was established. *These four events were not unrelated.*[17]

It develops that the plot set in motion in 1913 led to every major event since that time. ("From this date forward, we were to be lied to, brainwashed and betrayed.") The most recent "planned events" have "set the

---

[16] From 1348 through 1350 it became general practice to torture and kill Jews in afflicted cities. Several Jewish communities were completely wiped out in this fashion: in Mayence alone 12,000 Jews "threw themselves into flames kindled to burn them." (H. V. Haggard, *Devils, Drugs and Doctors* [New York: Harper & Brothers, 1946], p. 208.)

[17] R. Maguire, "The Gravestones of 1913," *American Mercury* (August 1957), reprinted in Tract No. 8, undated. (Italics added.)

stage for the greatest tragedy since the crucifixion." (The crucifixion, needless to say, was engineered by the same forces, at an earlier stage of their development. *American Mercury* contains in each issue an article entitled "Termites of the Cross," which summarizes the efforts of the "Hidden Hand" [the Jews] to combat the teachings of Christ.)

The complicated nature of international affairs is frequently deplored in right-wing literature. One publication, for instance, carries the headline "The Whole World is Confused." It develops that "the only people not confused in the world today are the Elders of Zion. Bernard Baruch is not confused. Felix Frankfurter is not confused. Rabbi Hillel Silver is not confused. . . ."[18] A 1961 issue of *Common Sense* starts its lead article with the words "Who understands the Berlin Problem? Very few of us on the far right."[19] World events, in other words, may appear difficult to understand, *until* the conspiracy premise has provided a unifying solution for them. At this point, everything falls easily into place, the person comes to feel enlightened, and experiences the exhilarating feeling of living in a coherent —if dangerous—world. He experiences the need to share his discovery with friends *in part because he holds himself in possession of a formula which can dispel confusion.*

A related satisfaction is the assumption that the conspiracy formula *is available only to an enlightened elite.* As we have seen, this exclusiveness of the ideology is repeatedly stressed in sectarian literature. Those who write about the Great Conspiracy are "intelligence experts" or persons who have dedicated a great deal of time to the study of their obscure subject. This is necessarily the case because conspiracies are covert, and because they control, censor, and intimidate the public. Thus persons who have been made aware of the machinations of conspirators have access to a body of information with which they, *and they alone,* can save their ignorant fellows. All but those who share the secret are puppets pulled by invisible strings walking blindly to their destruction. Even if the enlightened, too, are to perish in the holocaust, they at least will not be sacrificed blindly and passively. *It is they who can read between the lines of the handwriting on the wall.*

Persons who hold a conspiracy belief frequently provide evidence of their superior *diagnostic and prognostic skill.* An illustration of sophisticated diagnosis, for instance, is a leaflet handed to audiences at the Bolshoi Ballet during a recent cultural exchange visit. This leaflet originated with a group

[18] *The Key to Freedom* (Union, N. J.: Christian Educational Foundation, undated), p. 4.
[19] *Common Sense* (September 1, 1961), p. 1.

called the "Committee to End the 'Alice-in-Wonderland' Atmosphere in Which Free Americans Unwittingly Finance the Destruction of Their Free Society and Enjoy Themselves While Doing It." The reader is informed that he has subsidized the Russian economy by spending dollars for his tickets, has provided free access to the United States for Russian spies, and has endorsed the premises of Russian propagandists.[20]

Another illustration is a pamphlet distributed to employees of the Michigan Bell Telephone Company. In this pamphlet, company personnel are instructed "how to spot Communists." They are told, for instance, that

> Wherever you find a Communist, you find an advocate of *peace*. "Peace" is one of the golden words of their vocabulary. They have "peace" movements of every kind; they have peace campaigns, peace prizes, peace conferences, peace processions. Every Communist is a devotee of peace.[21]

The person studying the pamphlet is helped to identify the "pseudo-liberal" who acts as a front for the "sympathizer" who in turn represents "fellow travelers" manipulated by the Communist Party.[22] This type of information gives the student of conspiracies an advantage over the naive observer, who would be unable to place liberal causes (such as pacifism) in proper perspective.

The prognostic ability of persons who are familiar with conspiracies permits them to anticipate the progressive victory of conspiratorial forces. A 1962 issue of *Common Sense*, for instance, carried the headline "Will We Win the Cold War?" The answer to this question was

> I DOUBT IT—and this statement is intended to provide in simple and clear language the reasons why we are not winning it.
>
> For sixteen years we have been fighting, and the communist advance is rolling merrily on. Is there at present a ground-swell awakening to a realization of the real peril? Certainly not sufficient unto the cause thereof. In reality the awakening is under the control of the enemy.[23]

General Edwin Walker, in a speech transcribed in another issue of *Common Sense*, was able to point out that the Berlin Airlift

[20] *Congratulations* (Multilith leaflet, no statement of origin, undated).

[21] Michigan Bell Telephone Company, Public Relations Department, Employee Information Section, *How to Spot Communist Traps* (Chicago: Enterprise Publications, undated), p. 4. (Reprinted from F. Schwarz, *You Can Trust the Communists* [Englewood Cliffs, N. J.: Prentice-Hall, 1961]).

[22] *Ibid.*, pp. 10–11.

[23] *Common Sense* (April 15, 1962), p. 1.

was hailed as a victory in the Cold War, but it was actually a defeat, since in taking to the air we submitted to Communist control on the ground. Today, by allowing a wall to be built in Berlin, we have submitted to the Communist division of Germany.[24]

This type of information makes its possessor a member of a brave minority that can view itself as the last hope of civilization:

> The friends of Daniel have refused to bow down to the sound of the king's music.
>   They did not change their position but became conspicuous when everyone else did bow down. They *endured* and they *lived through* the fiery furnace in loyalty to their faith. I would say to you, stand up beside Daniel and be counted.[25]

Only persons cognizant of hidden forces can spot their manifestations and can reverse their cumulative victory. The belief in a conspiracy is therefore an exclusive and self-consciously important frame of reference.

Needless to say, the question still remains: Why should *some* persons be *selectively interested* in *threatening* implications of events? Why should they choose to attend to trends which provide *pessimistic* forecasts? Why should they feel constrained to look for *dangerous* forces and *evil* people in their environment? We shall now try to deal with these questions.

Mechanisms can often be most clearly examined when they operate in extreme form. It may therefore be useful first to trace the birth of conspiracy beliefs in individuals who are diagnosed as mentally disturbed.

The genesis of paranoid reactions

"Paranoid reactions" is a psychiatric label that refers to "cases showing persistent delusions, generally persecutory or grandiose, ordinarily without hallucinations. The emotional responses and behavior are consistent with the ideas held. Intelligence is well preserved."[26]

This definition stresses the fact that delusions of persecution are not completely incapacitating. Although persons suffering from paranoia are *limited* by their delusions, they may otherwise think clearly and function adequately.

It is this that must be kept in mind when one considers Freud's para-

[24] E. A. Walker, "Muzzling the Military," *Common Sense* (February 1, 1962), p. 2.

[25] *Ibid.*, p. 4.

[26] *Diagnostic and Statistical Manual: Mental Disorders* (Washington, D. C.: American Psychiatric Association, 1952), p. 28.

doxical discovery that paranoia is a disease in which the patient has "cured" himself—in other words, that paranoid reactions are not only *problems*, but also *solutions to previous problems*.

Freud documented the assumption that the principal alternative to paranoia is panic. He showed that the paranoid patient perceives danger in the world *mainly to avoid facing unspeakable, undefinable, and unbearable threats originating in his own unconscious.*

This relationship of paranoia to panic is obvious in the developmental sequence which usually precedes the onset of systematic delusions.[27] First, a typical pre-paranoid personality emerges. The *pre-paranoid* person has been described as tense, insecure and fearful. He perceives every social encounter as dangerous, and interprets every action of others as suspect and threatening. As a result, he finds himself constantly in a position where he has to retaliate against intolerable "affront."

This pattern is cumulative. If it runs its course, it leads to a precarious balance *in which the person maintains his integrity and self-esteem only at the expense of others.* He sees himself as pure and perfect, and views himself as infallible. But others, by contrast, are evil, defective, and perpetually in error. These convictions are related to each other. To perceive oneself as pure, one must suppress all evidence to the contrary, including impure feelings and impulses. One way of accomplishing this is to project impurity into the world, where it becomes embodied in others. Moreover, frailty is revealed in social interactions, and can be avoided if others are perpetually at fault.

This kind of strategy becomes progressively more difficult to sustain, especially since it involves constant strain and a perpetual battle to suppress evidence. Typically, the effort collapses in the face of dramatic personal failure. At this juncture, an acute crisis may ensue. It generally takes the form of a *period of terror*, in which the person feels cornered and threatened, and in which he undertakes a frantic *search for the object of his fear*. Everything around him becomes suspect; hidden signs of danger reveal themselves at every turn.

This is the problem that paranoid delusions tend to solve. The person's search eventually culminates with the discovery of "an imaginary organization, composed of real and imagined persons, whom the patient represents as united for the purpose of carrying out some action upon him."

[27] The following description of the pre-paranoid sequence has been abstracted from N. Cameron, "Paranoid Conditions and Paranoia," in S. Arieti, ed., *American Handbook of Psychiatry*, Vol. 1 (New York: Basic Books, 1959), pp. 512–519.

This imaginary conspiracy may vary in content, but it frequently includes minority groups and international political organizations.[28]

The creation of the delusional system is the "restitution" or "cure" referred to by Freud. The patient experiences a sense of profound relief: the transition from a diffuse, unspecifiable danger to a tangible enemy ends his tormented, all-consuming search. He now has a target for his feelings, and thinks that he knows what to do. He can relax, except for his careful vigilance against the forces of evil.

Conspiracies, in other words, may be the *final effort to maintain an unrealistic self-concept, on behalf of which one's own weaknesses, failures, and inadequacies have to be explained away.*

But how does the need for such favorable self-evaluation come about? Again, we must look for the answer in a relatively *extreme* personality type.

The authoritarian personality

Several years ago, a large-scale study of anti-Semitism revealed that persons who are prejudiced against Jews also frequently hold other attitudes in common.

Typically, they are prejudiced against persons other than Jews. They have a strong sense of loyalty to their own kind, whom they hold in high esteem, and they view all other people with suspicion and contempt:

> People are categorized primarily according to the groups to which they belong. . . . The major outgroups in America today appear to be Jews, Negroes, the lower socioeconomic class, labor unions, and political radicals, especially Communists. Other groups whose outgroup status varies somewhat are Catholics, artists and intellectuals; Oklahomans and Japanese (in the West); pacifists, Filipinos, Mexicans, homosexuals. Most other nations,

---

[28] Traditional scapegoats are ideal candidates for membership in imaginary conspiratorial organizations, because of their easy availability and their standard negative evaluation. The mechanism is illustrated in the following comic strip excerpt (from Walt Kelly, *Pogo* [Post Hall Syndicate], April 17, 1954):

Pogo: Ain't you ashamed? You owes *Mole* a apology. *You* packed Pup Dog in by mistake *and* you was sayin' *Mole* was a *kidnapper* . . . wanted him *lynched.*

Albert: But I was lookin' for s'picious critters . . . varmints what could do a *dirty trick* like *that!*

Pogo: But *you* was guilty—an' you blamed him unfair! Enemy or not.

Albert: What dogboned good is a enemy if you can't blame him for stuff like that there?

especially the industrially backward, the socialistic, and those most different from the "Anglo-Saxon," tend to be considered outgroups . . . it would appear that an individual who regards a few of these groups as outgroups will tend to reject most of them.[29]

This type of view can be classified as *ethnocentric*, because it divides the world into an idealized group—to which the person himself belongs—and an immense human garbage pail, comprising other people. Prejudice is one aspect of this basic attitude; another is the exaltation of the "we." Ultimately, of course, the latter becomes an *idealization of the person himself*: "A sample 'map' illustrating the ever-narrowing ingroup would be the following: Whites, Americans, native-born Americans, Christians, Protestants, Californians, my family, and finally—I."[30]

The ingroup provides the person with a standard against which he can measure himself and find himself perfect.[31] The ethnocentric person uses this standard by taking great pains to be conventional, proper, and conforming to the demands of his group. He is *authoritarian*, in the sense that he respects power (with which he complies, feeling this to be no reflection on himself), and he regards every other human attribute as a sign of contemptible weakness. Feelings—especially unconventional feelings—are taboo to him. They must not only never be expressed but must not even be experienced. As in the case of the pre-paranoid patient, feelings must be assigned to the outgroup:

> Thus it is not oneself but others that are seen as hostile or threatening. Or else one's weakness leads to an exaggerated condemnation of everything that is weak; one's weakness is thus fought outside instead of inside. At the same time there is a compensatory—and therefore often compulsive— drive for power, strength, success, and self-determination.[32]

[29] T. W. Adorno, Else Frenkel-Brunswik, D. J. Levinson, and R. N. Sanford, *The Authoritarian Personality* (New York: Harper & Brothers, 1950), p. 147. By permission of the publishers.

[30] From *The Authoritarian Personality* by Adorno, *et al.* (Harper & Brothers, 1950), p. 148.

[31] James Van der Zanden has illustrated the operation of this mechanism among members of the Ku Klux Klan. He cites Klan speeches that include statements such as "our kind of white are elected to rule the world and everything in it," and "Klansmen are the cleanest and most perfect people on earth." He also shows that Klan members seek to enhance their own status by depressing that of the Negro. (J. W. Van der Zanden, "The Klan Revival," *Amer. J. Sociol.*, 65 [March 1960], p. 460.)

[32] From *The Authoritarian Personality* by Adorno, *et al.* (Harper & Brothers, 1950), p. 474.

In other words, it is *others* who have *impulses which emasculate and degrade them.* Since the ethnocentric person is free of such impediments, his qualifications for status and success are obviously superior. The catch lies in the fact that despite his obvious qualifications and ambitions, his deserved success may not materialize. How is this explained by him?

This question furnishes a bridge from the authoritarian outgroup to the paranoid "conspiracy": It is obviously "they" who stand in the way of one's merited advancement. It is "their" machinations that have changed the nature of society to prevent the victory of the best. It is "their" menace that lurks perpetually in the background, qualifying the obvious validity of power.

Authoritarian and pre-paranoid persons, both experience the consequence of two relationships: (1) unrealistic self-evaluations lead to experiences of failure and (2) failures reflect on high self-evaluations. This kind of self-destructive circle requires an escape, which is provided by the opportunity of assigning blame to others.

But where does the need for self-idealization originate? Studies of authoritarian personalities provide insight into an important source. They show that *authoritarian persons frequently come from a type of home that represents a prototype of the authoritarian world:*

> When we consider the childhood situation of the most prejudiced subjects, we find reports of a tendency toward rigid discipline on the part of the parents, with affection which is conditional . . . upon approved behavior on the part of the child. Related to this is a tendency apparent in families of prejudiced subjects to base interrelationships on rather clearly defined roles of dominance and submission, in contradistinction to equalitarian policies. Faithful execution of prescribed roles and the exchange of duties and obligations is, in the families of the prejudiced, often given preference over the exchange of free-flowing affection.[33]

It is in the context of this childhood that the authoritarian discovers the need to suppress impulses, the requirement of perfection, the importance of power and status, and the intolerable character of deviation. This information is acquired with such pain and immediacy that it forms the basis of his subsequent approach to all problems of life.

> Thus a basically hierarchical, authoritarian, exploitive parent-child relationship is apt to . . . culminate in a political philosophy and social outlook which has no room for anything but a desperate clinging to what appears

[33] From *The Authoritarian Personality* by Adorno, *et al.* (Harper & Brothers, 1950), p. 482.

to be strong and a disdainful rejection of whatever is relegated to the bottom.[34]

Less extreme early experiences (such as those offered in many middle-class homes) are responsible for less severe forms of the same basic pattern. *With varying degrees of self-righteousness and inflexibility, persons bred by conventionality and status-consciousness see society as a neatly ordered hierarchy, in which they and their ingroup occupy a select place. To the extent to which this preferential position is endangered, there is a presumption of foul play.*

Endangering may take many forms, from economic dislocation and political or military setbacks to the questioning of one's values. The following brief review of a recent episode in American history shows several of these factors at work.

The authoritarian episode

The social movement that the cartoonist Herblock labeled "McCarthyism" began in February of 1950. It was during this month that United States Senator Joseph McCarthy made two speeches denouncing "card-carrying Communists" in the State Department.

A subcommittee appointed by the Senate (the Tydings Committee) questioned McCarthy's charges, but many members of the general public believed him. Almost from the start, the Senator evoked a sympathetic response among "patriotic" organizations. McCarthy Clubs soon sprang up all over the country.[35]

After firing his opening blasts, Senator McCarthy mounted a bitter assault on "New Deal" officials, whom he depicted as heading a conspiratorial network intent on destroying the United States. He charged that Secretary of State Acheson, with the help of Professor Owen Lattimore, planned the Communist takeover of China. There was a "plan conceived by Mr. Acheson's architects to deliver vast areas and millions of people into Communist slavery."[36] When the Korean War broke out, McCarthy revealed that "American boys are dying in Korea because a group of untouchables in the State Department sabotaged the aid program that Congress had voted for Korea."[37]

[34] From *The Authoritarian Personality* by Adorno, *et al.* (Harper & Brothers, 1950), p. 971.

[35] J. P. Chaplin, *Rumor, Fear, and the Madness of Crowds* (New York: Ballantine, 1959), p. 149.

[36] *The New York Times* (May 16, 1950).

[37] *The New York Times* (July 2, 1950).

He accused President Truman and Secretary Acheson of having created "death traps" by "sabotaging rearming."[38] In a typical attack on the State Department, McCarthy demanded that the President "fire the pied pipers of the politburo, fire the headmaster who betrays us in Asia, fire the collectors of corruption, those prancing mimics of the Moscow party-line in the State Department."[39]

The Senator's approach proved politically profitable. In the 1952 elections, he was returned to his seat by a considerable margin, and acquired the chairmanship of the Senate Permanent Investigations Committee. Armed with this new weapon, McCarthy initiated a campaign which permeated every segment of American life. He not only personally destroyed individuals and organizations but inspired others to suspect, to investigate, and to black-list. Witch-hunting committees of all kinds sprang up, and public and private enterprises began to examine the loyalty of their personnel.[40]

In addition, distrust, suspicion, and panic permeated all social interactions, and few Americans ventured to openly question the premise of domestic Communist subversion.

Finally, in 1954, a televised battle between McCarthy and the U. S. Army exposed the Senator's tactics at their worst. The spectacle disillusioned most of McCarthy's moderate followers, and left him politically isolated. In a relatively short time, the internal Communist conspiracy began to recede as an object of concern (except for political extremists).

Precipitating events

Can the McCarthy episode be blamed on psychological defeats or failures? Did events take place at this time *that Americans could interpret as reflections on their integrity and status?* The answer to this question is clearly affirmative.

A few years prior to McCarthy, World War II had ended, but the Cold War had immediately begun. This in-between state was punctuated with several setbacks, including Communist victories in China and Czechoslovakia. It became increasingly obvious that "we had spent billions in war and foreign aid, but Communism, nonetheless, was picking up all the marbles."[41]

---

[38] *The New York Times* (August 3, 1950).
[39] *The New York Times* (June 6, 1950).
[40] R. Rovere, "McCarthyism in Retrospect," *New Republic* (May 18, 1959), p. 14.
[41] N. A. Kenny, "Senator McCarthy, a Summing Up," *Catholic World* (September 1957), p. 445.

A major trauma occurred when the U.S.S.R. exploded its first atom bomb, several years earlier than the experts had predicted. To add insult to this injury, the espionage trials of Hiss, Gouzenko, and the Rosenbergs raised the suspicion that American atomic secrets had contributed to the Russian feat.

The Korean Police Action proved to be a culminating blow for persons frustrated by the "years of shock."[42] Initially, this military confrontation raised high hopes and enthusiastic expectations. At last—the feeling ran— Communism will be decisively (though belatedly) defeated. Now that the Administration had decided to act, American superiority would be clearly obvious. President Truman was rewarded for his Korean decision with unprecedented esteem.[43]

There followed a succession of defeats, and finally the stalemate produced by Chinese intervention. Public opinion reacted incredulously and with bitterness. What had begun as a confident test of our undisputable superiority ended as yet another Communist gain.

Into this predisposing situation emerged Senator Joseph McCarthy and his Communist Conspiracy. McCarthy's "stab in the back" formula dealt directly with the events of the preceding half decade, and provided an explanation for them which was not only *coherent* and *face-saving,* but also an obvious *depository for accumulated feelings.* The Senator's image of Secretary Acheson, for instance, was of a deliberate, treacherous fiend, who imposed on a simple, trusting public. Implicitly, the purity of our motives made the internal Communist danger possible.

McCarthyism became a symbol of American *resolution* and *strength.* Many of the Senator's followers stressed his militancy and forcefulness. Many admired him as a fighter without "kid gloves" in an arena in which frustrating inaction had been the rule.[44] McCarthy was visibly doing something to combat danger to American status.

The need to redeem the image of the ingroup was not equally distributed in all segments of the American public. One group that was overrepresented among McCarthy followers was that of *small-business men.* These men had been gradually displaced from their role in the American economy. Materially, they encountered increasing difficulty in making ends meet. Ideologically, their nineteenth-century conservatism, with its empha-

---

[42] This term is used in E. F. Goldman, *The Crucial Decade* (New York: Knopf, 1956), p. vii.

[43] J. M. Fenton, *In Your Opinion* (Boston: Little, Brown, 1960), p. 89.

[44] *Ibid.,* p. 136.

sis on individualism, had become an anachronism in an age of bigness and complexity.[45] McCarthy's philosophy had the advantage for them of being supremely *simple*. More important, the Senator's references to evil forces in government enabled them to explain their own fate. For them, the "Communist menace" was transmuted into the menace of *cosmopolitanism, bureaucratization and collectivism*—all rolled into one.[46] McCarthy gave them the hope that his purge of Communists could turn back the clock of twentieth-century industrialization.[47]

Another group of Americans over-represented among McCarthy's followers were Catholics. This is easily explained through McCarthy's own Catholicism. Whereas for other Americans, McCarthy merely shared the ingroup of Americanism, Catholics had an enhanced opportunity of identifying with the Senator. They could thus more directly build their own status at the expense of McCarthy's Communist enemies.

The transactional basis of conspiracies

Clearly, conspiracy beliefs are prevalent among groups of people with a special kind of problem. Such beliefs tend to come into being at the intersection of self-regard and defeat: the urgency of the need to preserve one's self-image must be combined with the bitterness of experienced failure. In the case of Nazi Germany, for instance, traditional Germanic family structure and the aftermath of World War I converged to create the myth of the Jewish betrayal at Versailles. Among American fascists, authoritarian personalities in a marginal social position reacted to post–World War II problems by attributing them to the Jewish-Communist conspiracy. The internal Communist menace of the average McCarthyite was a *milder product of less extreme transactions of the same kind.*

The personal reactions of marginal men are converted into social movements when these men face shared frustrations with jointly elaborated conspiracy beliefs. Few types of social movements are as closely knit and interdependent as those of conspiracy advocates. It may be of interest to briefly illustrate the mechanics of this interdependence:

[45] M. Trow, "Small Businessmen, Political Tolerance and McCarthy," *Amer. J. Sociol.*, 44 (November 1958), pp. 270–281.

[46] *Ibid.*, pp. 276–277; McCarthy's anti-Communism carried similar connotations to many of his rural supporters in the Midwest.

[47] It is not altogether irrelevant to add that small-business men may possibly come in disproportionate numbers from somewhat authoritarian homes. At least, it would not be surprising to find that for lower-middle-class parents status constitutes a relatively cherished value.

Operation Water Moccasin

In early 1963 the American Army staged an exercise in counter-guerrilla warfare near Claxton, Georgia. This maneuver, which was called "Operation Water Moccasin III," was witnessed by military observers from Canada, Formosa, France, England, Guatemala, Indonesia, Iran, Italy, Japan, South Korea, Liberia, Pakistan, the Philippines, Spain, Thailand, Turkey, and South Vietnam. Altogether, 124 foreign observers attended, as the Army's guests.

A few weeks after the beginning of the exercise, the Claxton *Enterprise* published an editorial complaining that "Our office has received numerous letters . . . all expressing a grave dread over the operation."

The *Enterprise* reported that

> One Congressman went so far as to suggest that the United States was training "barefooted Africans as guerilla warriors," to be used to subjugate other African nations.
>
> Another had it figured that the United States was sending in foreign troops to be trained to overthrow our government. Another decided we were being trained on how to surrender our cities to insurgents.
>
> Still another imagined all of this area being "invaded by hordes of Mongolians" who were overrunning the entire area.[48]

On May 2 Senator Thomas H. Kuchel of California read to the Senate some of the mail he had received on the subject of Operation Water Moccasin.[49] One of the Senator's constituents had written: "The news has just broken, although there had been rumors for a week or more, that Georgia is the place for 16,000 African soldiers, being trained by the U. N. for guerrilla warfare. Complete with nose and ear rings. This time, the U. N., and our State Department, have gone too far."

Another correspondent inquired, "It is unconstitutional to quarter American troops in American homes, so how come these pagan, ruthless, brutal, Godless savages?"

A third dealt with the same allegation, and added, "I also understand there are Oriental troops in Mexico at this moment waiting to 'occupy' parts of California for their training."

A recurrent theme in Senator Kuchel's mail was the danger that American sovereignty had been sacrificed to the United Nations. For many

---

[48] T. H. Kuchel, "The Fright Peddlers," *Congressional Record*, 88th Congress, First Session (May 2, 1963), reprint, p. 2.

[49] *Ibid.*, pp. 2–5.

persons, it seemed, Operation Water Moccasin involved a U. N. Army of Occupation:

> These so-called war games are in reality a deceitful way of bringing in the troops that will be used to enforce United Nations law on U. S. citizens. What are you doing about this? Let's get out of the godless United Nations and kick it out of the United States of America.

Two of Senator Kuchel's correspondents cited as their authority an official of the John Birch Society who had recently completed a speaking engagement in California. Others enclosed a leaflet entitled *The United States Has No Army, No Navy, No Air Force*. This publication (originating with a group of Methodist laymen in Texas) claimed that American armed forces had been placed under the command of a Russian officer in the United Nations. Senator Kuchel reported that "I have received so far more than 2,000 letters demanding abolition of the U. S. Arms Control Agency on the grounds cited in the leaflet. Indeed, several hundred constituents have sent to me this leaflet or variations of it."

When the Senator wrote to some of his correspondents, he received "more leaflets in return, even wilder than the first batch. Plus, new or renewed accusations as to what is prompting my answers."

This second set of publications again stressed the danger of U. N. control of the U. S. They featured "that Russian colonel again, ever ubiquitous in 'running the U. N.'s military operations' and getting ready to take over our Armed Forces, plus our jobs, our homes and our very selves."

Senator Kuchel traced the Plot of the U. N. Russian Colonel to a tract published in the early 1950's by a California group (the Cinema Educational Guild) that is both virulently anti-Semitic and anti–United Nations. The details of the conspiracy had been adapted and disseminated by a variety of right-wing organizations. The same situation prevailed with respect to Operation Water Moccasin. *Common Sense*, for instance, had published the following article on February 15, 1963:

Where There's Smoke

> There are strong rumors that the American government is "leasing" on behalf of the United Nations, some million and a half acres of land in Georgia, comprising some nine counties, to be a military installation with a U. N. force in command. This military post will be installed for the purpose of Counter-Insurgency in the South.

Disarmament   Occupation
Then What? ? ?

If you have any information on this diabolical plan, please communicate with us.[50]

This notice dramatizes the function that conspiracy-oriented publications serve for their readers. Whereas the average "consumer" of conspiracies suffers from a condition analogous to the pre-paranoid state—anxiety, foreboding, a sense of danger, and a deep suspicion of foul play—he is usually unable to supply the documentation and logic for a full-blooded Plot. *His membership affiliations represent a source of ready-made conspiracies complete with authoritative references and eye-witness reports.* These conspiracies are tangible, but are also sufficiently comprehensive to permit selective emphasis. The same movement can satisfy persons primarily concerned about taxation and individuals involved in the fight against fluoridation; it can accommodate rabid anti-integrationists and anti-Semites. The only concession demanded of every believer is endorsement of the premise that his favorite enemy forms part of the more comprehensive conspiracy.

The authors and publishers of conspiracy schemes—the leaders of conspiracy-oriented movements—get confirmation of their views through the support they receive from "conspiracy consumers." They are also provided with a communication network, and with raw material in the form of rumors, suspicions, and other grist for their conspiracy mills.

This division of conspiracy-oriented movements into leaders and followers, or "conspiracy producers" and "conspiracy consumers," becomes obvious whenever a conspiracy-centered movement embarks on an active campaign. We shall briefly illustrate this process, and then turn to our concluding discussion.

The authoritarian campaign

Robert Edward Edmondson was one of the leaders of the American ultra-right. Although most of his writings centered around the assumption that fluoridation of water was a Communist plot, he was also active in promoting belief in a Jewish-led general conspiracy.

After Edmondson died, in April 1959, his home-town newspaper, the Bend (Oregon) *Bulletin*, published an editorial venturing the suggestion that "Edmondson was one of the last of a dying breed." Six days after this

[50] *Common Sense* (February 16, 1963), p. 4.

editorial, the *Bulletin* received the first letter in a campaign which continued over the next eight weeks.[51]

The first portion of this campaign consisted of personal messages, most of them full of sharp invective. Criticisms of the editor were generally interspersed with discussions of various aspects of the Jewish-Communist conspiracy. The *Bulletin* reproduced six of these letters, and then published an editorial entitled "This is the Shutoff":

> Effective today, the Bulletin has ceased to publish further letters on the life and times of the late Robert Edward Edmondson. It has become apparent that the letters are an organized campaign, carried on by some of the late Mr. Edmundson's friends in some of his "causes." Particularly, it is noted, the letters come mostly from the anti-Semites, who were for Hitler when Hitler was massacring the Jews, who see in international Communism only a Jewish plot to make slaves of the rest of us.
>
> We don't like Communism either.
>
> But we fail to find in it a plot by members of the Jewish faith to gain power over the rest of the world.
>
> And we can find no recognized authority on Communism who disagrees with us. Ordinarily the *Bulletin* publishes all letters to the editor received. Since the current batch is merely repetitious of a thoroughly discredited theory, we feel further publication of them will serve no useful purpose.[52]

Several of the correspondents who were being "shut off" had been well-known leaders in extreme right-wing organizations. One letter, for instance, had been written by the female author of monographs such as *Alien Minorities and Mongrelization*. Another letter came from a retired general who had bombarded periodicals with anti-Semitic proclamations. A third letter was from the publisher of a weekly newspaper which had viewed American entry into World War II as a Jewish-inspired plot.

At almost precisely the time the *Bulletin's* "shutoff" editorial appeared, the April first issue of *Common Sense* arrived in the hands of its subscribers. This issue prominently featured two of the letters that had been written to the Bend *Bulletin*. It also reprinted an article by Edmondson on the Jewish origin of the Supreme Court desegregation decision.

For the next three weeks, the Bend *Bulletin* was flooded with mail. This mail, however, included few letters. It consisted mainly of leaflets, pamphlets, flyers, reprints, bulletins, tracts, clippings, and copies of news-

[51] For an extended analysis of this mail campaign, see H. Toch, S. E. Deutsch, and D. M. Wilkins, "The Wrath of the Bigot: An Analysis of Protest Mail," *Journalism Quarterly* (Spring 1960), pp. 173–185, 266.

[52] Bend (Oregon) *Bulletin* (May 12, 1959).

papers. Most of this material dealt with one or more aspects of the Conspiracy, such as integration, Communism, the Jews, taxation, fluoridation, the New Deal, the United Nations, foreign aid, and summit meetings. Combinations varied from Jewish-Communistic ("Communism fits the Jewish character") to Jewish-Negro ("They are pushing the nigger organization, the NAACP") and Communist-Negro ("the Communist Conspiracy . . . mongrelizing the American White Race.")[53]

There is little doubt that this flood of literature was set off by the open letters in *Common Sense*. Of the few persons who wrote their own messages, several referred to their predecessors or to *Common Sense*; two even enclosed copies of the paper.

The mail campaign thus consisted of two distinct but related stages. In the first phase, the leaders of extremist movements publicized the fact that the editor of the Bend *Bulletin* had revealed himself as a "dupe" of the Conspiracy. They wrote to the "renegade" editor, exposed the implications of his position, and expressed their contempt for him. Once this had been done, members of the rank and file *certified that they had incorporated the new enemy into their catalogue*. They also expressed their hatred, but they did this by simply transmitting copies of literature from their files. In other words, *they adopted a prediagnosed threat, and countered it with "canned" messages*. Their own role was limited to that of endorsement and promotion. The implication of their attack was something like this:

> You have been named by reliable authorities as a person who is a danger to people like myself, and whom I have to fear and hate. The enclosed exposure of your cause will demonstrate to you that we know how dangerous you are. This material is so carefully prepared, thoughtfully composed, and aptly expressed that I couldn't say it better myself.

The economy of this strategy is obvious. The conspiracy "consumer," who is filled with fear and suspicion, casts about for indications of causality and responsibility. He is supplied with these in usable form. In turn, the conspiracy "producer" becomes an acknowledged expert in the enterprise of locating and classifying hidden dangers. He benefits from the conspiracy consumer's sharing his discoveries, partly because this enhances his role as an expert, and partly because it furnishes him with manpower for his campaign. Consumers and producers thus serve each other's needs. Their joint activities—which consist of circulating the same material over and over—increase their ability to convince each other. Like the Mongolian strategy of

[53] Toch *et al.*, "The Wrath of the Bigot."

charging from several directions with a maximum of noise, the outcome is an illusion which may not fool the enemy, but does raise the morale of attacking troops.

The ingredients of conspiracy

The function of a conspiracy-oriented movement is not to do battle with conspiratorial forces, but to provide reassurance and security to its own members. At first glance, this statement implies a contradiction in terms. Conspiracies, after all, are concentrated manifestations of evil. The view espoused by the ultra-right, as we have seen, presupposes that all our institutions are controlled by destructive agents. On the face of it, this kind of conception seems far from reassuring, especially since no hope of relief is provided. The writers we have quoted see themselves completely enveloped by the enemy, and they propose no real counter-measures. Except for far-fetched contingencies and calls to arms, their positive suggestions are limited to keeping informed and spreading the word.

This injunction only enhances the voice of doom, because it ensures maximum circulation for conspiracy exposés. Sensational revelations can be relished and passed on, like marbles, jokes, recipes, and choice pieces of pornography.

Why should an individual wish to dispose of a cast of potent friends, with which he can people the world? What use can he make of plots directed against himself and his kind? What is there to be gained from the assumption that the cards are hopelessly stacked against him?

It is relevant, of course, that the Conspiracy Premise does have intrinsic advantages. It is simple and coherent in form, and it offers an exclusive view of a trend that calls for no taxing response. The conspiracy-believer can become a sophisticated spectator to the destruction of a senseless world, and of the dupes who inhabit it.

But even this would have to be *selectively* appealing. A person engaged in efforts to remedy social deficiencies, for instance, would not be able to afford the passivity and pessimism of this view; people seeing peace and prosperity around them would find no data needing explanation. *And even the dissatisfied individual in a complex world might prefer the discomfort of his condition to the inevitability of craftily engineered doom.*

Conspiracy beliefs respond to a real need *only* for persons *who cannot preserve their self-esteem unless they conceive of themselves as victims of a plot.* If no conspiracy were available to them, such persons would have to re-examine their assumptions with the foreknowledge that these were invalid. They would have to re-evaluate their own worth in the face of accumulating evidence of impotence. In the extreme case of the psychiatric patient and the authoritarian bigot, the risk consists in facing aspects of oneself that one cannot tolerate; in the person of the McCarthyite, the main danger is that of recognizing that the world has passed one by. In both instances, efforts to rationalize failures have reached a point of diminishing returns. Neither primitive conservatism and vested simplicity, nor self-assigned purity and a dichotomous view of people can be preserved in a complex and progressing world. These types of conceptions can survive only if the real world can be explained away.

In other words, *conspiracies are amendments to untenable schemes, which salvage them in the face of clashes with reality.* The frantic effort of conspiracy-oriented movements is the final rallying cry of overextended anachronisms.

4 ▷ GAIN THROUGH COMMUNITY

SOCIAL movements are always *collective* efforts to solve problems, but sometimes the collective aspect seems to be almost irrelevant. In other instances, it appears to be crucial. The present chapter will provide one or two illustrations of social movements in which community of membership is the *chief means* to the movement's goals. In these movements, each member solves his problems with the help of others; in turn, he forms part of the solution to the problems of other members. Although this process occurs in various kinds of movements, we shall illustrate it with social movements that aim at producing changes within their members, rather than directly in society at large. In other words, we shall deal with movements which collectively promote individual change.

The collective solution of personal problems presupposes that the person has a problem that can be fruitfully shared with others. The individual may realize that his difficulties are unique, but he must also feel that they are sufficiently similar to the concerns of others to be jointly attacked. He must further be convinced that the "collectivization" of his problem would be fruitful. This conviction is usually late in coming. We shall see that collective solutions of private problems tend to be resorted to when other solutions fail. Routinely, people come to a social movement for help when they conclude that individual corrective efforts are inadequate to the task.

Serious games

Our first illustration is one which to an outsider may appear trivial, but which for the persons involved may have excruciatingly tragic implications. The problem is that of chronic obesity. This condition not only impairs a person's physical well-being and his appearance, but also tends to throw a dark shadow on his relationship to other people. This is the case because—in our culture—overweight persons are often viewed as sloppy, irresponsible, and ungainly. Worse, to some extent the fat person may subscribe to this evaluation of himself.

There are several organizations composed of corpulent individuals who try to help each other lose weight. One of these groups is Fatties Anonymous, which is patterned after Alcoholics Anonymous. Somewhat more original in method is TOPS, a flourishing social movement with headquarters in Milwaukee.

TOPS (Taking Off Pounds Sensibly) was founded in 1948 by a stout woman and her sympathetic physician. In 1958, TOPS included 800 groups with a total of 15,000 members. By early 1964, membership increased to 71,566 persons distributed among 2,874 chapters located throughout the United States (as well as in Canada, South Africa, and Japan). Chapters vary in size from 4 to 150, with the average group comprising 30 men or women. There are also alumni groups called "KOPS" (Keeping Off Pounds Sensibly), which are designed to prevent relapses.[1]

TOPS was founded on the principle that "The desire to lose weight could be encouraged into the will to lose it by the simple psychology of competitive play."[2] In contrast to most self-help groups, TOPS is deliberately light-hearted. Chapter names often reflect a playful spirit:

> Cheerful Cherubs
> Blubber Busters
> Melting Pots
> Happy Losers
> Diligent Dieters
> Adipose Chasers
> Snack Snubbers

[1] For recent membership figures and other information, I am indebted to Rae L. Getter, editor of *The* TOPS *News* (personal communication).

[2] "Tops, Born in Wisconsin, Depends on MD Guidance and Counsel," *The Medical Forum Magazine of the Wisconsin Medical Society* (January 1958), p. 79.

Pound Peelers
Pounds Aweigh
Waistaways
Alter-Ego
Cal Cutters
Don't-B-Eatnicks

Weekly sessions are held in a variety of locations, ranging from homes to meeting halls. At the beginning of the agenda, each member must be weighed by an official Weight Recorder. Weights are recorded on Weight Charts, and losses or gains for the week are computed. Members weighing less than they did at the previous meeting are designated "TOPS," and are decorated with a cardboard heart specifying the amount of weight lost. Members whose weight has remained constant are labeled "Turtles." Members whose weight has increased become "Pigs" and have to wear a pig-shaped label or a bib.

The ceremonial is conducted by the chapter Leader, the Weight Recorder, the Crying Towel Bearer, and the Piggy Bank Bearer. At the start of proceedings, the following dialogue ensues:

> *Leader*: Who pounds at our door?
> *Recorder*: Not who pounds. What pounds?
> *All*: Surplus Pounds!
> *Leader*: Pounds Off!

There follows a procession, in the course of which members join hands and sing the following pledge:

> The more we get together
> Together, together—
> The more we get together,
> The slimmer we'll be.
> For your loss is my loss;
> And my loss is your loss;
> The more we get together
> The slimmer we'll be.

Names and weight statistics are then read off. Turtles are required to shed a symbolic tear for the Crying Towel Bearer. Pigs must deposit fines into the Piggy Bank, but are encouraged by the Piggy Bank Bearer with the words "They'll all do better, so don't you fret." Meetings culminate with the crowning of the Queen (King, Princess, etc.) who has lost most weight.[3]

[3] E. Manz, *How to Take Off Pounds Sensibly* (Milwaukee: TOPS, 1955).

TOPS members frequently take time to discuss possible reasons for weight gains and losses. In this manner, individual experiences can be pooled for everyone's benefit. Other procedures may vary from one chapter to another. For instance, some chapters make it a practice for each person to have a "secret pal," to lend her encouragement and support between meetings. Other chapters may provide a "pig plate," which the most delinquent member must use at home. Inter-club activities (such as "lo-cal" luncheons) are also common.

The high point of the year is the three-day national convention, which takes place in the spring. At this meeting, members have the opportunity to discuss and to plan weight reduction methods. The convention reaches its climax with the selection of a TOPS Queen and her royal family. The candidates are the chapter Queens (Kings, etc.), for whom an annual weight loss of 100 pounds is not unusual.[4] Royalty is also selected at the state level. The "good loser" can be rewarded in more than one formal competition and in one of eight categories, ranging from children under 13 to adults weighing 400 pounds and over.

Competition is clearly one of the main tools used to help TOPS members lose weight. But competition is a two-edged weapon, which can create terrible unhappiness and can kill motivation. This possibility is precluded in TOPS by combining competition with (1) group supports, and (2) playfulness.

Rewards are sufficiently real to serve as incentives, but their symbolic or make-believe quality makes it possible to face failure with good humor. Inadequate weight loss leads to a mock reprimand and a not very serious stigma. Misfortune is further neutralized by being combined with the assurance of hope, the encouragement of interested friends, and a shared realization of the difficult nature of the enterprise. Moreover, the task is not prohibitive. It is not only physically impossible to be a perpetual pig, but an occasional weekly crown is a manageable attainment.

The playful aspect of TOPS removes the drabness and grimness of last-ditch battles against well-established habits; it also makes meetings attractively relaxing and non-threatening. Further, it converts relatively rigid adults into comparatively malleable children.[5] The crux of the "game" is

---

[4] *The TOPS News*, April 1963, cover. In 1963, 29 TOPS members were listed as having recorded a loss of over 100 pounds.

[5] It has been shown in other contexts that the promotion of regression in adults increases their susceptibility to change. The effectiveness of this method—in its extreme form—may be seen among inmates of concentration camps.

that it enables participants to accomplish ends which they cannot otherwise attain.

But the feature of TOPS that clearly makes it a social movement is not the use of props. It is the reciprocity of relationship among members. It is the sentiment expressed in the lines

> For your loss is my loss
> And my loss is your loss.

With this feeling of shared responsibility, each member's problem becomes a group objective; in turn, each person comes to feel that his efforts contribute to the attainment of a common goal. One's own individual loss of weight thus becomes a side product, which the member cheerfully "plows back" into the total enterprise. His victory gains meaning from the incentive it provides for others, and from the validity which it adds to the game.

The mutuality of support

One of many social movements that contrast with the cheerful competition of TOPS is a tense enterprise known as "Recovery, Incorporated." Recovery is composed of self-styled "nervous" people—most of whom have been diagnosed as emotionally disturbed, and many of whom have been patients in mental institutions. The typical Recovery member views himself as handicapped by some combination of *symptoms,* which may include

> . . . dizziness, heart palpitations, tremors, feelings of unreality, nausea, diarrhea, constipation, sweats, throat "locking," sleeplessness, fatigue, headache, miscellaneous aches and pains. Particularly distressing to the nervous patient are his panics and depressions, fear of harming himself and others, fear of physical collapse or of losing his mind, fear of being alone or of being with people, fear of the sustained handicap.[6]

The purpose of Recovery is to help its members alleviate their symptoms so that they can lead comparatively normal lives. Recovery does not offer to cure mental disorders, nor does it promise happiness, prosperity, or well-being. It does offer *relief,* however, and does promise that hitherto incapacitated persons can be kept afloat through the adversities of life. Given the fact that Recovery is composed of self-tortured people—many of whom have regularly commuted in and out of hospitals—it is obvious why these offerings should suffice as incentives to membership.

The problems of Recovery members may be of subjective origin, but

[6] *Recovery, Inc.* (Chicago: Recovery, 1958), pp. 9–10.

they are also real. A prospective member, for instance, may feel unable to leave his home alone, or he may expect to die at any moment, or he may react to every frustration with unbearable physical pain. A case history in a magazine article is fairly typical of the problems brought to the movement:

> Abigail used to have an obsession about dirt, and a compulsion to wash her hands. At the peak of her illness she might wash as long as two hours and consume up to four bars of soap. She refers to this as her "Lady Macbeth Period." . . . She was hospitalized three times, and finally underwent a delicate brain operation. . . . Upon coming out of the anesthetic, she immediately demanded a bar of soap.[7]

When this member arrived at her first Recovery meeting, she sported hands "swollen to twice their normal size." She had become socially isolated, and she could not work. After several months of membership, she began to be able to "stay away from soap." With time, she reduced her washing to normal limits. She returned to work, and began to lead an active social life. By conquering her symptom, she had achieved the objective of *"averageness"* stressed in Recovery literature.

Recovery was founded in 1937 by Dr. Abraham Low, a Viennese neurologist and psychiatrist who had come to Chicago in 1922. At its inception, the purpose of Recovery was to enable Low's patients to effect the transition from formal therapy to the community. In 1952, Low authorized the group to expand into a national organization. Ten years later, over two thousand persons attended weekly meetings in the state of Michigan alone.[8]

Although Low died in 1954, Recovery, Inc., continued to follow his specifications closely. The phraseology used in Recovery meetings was originated by Low, and the procedure never deviates from the steps prescribed by him. The extent of Low's authority in the movement is symbolized by the weight attached to his concept of *sabotage* ("a statement casting doubt on the validity of the physician's diagnosis and authority").[9] In practice, sabotage includes any deviation from Low's prescriptions.

In order to avoid sabotage, the Recovery member must apply Dr. Low's "Will Training" literally. Will Training is based on the assumption that symptoms can be eliminated through the exercise of will power. The

---

[7] R. S. Larson, "People in Search of Sanity," *Catholic Digest* (November 1959), p. 62.

[8] Lansing (Michigan) *State Journal* (October 28, 1962).

[9] A. A. Low, *Mental Health Through Will Training* (Boston: Christopher, 1950), p. 24.

patient is taught to "*spot*" symptoms—which means that he must focus his attention on them and reduce them to size. According to Dr. Low, "You can throw off any nervous symptoms at any time if you spot them as distressing but not dangerous. The symptom will return, but in the end you will bring it under control."[10]

The patient is helped in his task by being provided with a vocabulary that enables him to perceive symptoms as subjective products. For instance, a patient may "spot" the onset of "angry temper," implying "I *persuade myself* that a person has done me a wrong." Or he may "spot" an attack of "fearful temper," which would mean, "I *am afraid* that I have sinned, I *feel* that I am wrong."[11] The patient is also taught to avoid the temptation of "working himself up" and to "command his muscles" to eliminate the symptom. In the event of success, he is expected to "endorse" himself for applying Dr. Low's scheme.

During regular Recovery meetings, patients relate instances of recent victories over their symptoms. These "examples" end with descriptions of how the member would have reacted in comparable situations before coming to Recovery. At the conclusion of each "example," other members "endorse" the narrator for his success. A typical "example," delivered at a public panel, is the following:

> My husband and I are to visit my father at Easter time. My husband thought it would be a good idea for me to get a new dress and a new hat for the occasion. I agreed. So I went, alone, to a department store to make my selections. I had a severe lack of spontaneity; difficulty in concentrating; preoccupation; a sense of fatigue. I felt depressed and I felt like procrastinating. However, I spotted that I was fearful of shopping, alone, because of the discomfort of my symptoms. I commanded my muscles to walk into the ladies' ready to wear department. I picked out a dress that I thought looked nice on me. I endorsed myself for making this effort. But I was still quite tense—with a strong impulse to procrastinate—when it came to buying the hat. I then made a decision. I told myself that I will absolutely make an all out effort to get myself a hat. After making this firm decision I immediately began to relax, even before I started to look at this year's Easter bonnets. I did purchase a hat, again endorsing myself for my efforts. My husband, by the way, likes both the hat and the dress on me very much.
>
> Before Recovery I would not walk into a store, alone, to buy anything. My husband would have had to go with me. Now, with Recovery training,

10 *Ibid.*, p. 135.
11 *Ibid.*, p. 22 (italics added).

I am proud of the fact that I can depend on my own *self* management.[12]

Recovery publications frequently list "examples" that are regarded as models of the application of Low's method. A typical illustration reads:

> The other morning I was shaving and suddenly I realized that I was looking at the lower portion of my face and for some reason I was afraid to raise my eyes to look into the mirror directly into my own eyes. This may sound ridiculous but there was a great deal of fear in my mind at the thought of raising my vision. I began to feel very tense, had a fullness in my stomach and at that moment I really felt hopeless.
>
> I continued to shave and then I remembered that Recovery says to "do the thing you fear to do." This was such a hard thing for me to accept just then, but I knew that I had to look myself in the eyes. I am a grown man, tall and of pretty husky build, but I can tell you that it took a lot of courage to do this simple thing. As soon as I had faced the fear with my muscles and gazed into my own eyes in the mirror, the idea came to me, "this is silly." I started to laugh at myself. I thought, "This is an example I would never want to give on a panel." Then I spotted that regardless of what other people would think, I knew just how much effort had gone into this practice for me and I endorsed myself and felt quite proud of my accomplishment.
>
> Before Recovery training, I used to look at myself in the mirror and ridicule each feature until I couldn't stand the sight of my own face. I had the obsession that no one accepted me, and preoccupation and depression were my worst symptoms. I spent two periods in a mental hospital for a total of fifteen months. I still do not have the conviction that I am a desirable person, but I think I am gaining more sense of Averageness through my Recovery Training.[13]

Members of every Recovery group meet once a week (although any person may attend the meetings of several groups). Occasionally, sessions open with the playing of one of Low's recordings, but more usually the meetings start with everyone reading aloud from *Mental Health Through Will Training*. Each member is supposed to read one paragraph, and refusals are interpreted as "sabotage." Reading aloud tends to be unpleasant for the members, despite the fact that they have done it before, know the book by heart, and are familiar with each other. Reading is followed by the discussion of "examples." The discussion may consist of criticism, if the narrator

---

[12] *The Recovery Reporter*, (March–April 1959), p. 3. By permission of Recovery, Inc.

[13] Brighton (Michigan) *Michigan Messenger*, Vol. 1, No. 6, undated, p. 2.

reports failure. In all other instances, examples evoke endorsements, and these are frequently elaborated.

Recovery meetings are conducted by group leaders, who are "nervous patients" themselves. Leaders are presumed to have achieved "averageness," and they do not regard themselves as "cured."

Despite the standardized fashion in which meetings are conducted, the key to the success of the movement lies in these groups. Here, participants derive a variety of benefits from each other. A Jesuit priest who belongs to Recovery lists these gains as follows:

A new Recovery member learns that he is not the sickest person in the world, as he thought he was. Secondly, he learns that what others have done, he can do also in solving his nervous problems; he learns specific ways for handling problems of his own that are similar to the ones described in the meeting. He respects a certain authority in those who have experienced what he has experienced; for this reason he will take advice and even reprimands from a fellow patient which he is not yet disposed to take from his own doctor. He gets relief from aerating and ventilating his symptoms. He leaves the Recovery meeting with more confidence in himself to cope with his symptoms, and he gets a morale boost that will last him through the week.[14]

The process is a reciprocal one. Each member helps others to control their symptoms while they reinforce his efforts to cope with his own. One of the songs popular at Recovery parties (sung to the tune of "Alexander's Rag Time Band") contains a stanza that reads:

> I'm glad we met
> I won't forget
> That you helped me to get well
> And if it's true
> I helped you too
> Then for both of us it's swell.[15]

Members contribute to the group, first, by helping to *define its problem*. The repeated listings of similar symptoms (in sterotyped language) dispels the feeling that each member's troubles are unique to himself. Instead, the feeling grows that the group has *shared* problems, which are susceptible to a *joint* solution. Members also remind each other of the *reality*

[14] M. L. Duggan, *Recovery, Inc.; An Answer to Nervous Problems. An Interview with John J. Higgins, S. J.* (St. Louis: Queen's Work, 1955), p. 10.

[15] From a mimeographed collection of songs distributed at local anniversary celebration of Recovery, Inc. (1961).

ommon problem. Each time a member completes the inevitable Before I had my Recovery training . . . " he implies that the .....ernative to Recovery is always misery.

Another contribution of members to the group is their weekly *testimonial* to the Recovery method. The stream of vignettes that pours forth around the table reiterates that recovery works. And each member, by providing examples, *constitutes an example himself*. His victorious presence contributes to the resolution of his peers and builds the determination of novices and laggards. Conversely, group reactions to examples reinforce the convictions of the narrator. As he is endorsed for having applied the prescribed techniques, he becomes less prone to question their validity.

The Recovery group is thus a concentrated pep rally, which sustains each member's enthusiasm in solving his problems. Between meetings, the member fights his battles in confidence, knowing that success is almost inevitable. He knows that he is in possession of weapons that he can use with *absolute trust*. Although his own goals may be uncertain, and his own experience may deceive him, the unanimity of his group and the univocacy of their reports provide incontrovertible evidence. The ritual has become indistinguishable from spontaneous unanimity.

Every Recovery meeting covers the cycle from problem to solution. The member is presented with "before" and "after" pictures. He sees— time after time—that the Recovery method bridges the gap. The member's own problems soon become just another example, and his own achievements add further validation to accepted techniques. In this fashion, *individual* solutions of *individual* problems become transmuted into a *shared* victory.

The psychological vise

Two factors contribute to the willingness of an individual to try to pool his private problems with those of other people. One requirement is his inability to cope with the problem on his own. The other factor is the subjective intolerability of the problem. Bill W., the founder of Alcoholics Anonymous, speaks of the prospective A.A. member as a man "caught as in a psychological vise." Bill W. explains the A.A. dictum that an alcoholic must have "hit bottom" before being attracted to A.A. membership:

If the jaws of [alcoholism] do not grip him tightly enough at first, more drinking will almost invariably turn up the screw to the point where he will cry—"enough." Then, as we say, he is "softened up." This reduces him to a state of *complete dependence* on whatever or whoever can stop his drinking.[16]

The remainder of A.A.'s task is to demonstrate to the thus predisposed person that he can profit through membership in the movement, and to involve him in active participation. Some predisposed persons may drop out because they are unable or unwilling to become part of a group. Alcoholics Anonymous has been found most successful with persons who feel able to share intimate reactions with others, and who feel comfortable in social situations. The congenial A.A. member is also likely to be a person who has experienced satisfying relationships with *some* groups in the past.[17]

Even with a predisposed and group-oriented member, however, the first steps of recruitment are critical. Appeals or techniques that may work with one member may be anathema to another:

> "I had a lot of trouble getting the program in the beginning," one A.A. remarked after he had been sober for a number of years. "I wanted to stop drinking but it just seemed that I couldn't. All the time, I knew that Jim, my first sponsor, was disappointed in me. What he didn't know was that I was disappointed with myself. I wanted desperately to make the grade in A.A. After one particularly bad slip, I was positive that I could get the program; I suddenly saw A.A. in a new light. But when I called Jim, he didn't seem particularly interested; he just said he'd look for me at the next meeting of the local group and I could tell he didn't really believe I would be there. I know I had given him the same story several times before, but this time I meant it; it made me angry when he sounded so skeptical. So I got drunk again and it wasn't until a year later that I finally came back to A.A. and got the program. Jim and I are good friends now and I can understand his attitude when I called him that time, but I can't help thinking that if he had stayed with me a bit longer. I *might have been in A.A. a year earlier*."[18]

Thus, A.A. (which uses sponsorship as an aid in the transition into membership) types approaches as "hardboiled," "casual," and "protective," and indicates that each of these is useful with *some* members.[19]

Beyond variations such as these, *all* prospective members of any "problem solving" movement are exposed to experiences which *are almost uni-*

[16] B. W., *Alcoholism the Illness* (New York: Alcoholics Anonymous, 1957), p. 12.

[17] H. M. Trice, "The Process of Affiliation with Alcoholics Anonymous," *Quarterly Jr. of Studies on Alcohol*, 18 (March 1957), pp. 39–54; J. Jackson and R. Conner, "The Skid Row Alcoholic," *Quarterly Jr. . . . . 14* (September 1953), pp. 468–486.

[18] *Sponsorship* (New York: Alcoholics Anonymous, 1953), p. 8.

[19] *Ibid.*, p. 7.

versally appealing. One of these is the use of each member as an "expert" and as an effective agent for the rehabilitation of others. A local publication of A.A. tells its readers that

> you were selected because you have been the outcasts of the world, and your long experience as drunkards has made, or should make you humbly alert to the cries of distress that come from the lonely hearts of alcoholics everywhere.[20]

A.A. stresses that the former alcoholic's role in rehabilitating others is vital for his own continued rehabilitation. The meaningfulness and importance of the "expert" and "professional" roles combine with the satisfaction of being "uniquely useful."[21]

Another appeal of self-change movements is that the member's problem is kept in the foreground. He is therefore faced with constant evidence that the movement's concerns coincide with his own. He is also constantly reminded of the severity of his problem, thus keeping alive his predisposition. Every A.A. meeting features speakers who luridly portray the depth to which their drinking had forced them to sink. The physical discomforts, the breakdown in social relations, the financial problems are exemplified in innumerable permutations: the fruitless efforts to stop drinking are enumerated. The prospective member is reminded again and again that he suffers from a destructive chronic illness, with which he is unable to cope unaided.

From the listings of these experiences the prospective member also gains the impression that his fellow-members share his own perceptions and feelings. The experiences he hears ring sadly familiar; the reactions that are detailed sound precisely like his; the very language used is that of the alcoholic. *These communalities provide a basis for communication.* The new member feels that he can understand and can be understood. There is also the common bond of facing the same danger, which makes A.A. able to proclaim that "We are united by our common problem, alcohol."[22]

Lastly, personal testimonies and the physical presence of persons who have solved their problem through membership testify to the *validity* of the method. The new member gains the impression that the movement has worked for others like himself. He *knows* the problem, and he *sees* the

[20] *Power Beyond Estimate* (Lansing, Mich.: Alcoholics Anonymous, undated), p. 2.
[21] B. W., *Alcoholism*, p. 7.
[22] *This is A. A.* (New York: Alcoholics Anonymous, 1953), p. 7.

solution. He is told that the techniques used by the movement (twelve steps, in the case of A.A.) are the only effective path to the goal. He is unable to refute the evidence.

The proof of the pudding

When a self-change movement claims to be effective, this claim comprises *three separate assumptions*. The first of these is that *a social movement* can solve the person's problems, although he may not be able to solve them himself. The second claim is that *the movement in question* can solve the problem. The third proposition is that *the specific techniques of the movement are the best or the only techniques which can accomplish the job.* Thus, A.A. assumes that its spiritual overtones (which are not stressed to the new member) are essential to continued abstinence, and Recovery proclaims that Low's guidelines must be literally followed to avoid symptoms.

The social movement's claim that it can help its members is *provable*, and frequently *proved*. Although the assumption that the movement's techniques are the best means to this end is usually *false*, it is a *useful* assumption, because it increases the confidence of members. What could be correctly claimed is that *every social movement which enables its members to solve their problems must incorporate features that are essential to its effectiveness.* Although it may not be the only road to Rome, it does know the way. Possibly *despite* dogmatically defended arbitrary variations, every effective movement provides the necessary support for the efforts of its members.

It is not unreasonable to assume that psychologically sound supportive techniques recur from movement to movement. Even a review of such widely different groups as TOPS and Recovery shows that in some respects similar objectives are served.

Recurrent benefits

One service every self-change movement seems to provide is to build a fire under its members by stressing the intolerability of their fate. By spelling out the undesirable consequences of the member's condition, the movement defines his problem. The result is to *reinforce the member's conviction that he must take action.*

The next step is to demonstrate that action is feasible, and that the goal is *attainable*. Social movements are admirably suited to show the feasibility of solutions, since they comprise persons in various stages of being changed. The practice of frequent testimonials, which seems to be almost universal among self-change movements, draws each member's attention to the successes of his fellows. Once someone has accepted the assumption that his problem is the same as that of others, their accomplishments assure him that his own improvement is also attainable.

The probability of a solution is further increased by *circumscribing the goal* so as to make it relatively easy to attain. Recovery, for instance, discourages its members from aiming at "exceptionality." A.A. makes the minimum demand of a resolution to stay sober for 24 hours. In TOPS, weight is gauged every week, and the objective becomes that of tipping the scales less forcefully seven days later.

Social movements also *retain their members on the road toward the goal*. They accomplish this through *incentives* and *encouragement*. Members are made aware of their progress through concrete indications of achievement (such as weight charts in TOPS, and Recovery endorsements). It is also a general practice to rebuke more or less sympathetically any member who strays. Lastly, the progress of the whole group provides each member with *norms* against which he can gauge his own achievement.

A final incentive is that members become "hooked" through the *cycle* of their participation. Each member learns that his achievement is a necessary condition for the success of others. As he benefits from his relation to other members, he becomes aware of their indebtedness to him. This converts his problem-solving efforts from selfish necessity to an act which has satisfying social consequences. In this connection, every member also discovers that he quickly benefits from efforts to help his fellow members. To the extent to which such help is successful, it adds vigor to the helper's efforts to help himself.

Another consequence of the nature of self-help movements is the fact that the solution of personal problems is placed in a wider context. *Each individual's efforts to solve his own problems become part of his efforts to solve a social problem*—one with which he is intimately familiar, and about which he has reason to be concerned. Since the member has learned to see himself as an example of a general problem, he can view his efforts as directed at both the particular and the universal goal. Every ounce of weight lost by a TOPS member also decreases the total amount of surplus fat in the universe; every day of sobriety achieved by an A.A. member reduces the prevalence of alcoholism. And multiplied by the achievement of the member's entire group (for which each individual is responsible) this relationship can be objectively confirmed.

When a person resorts to a social movement for the solution of a private problem, his actions have inescapable social consequences. To the extent to which he participates in the collective effort, he changes society as he changes himself.

5 ▷ THE EXPLOITATION OF PREDISPOSITIONS

In the last three chapters we have reviewed three types of social movements, each of which seemed to provide a solution to some kind of problem. We could add more chapters containing parallel accounts: we might examine revolutionary movements, fraternal groups, religious revivals, agrarian revolts, and an infinite variety of other movements. In every case, we could show that different needs are differently responded to. In every case, we could outline how a group of people encountered appeals that proved attractive to them.

But is there a gap in this scheme? Does the transaction of problem-and-solution come into being by a happy coincidence? Is it correct to assume that the situations that evoke needs will also inspire answers to these needs? Or must the availability of appeals concern us as a separate problem?

Many students feel that social movements must be regarded as *deliberate* products, and that a key to the understanding of a movement is the study of how it was concocted. In this view, it is important to determine who drafted the movement's platform, planned its organization, and shaped its propaganda. The *details* of the planning are also seen to be important, because these are the presumed means whereby people are seduced into membership.

Eric Hoffer asserts that "a full-blown mass movement is a ruthless affair, and its management give an appearance of spontaneity to consent obtained by coercion."[1] Herbert Blumer, a pioneer in the sociology of social movements, tells us that the *process of agitation* should be our main concern. He points out that

> The gaining of sympathizers or members rarely occurs through a mere combination of a pre-established appeal and a pre-established individual psychological bent on which it is brought to bear. Instead, the prospective sympathizer or member has to be *aroused, nurtured,* and *directed,* and the so-called appeal has to be *developed* and *adapted.* This takes place through a process in which attention has to be *gained,* interests *awakened,* grievances *exploited,* ideas *implanted,* doubts *dispelled,* feelings *aroused,* new objects *created,* and new perspectives *developed.*[2]

This listing implies that people are brought to social movements through the skill of leaders and agitators, rather than because of pre-existing problems. It further suggests that social movements cannot be understood without a backstage view of the origin of appeals.

Blumer's prescription is not easy to apply because the "stagers" in most movements share the problems of other members, so that it becomes difficult to distinguish the agitators from their clients. There are some movements, however, where the distinction becomes possible, because appeals seem to originate with people who are primarily interested in other ends than the solution of the problems of potential members. The present chapter will concern itself with these kinds of ventures.

The framework for exploitation

In the situations with which this chapter will deal, needs are responded to for the sake of profit, and people are induced into participation by deliberate appeals to their known interests.

We shall try to show that even in instances of flagrant profiteering, the vital fact remains that the needs that are appealed to are real needs. They existed before their exploitation; they can be traced to deficiencies in social institutions. Moreover, even appeals that are contrived have to become "appealing": If needs did not precede appeals to some measure, attempts to appeal would be cries in the wilderness.

What is of interest, in other words, is not that social movements are

---

[1] E. Hoffer. *The True Believer* (New York: Harper & Brothers, 1951), p. 129.

[2] H. Blumer, "Collective Behavior," in J. B. Gittler, ed., *Review of Sociology* (New York: Wiley, 1957), p. 148 (italics added).

contrived, but that they are contrivable. What matters is that concrete, painful, urgent problem situations exist, to which pseudo-solutions (or real solutions) may be furnished. The exploiter in such situations is not the originator of the problem, nor is he responsible for the eagerness with which his solutions are responded to. He is at best an individual who has sensed an existing social deficit, and is aware of some prerequisites for an appealing solution. His success is a function of the unhappiness of his clients, and of the vividness of their dreams and aspirations. The effectiveness of his exploitation increases with the acuteness of needs and the intensity of hope. It also improves with the degree to which he accurately diagnoses the underlying problem.

The presumption of exploitation

Although exploitation is a dramatic form of human relationship, it is difficult to locate and hard to identify accurately. The people who are directly involved are not good sources of information. Victims tend to be unaware that they are victimized, or they would (usually) object to the arrangement. Exploiters, by the same token, are in no position to discuss their activities, since this would imperil their rapport with their clientele.

As a result, exploitation must generally be inferred circumstantially rather than directly. The *presumption of exploitation* tends to derive from one of several related premises. The first of these is the inference that *behavior which is convenient for leaders is usually engineered by them*. In other words, if a group of persons behaves in a way that has favorable consequences for individuals in authority, it is assumed that this result has been intentionally achieved. The social philosopher Critias, for instance, deduced that gods were the invention of a clever ruler, from the premise that gods are helpful in controlling people.[3] Karl Marx similarly inferred that religion is "the opiate of the masses."

A slightly different version of the same assumption has it that if a group of people behaves in a way which (in the observer's judgment) is *not in their own best interest*, manipulation can be inferred. Thus, again according to Marx, "non-proletarian ideologies" may become prevalent among workers, suggesting outside inspiration. Similarly, medical practitioners and health food enthusiasts view each others' clients as dupes who are destined for an early grave.

A third, related premise is that people who are *drawn into irrational or*

[3] E. Hayden, *Biography of the Gods* (New York: Macmillan, 1941), p. 49.

illogical solutions to their problems are being exploited. This argument sometimes is applied to unpopular movements in an effort to classify members as instruments of evil. An illustration of this device is the following biblical account (Peter II, 2:1-3):

> But there were false prophets also among the people, even as there shall be false teachers among you, who privily shall bring in damnable heresies, even denying the Lord that brought them, and bring upon themselves swift destruction.
>
> And many shall follow their pernicious ways; by reason of whom the way of truth shall be evil spoken of.
>
> And through covetousness shall they with feigned words make merchandise of you: whose judgment now for a long time lingereth not, and their damnation slumbereth not.

This type of inference is at best risky. Inferring exploitation from the contention that people behave in a way that does not make sense or is wrong assumes that the observer knows how people *should* behave, but don't; in practice, this most frequently presupposes a model of spontaneously rational, practical, and self-oriented behavior which applies only to some people in some situations.

Moreover, even where people do behave in a way that is unnatural or unusual for them, this does not prove that someone is directly responsible for the change. And where someone is responsible, this does not mean that he intended to profit from his impact, or that he practiced deception. Effectiveness does not require intent, and intent does not imply maliciousness.

It may be an established fact that a certain leader has derived profit from his followers: He may own a number of very expensive automobiles; he may live in a palatial home, cohabit with a harem, and eat exceedingly well. None of this excludes the possibility that material gain was never his primary concern; he could easily have reluctantly availed himself of opportunities thrust upon him by his followers. It is similarly possible that quack remedies could be purchased from a willing supplier who did not even momentarily suspect that his medication was not the miracle cure he advertised.

To be sure that a group of persons is being exploited, we must know that (1) someone has induced them to behave as they do (by appealing to their needs); (2) the instigator is deriving benefits from his efforts; and (3) his actions were deliberate, and motivated by the desire for profit.

It is not easy to find groups in which we can be certain that these requirements are met. To maximize our chances, the illustrations in this chapter will be drawn from obviously commercial enterprises that also happen to be social movements.

We shall deal with two types of businesses that double as social movements. The first is the sort of enterprise that lays claim to rendering commercial services but covertly promotes a social movement. The second type is the converse: It advertises itself as a social movement, but its "members" become tools of a business enterprise. In both situations, human needs are appealed to on false pretexts, and the stated objectives differ from the intended consequences.

Latent social movements

In May 1960, *Time* reported that John Milton Addison had announced his candidacy for the governorship of Texas. Some of Addison's most fervent political supporters were persons who had invested their savings in his uranium mining concern. Although Addison's business enterprise was a relative failure (an investment of $1,250,000 had produced $289.93 in uranium ore), he had secured the continued loyalty and support of his investors with periodic revival-style meetings. *Time* quoted Addison as shouting:

> "You understand I can take your money and tear it up, burn it, throw it away, or spend it on wild, wild women—don't you?" (Screams of "Yes!") "And you want it that way?" ("Yes! Yes!")[4]

Obviously, Addison's business associates were seeing him as more than a vehicle to profit. The reason for their loyalty may have been partly an impatience with ordinary business incentives, and partly the desire to benefit from revolutionary scientific changes. But whatever the details, Addison's commercial ventures (and later, his "Clean 'Em Out Right" Party) were viewed as a refreshing and satisfying deviation from conventional rates of progress. Although superficially Addison's followers were investors in a business enterprise, their investments represented manifestations of hope. The prospect that motivated their commitment was the belief that Addison— as one follower put it—"can do wonderful things on this earth."

Latent social movements like that of John Milton Addison are *business enterprises with latent appeals.* The relationship between such a business and its clients includes all the elements of a transaction between a social

[4] *Time* (May 30, 1960), p. 12.

movement and its members. The *ostensible* purpose of the relationship is the rendering of a routine service in exchange for profit. This, however, is a fiction which hides the fact that solutions to basic social problems are promised. It can usually also be shown that these promises are made by individuals who are fully aware of what they do.

Arthur Murray, the head of a chain of studios whose manifest purpose is to teach people how to dance, describes himself as a supplier of "sociability." Although Murray has denied that he caters to "lonely hearts," he has pointed out that his students are not confined to persons seeking dancing lessons. Mr. Murray has listed diversion, exercise, and social life among the rewards obtained at his studios. He is quoted as having estimated that 50 per cent of his prospective customers are attracted by the opportunity for social life.[5]

Dance studio advertisements proclaim that "The saying that 'Saturday Night is the loneliest night of the week' is not true for Arthur Murray students."[6] This appeal, coupled with descriptions of studio parties, appears designed to attract persons willing to take dancing lessons in order to gain companionship. Advertisements contain testimonials from students, including such statements as

> An evening spent at Arthur Murray's is a highlight of a person's life.
> My attitude toward life has changed from gloom to cheer since I enrolled. . . .
> I love it so that I simply live for it.[7]

These statements are revealing because they show that "dancing lessons" have acquired a disproportionate importance to people. It becomes obvious that Saturday night may indeed have been the loneliest night of the week for many Arthur Murray students. At the very least, some persons who are unable to secure companionship and attention elsewhere can derive these commodities (at a price) from the dance studio:

> There is Sybil, age 40, a secretary: "I took Sybil to Tavern on the Green for a studio party," her handsome young instructor said. "Out of the clear blue

[5] E. Katcher, "Inside the Arthur Murray Studios," No. 10, New York *Post* (October 10, 1957). This section contains excerpts from the series entitled "Inside the Arthur Murray Studios" by Gael Greene and Edward Katcher in the New York *Post*. Copyright 1957, New York Post Corporation.

[6] Arthur Murray advertisement.

[7] Katcher and Greene, "Arthur Murray Studios," No. 11, New York *Post* (October 11, 1957).

sky, she starts to cry. It seems it was the first time she'd been to a party and danced more than one dance."[8]

"I'm a lingerie buyer, here for the week with nothing to do evenings," she said. . . .

Mae was a lifetime Arthur Murray student—that entitled her to 1,000 hours of instruction plus two hours a month for the rest of her life.

"I can take my lessons anywhere," she added.

"Where else can a single woman go in New York City?" she asked. "I can't go to nightclubs or fancy restaurants. So I come here."[9]

"The dance studio gives you a dollar to buy a birthday cake and a card for your pupil. It's a nice little touch. You'd be surprised how much it can mean.

"One man—it was his 67th birthday. He was so pleased when he saw the cake his teacher had bought, he cried. It was the first time in his entire life he'd had a birthday party. Imagine . . . and he was 67 years old."[10]

In addition to companionship and attention, the studio may also offer glamour. Dancing teachers may be instructed to appear physically glamorous, and small details in the decor and routine may be designed to give the same impression. Even the language used in the studio may carry exotic overtones—starting with nomenclature (such as "magic step") applied to the studio's version of dancing.

The needs of students can be assessed by experts, as the first phase of an effort to represent dance courses as uniquely meeting psychological requirements. Teachers—who are usually also sales persons working on a commission basis—may be directed to explore the feelings of their students and to cater to them.[11]

The extreme application of this principle is illustrated by the publicized case of a sixty-year-old widow who had won a "free dance analysis":

After that it was just one great bewildering whirl of salesmanship. She withdrew $7,300 of her savings to buy a lifetime course, put two mortgages on her home to buy the $9,000 gold medal course and then the $12,000 lifetime executive course. By mid-July she had paid out over $25,000, had a nervous breakdown from worry over paying the rest. What sales technique had been used on Mrs. Frisch? Just sheer flattery. Admitted her instructor: "She idolized flattery."[12]

[8] *Ibid.*
[9] Greene, "Arthur Murray Studios," No. 2, New York *Post* (October 11, 1957).
[10] *Ibid.*, No. 6, (October 6, 1957).
[11] *Ibid.*, No. 7, (October 7, 1957).
[12] *Time* (April 11, 1960), p. 103.

What converts such an instance of salesmanship into something we can classify (even remotely) as membership in a social movement? Flattery, after all, is a standard means of persuasion. The assessment of individual needs to permit a personalized sales pitch is a routine business procedure. Even the creation of atmosphere and the use of euphemisms to describe one's product are routine ways of putting one's best foot forward. It is obvious that the Arthur Murray organization tries to attract and hold students. But how are students transmuted into members?

The transformation occurs when two factors combine to cement the ties between the dance studio and some of its habitués. The first of these factors is the advertised *appeal* (subsequently reinforced through personal contact) which makes dancing a way of gaining companionship and attention. The second factor is the existence of circumstances in our society—especially for older persons, and particularly for older women—which limit their personal contacts and their social activities.

A social movement (of sorts) arises, in other words, because persons join in an effort to solve a problem created for them by a recurrent social deficit. The *situation* here is *social isolation*, the *problem* is *loneliness*, and the *solution* is *companionship in a framework that carries respectability and meaning*. The dance studio furnishes personal relationships that include physical proximity and an aura of intimacy—but does so with a didactic rationale. The quasi-intimate association of dancers becomes a pretense rehearsal for a play that never takes place. The learning of sociability is presumed to have outside application, but in practice its exercise can be confined to the studio itself.

If such facts were made explicit, many prospective dancers might not be able to justify taking their first step. The ideology therefore is never created, and the appeals remain latent. Such is commonly the character of *latent* social movements, which makes them hard to classify as social movements at all. Moreover, in the case of the dance studio, the goals of membership are so short-range—confined, as they are, to a few hours of make-believe in otherwise drab lives—that the term "social movement" applies even more remotely. However, we do observe the effort to cope with loneliness, and this fact retains the dance studio within the borderlines of our discussion.

An illustration of more direct attempts to cope with loneliness is a set of business ventures that have acquired the label "lonely hearts clubs." These enterprises occur in infinite variations, and the model for them is the marriage broker of antiquity. The brokerage function may be exercised directly, in the form of personal introductions, or indirectly, by providing facilities for mixing, or (most frequently) by circulating lists of prospective partners to their counterparts.

A very conservative estimate has it that there are some 500 lonely hearts clubs operating in the United States today.[13] Guesses at their membership range from 100,000[14] to 4,000,000[15] persons, with the true figure probably lying somewhere in between. Evan Moore, the owner of a large correspondence club, reports a list of 30,000 members[16] and claims some 42,000 inquiries a year.[17] Clara Lane, director of Friendship Center, has introduced 40,000 people to each other in ten years.[18]

The large clientele of commercial marriage brokers reflects the absence of formal community arrangements for the establishment of acquaintances. When K. M. Wallace, who operates a computerized lonely hearts club, asked his members why they had joined, nine out of ten indicated that they had experienced insufficient opportunity to meet people on their own.[19] Clara Lane points out:

> As I see it, I'm simply filling a void created by the fact that America has drifted away from the kind of community life I enjoyed when I was a farm girl living near Davenport. Then, I knew every boy in the county. Today, millions of American girls don't even know the boy next door.

As an example, Miss Lane cites the fact that "Last spring I introduced a man and a girl who, it developed, lived only three doors away from each other in Fairview, N. J."[20]

With the traditional facilities for social intercourse—such as churches—becoming less effective as community centers, with physical and social mobility disrupting stable groupings of people, and with increasing emphasis on personal independence, social informality, and career considerations, a large number of Americans have become social isolates. Of course, the pattern of social isolation varies. Young farmers may discover that neighboring farms contain no prospective brides, while farmers' daughters contribute to

[13] A. Henley, "Wanted: Eight Million Wives," *True Love* (May 1961), p. 43.

[14] *Ibid.*

[15] F. Kasky, "Truth about Mail-Order Marriage: Lonely Hearts Clubs," *Colliers* (April 1949), p. 21.

[16] T. Sugrue, "I Sent a Letter to My Love: Matrimonial Correspondence and Lonely Hearts Clubs," *American Magazine* (February 1937), p. 121.

[17] G. Palmer, "How They Get Married by Mail," *Good Housekeeping* (October 1941), p. 185.

[18] C. Lane, "Cupid Is My Business," *American Magazine* (February 1949), p. 30.

[19] K. M. Wallace, "We Ran a Lonely Hearts Club," *McCall's* (March 1956) p. 157.

[20] Lane, "Cupid," pp. 30–31.

the pool of unmarried secretaries in New York and Washington. Clara Lane reports a letter from a girl recently arrived in a small town, who

> ... wrote me that she felt "buried" there, with only farm boys to date. I wrote back and told her that if she wanted to feel really buried she should come to New York.
> Our bulging cities today are teeming with lonely, rootless people. And hundreds of our smaller towns are filled with transients, commuters, and migrant newcomers. We have become a nation of strangers.[21]

Persons who feel the pressure of impending isolation explore every available avenue of respectable encounter. Within the limits of facilities open to them, and within the range of their financial and psychological resources, they

> go to neighborhood bars and strange bars. They go to theatres, concert halls, wrestling matches, public libraries—anywhere people will gather. . . . Those with more outgoing personalities patronize dance halls, attend evening classes in music appreciation, painting, dramatics and current events, go on cruises, visit nearby resorts, or join ski clubs, photography clubs, political clubs, even nudist colonies.[22]

Much of this struggle is doomed to failure, because the institutions resorted to are not designed to foster companionship and community. As a result, according to Miss Lane, "many will have to remain lonely, *or muster their courage and come to someone like me.*"[23]

Commercial introduction services are the last resort for persons who have explored more respectable means of coping with loneliness and who have failed. The fact that people use agencies that are suffused with "a certain air of questionable morality"[24] reflects the intensity of their problem.

The candidate for membership in a lonely hearts club may have to select his club from the classified advertising pages of a pulp magazine which may also feature requests for "a shapely girl who is no prude" or for "a lady of substantial means," or may advertise aphrodisiacs, witch charms, cheesecake photographs, "girlie" films, astrological forecasts, and pep pills. Subsequently, the prospective member must overcome resistance to mailing a picture and a set of vital statistics for publication in a catalogue. Even later, total strangers—whose intentions are unclear and whose backgrounds are

---

21 *Ibid.*, p. 31.
22 Henley, "Eight Million Wives," p. 42.
23 Lane, "Cupid," p. 31 (italics added).
24 G. Mason, "Wives by Mail," *Scribner's Magazine* (May 1931), p. 533.

ambiguous—must be responded to, and eventually must be encountered in person.

If these hurdles are overcome, it generally reflects the degree to which loneliness has become intolerable. And the operators of lonely hearts clubs are aware of the depth of misery to which they cater. One matrimonial magazine, for instance, reminds its readers,

> *The saddest words of tongue or pen*—"*It Might Have Been*" . . . just because you have not as yet found your ideal is no reason for you to give up and go on your lonely, desolate and thoroughly miserable way. There are plenty, yes hundreds, of persons just waiting to hear from you—handsome, beautiful, wealthy, home-bodies, sports lovers—they are of assorted descriptions and from every walk of life—perhaps just down the street or in some adjoining city or nearby state. But the first move is up to you—*Are You Up To It?* I am sure you are!
>
> *The First Move?* Why naturally, it is to fill out the application below and mail it in.[25]

The candidate's vividly depicted unhappiness is contrasted with the unlimited pool of "love and romance" in the universe, and with the "lifetime of enthralling pleasure and complete happiness" which marriage could offer. Frequently sample listings are provided, to illustrate the availability of a large assortment of lonely persons of the other sex. Many clubs stress the confidentiality of membership, emphasize their attention to individual requirements, and state their ability to furnish special categories of partners. Some clubs may even go out of their way to reassure candidates about the respectability of membership.[26]

Such reassurance, however, is frequently superfluous. To the candidate for membership in a lonely hearts club, long shots seem reasonable. The state of mind of a person at this juncture is reflected in the following excerpted statements quoted in a membership list circulated by a Southern club (the name of the club was not stated):

[25] *The Western Heart* (May–June 1961), p. 9.

[26] The Get Acquainted Club, Denver, Col., for instance, points out in its prospectus that

> The object of this Club is to introduce and put in touch with each other, ladies and gentlemen who are lonely, sincere and sometimes timid and shy. Disregarding how particular you might be, there is no reason why you should be embarrassed at meeting people through our Club. We live today in a far different world than just a few years ago— People are *so* busy with their own personal problems that their social life as they once knew it is almost passe, and many of our nicest, highest type people use our method of introduction to search for compatible companionship.

(RJW, age 30): I'm satisfied with my home, but it's like living on an island to be all alone. A woman can't just walk up and get acquainted. Why don't you drop me a line?

(HC, age 36): Do you crave companionship, well believe me I do and altho I stay busy and have my own money there's times when it doesn't seem worthwhile. There must be someone.

(BJ, age 45): I just want a strong man to guide me and in return I'll give him a gentleman's home. I'll keep his house clean and wash and iron and I'll sing all day I'll be so happy.

(ERM, age 35): How would you like a partner? That's what marriage amounts to. Yes a nice man am I asking too much.

The urgent tone of inquiries such as these shows the strained nature of the isolate's position in a family-oriented world. Women who are expected to find exclusive fulfillment in marriage, men whose solitary condition is regarded as a reflection on their masculinity or as a defective sense of responsibility—such persons cannot afford to adjust to their status as isolates. And somewhat independently of these pressures, there is the *feeling* of loneliness—compounded of longing, desolation, self-pity, and a sense of incompleteness—"such a painful, frightening experience that people will do anything to avoid it."[27]

The extreme form of loneliness is that during which hope of ever not being alone is abandoned. It is at this stage, as Frieda Fromm-Reichmann points out, that loneliness can turn into psychosis, and can reach the level of intolerability where it can no longer be faced:

> The more severe developments of loneliness appear in the unconstructive, desolate phases of isolation and real loneliness which are beyond the state of feeling sorry for oneself—the states of mind in which the fact that there were people in one's past life is more or less forgotten, and the possibility that there may be interpersonal relationships in one's future life is out of the realm of expectation or imagination.[28]

For many persons, lonely hearts clubs seem to constitute a last-ditch effort to keep from losing hope—to stave off the conclusion that they will remain isolates. The member stays at a stage of loneliness where he can view his condition as painful but remediable—even if the probabilities are now low. This kind of picture is presented, for example, by the following description of a reporter's first lonely hearts date:

[27] F. Fromm-Reichmann, "Loneliness," *Psychiatry*, 22 (February 1959), p. 1.
[28] *Ibid.*, p. 5.

Without a doubt, here was a woman whose spirit was all but snuffed out by the storms of life and showed itself in her self-neglect.

Still, she was most pleasant and tried very hard—too hard—to make an impression. She admitted having looked everywhere for a regular boy-friend—dances, blind dates, even encouraged a few pick-ups. It all led nowhere. That's why she'd joined a lonely hearts club.[29]

The entrepreneurs who cater to needs such as these cannot be unmindful of the emergency function they serve. In the first place, they must have an awareness of the problem in order to sense its money-making potential. Clara Lane, for instance, tells us that "I could see the opportunities, from a strictly business point of view, because having lived in a series of cities, I had a pretty good idea of the amount of loneliness that exists in America."[30]

Second, it is almost impossible for the operator of a lonely hearts club not to become emotionally involved in the battle against loneliness. It has been reported that most proprietors of larger clubs become idealists, if they were not to begin with.[31] Daily experience dramatizes for them the fact that "loneliness is a terrible, corroding, humiliating experience." Clara Lane tells us that "If America can lick the problem of loneliness I shall be more than glad to fold my own business, and go back to milking cows on an Iowa farm."[32]

But America is not "licking" loneliness, and lonely hearts clubs continue to mitigate the hopelessness of the problem. They do so by providing lonely persons with an *awareness of each other*, with *means of intercommunication*, and with the *remote possibility of a restitution to community*. These commodities are furnished with full cognizance of their import, even in instances where the motivation is flagrantly mercenary. And the clientele of the clubs pay fees for services (such as advertisements or the channeling of correspondence), knowing that the apparent triviality of these commercial transactions thinly disguises the fact that personal happiness lies in the balance.

Ostensible social movements

In early April 1962 a justice of the New York County Supreme Court signed an order dissolving "Baseball for Europe." This enterprise was a foundation which had ostensibly given baseball fans the opportunity to

[29] Henley, "Eight Million Wives," p. 52.
[30] Lane, "Cupid," p. 31.
[31] Sugrue, "Letter to My Love," p. 120.
[32] Lane, "Cupid," p. 141.

enhance the popularity of America by sponsoring and subsidizing America's national sport abroad. The dissolution order came because the money which had been raised was not being employed as advertised. Although $21,000 had been contributed, less than one tenth of this amount had been invested in baseball equipment.[33]

An *ostensible social movement* is one that *enlists support for a collective cause, but really functions for the purpose of making a profit.* In such enterprises, the member operates under the impression that he is dealing with (or helping to deal with) a social problem. In reality, he is contributing time, effort, or money to a business enterprise.

Several illustrations of ostensible social movements may help us clarify their character. Our first example is the fan club.

Fan clubs—as the term indicates—are groups of admirers, organized for the purpose of giving expression to their admiration. The average fan club is a group of teen-agers— predominantly girls—and its idol is typically a youthful entertainer. The club may vary in size: members of the Ozzie and Harriet family, for instance, have 9,000 fan clubs which range from 12 to 15,000 fans. Shirley Temple as a child had 384 clubs with an average membership of 1,000. This included one club of 50,000 members "whipped up on the spur of the moment by a Chicago newspaper to exploit one of her pictures."[34]

Fan clubs need not be confined to teen-agers. The orchestra leader Lawrence Welk, for instance, has 100,000 devoted followers, led by a grocer's wife who invests 40 hours a week circulating publicity releases. It is not unusual for fans to spend a great deal of time promoting their idol. In return, they receive various degrees of personal attention. The director of Welk's fan clubs, for instance, explains that "Lawrence makes it up to me . . . he is never too busy to see me." More routinely, the reward may be an autographed picture, a recording, or some other token:

> In a contest last year to see which of the 10,000 members of Jimmy Rodgers' fan clubs could phone or write the most disk jockeys (at 10 points per call or letter, plus bonus points for charity donations, etc.) a boy from Richland Center, Wis. won hands down with 20,000 points. The contest lasted six months; his prize was a leather wallet and an autographed copy of the record album he had been plugging.[35]

[33] *The New York Times* (April 7, 1961).

[34] B. Johnson, "Facts Behind the Fan Clubs," *TV Guide* (January 23, 1960), p. 10.

[35] *Ibid.*, p. 11.

Fan clubs are sponsored by professional press agents for the purpose of obtaining publicity and public pressure on behalf of paying clients. For instance, a club that is convinced that it communicates with a Hollywood star may receive publicity releases from an agency such as United Fan Mail Service. ("With one secretary-typist signing club bulletins and editing club journals under 32 dummy names, UFMS conducts fan clubs for 60 . . . TV and movie stars.") Indications of the effectiveness of this kind of operation are easily obtained:

> A landslide of 15,000 letters written to a sponsor in response to instructions printed in one club bulletin ("Just sign your name and don't mention the club"), UFMS claims, saved one network show from being dropped in spite of its low ratings."[36]

This type of result suggests that fan club members are deliberately and successfully used to provide material for publicity campaigns. The idealistic efforts of teen-agers to establish contact with a flesh-and-blood hero would seem to terminate in slave labor for a cynical corporate enterprise.

This picture needs to be qualified with two considerations. First, the border between fan club and press agent is not easily drawn. *The two are engaged in a joint enterprise*, although their motives may differ. The average fan club member is aware that her efforts—if successful—promote the sale of records and enhance the standing of shows. The work may be a labor of love, but it derives part of its meaning from the concrete benefit it brings to the adored idol and to those blessed by his continuing presence on records or on the screen.

Second, the relationship between press agent and club member is more *reciprocal* than it appears to be. Not only do members permit themselves to be used, but—from their vantage point—they derive important benefits. Headquarters, after all, legitimizes their concern and provides them with eagerly awaited inside information. Headquarters also furnishes meaningful tasks through which devotion can be expressed. Without authoritative communications from Hollywood, the club member would lose her link to her idol. She would still be privileged to listen to his recordings, and she would be able to assemble available information—but the intimacy and the two-way nature of communication would be lost. And even though the communication is partly illusory, it is real enough to permit the teen-ager to establish a relationship that may serve as a landmark on the road from self-centeredness to social involvement.

[36]*Ibid.*

Given this kind of impact, exploitation cannot be defined as a one-way street. In fact, a closer look at "who gains what" may often make it difficult to tell *who* is using *whom.*

But what about situations in which psychological damage can be demonstrated? What about instances in which people are provided (in return for hard cash) with simple and sovereign illusions that prevent them from dealing with reality?

It is easy to show that *even when people are deceived*, deception may prove a blessing in disguise. What if "reality" has proved painful for people? What if it is too complex? What if the purveyor of lies also provides relief, peace of mind, and contentment? And what if deception is never discovered, or (in the event it is) if the pain of discovery is far less than the agony that has been spared? In other words, even where the exploited are harmed, the question of possible benefits must be posed. And it may, in fact, be *doubly* important, because it may help us to change situations which impel people to harm themselves. One illustration may suffice to make this point.

Aging is a multi-faceted problem. One of its components is the fact that increasing age tends to be accompanied by increasing physical infirmity. This correlate of aging becomes compounded as a problem when the afflicted individual looks to medicine for a remedy, and discovers that medical science does not pretend to reverse the course of entropy. He may learn from his physician that there is no way of restoring youthfulness and vigor, and that growing discomforts can merely be reduced to a more tolerable level.

In the face of this medical response, older persons have shown a tendency to be disproportionately receptive to promises of health based on oversimplified views of bodily functioning. Their susceptibility to health appeals has caused considerable consternation to the medical profession and to government officials. George Larrick, Commissioner of the Food and Drug Administration, has been quoted as complaining that

> These oldsters need little more than a vagrant suggestion to lead them to believe in the restorative powers of various nostrums. They are longing to read or hear about some wonder cure for the particular ailment that afflicts them, and with pathetic eagerness they embrace and employ it. It has been estimated that consumers waste $500 million a year on medical quackery and another $500 million annually on misrepresented vitamins, so called "health foods" and nutritional supplements.[37]

The nostrums the Commissioner refers to vary in the degree to which they are deceptive. At one extreme, there is concentrated sea water (at $3.00

[37] L. M. Stern, "The Gullible American," *The Progressive* (March 1963), p. 20.

a bottle) advertised as a cure for cancer, diabetes, and arthritis. Claims for sea water rest on its content of chemical trace elements, which exist in the sea in minute, worthless quantities.[38] A less extreme illustration is blackstrap molasses, a terminal product in sugar manufacture. This item has been popularized (and sold) by Gayelord Hauser, who also advocates the consumption of skim milk, brewer's yeast, wheat germ, and yogurt. Blackstrap molasses (prescribed for menopause troubles, baldness, low blood pressure, heart disease, indigestion, etc.) contains minerals, including iron, copper, and calcium. Such deposits of minerals, however, have been traced to scrapings from factory machinery and residues of limewater.[39]

On the least objectionable extreme of the health-food continuum are products which do contain legitimate nutritional supplements, but whose virtues are exaggerated. Thus, although it is a fact that wheat germ and brewer's yeast contain Vitamin B, it is also true that almost everyone derives enough Vitamin B for his needs from routine foods (such as enriched bread). Except for persons who suffer from relatively rare, specific deficiencies, experts agree that there are no health improvements to be gained from the ingestion of supplementary vitamins.

The promises of health-food advocates, however, are generally tied to premises that supersede specific claims for particular products. These premises may include the assumption that meats are toxic, that foods grown with chemical fertilizers transmit poison, that only fresh substances are digestible, that alkaline and acid foods should not be mixed (or should be mixed), that sugar is dangerous, that bulk is desirable, that only dry food is assimilable, and so on. The most common underlying premise is the glorification of food in its "natural" state, and the suspicion that anything "artificial" is toxic. America's leading publisher of health-food material, for instance, makes statements such as

> Man should observe a primitive simplicity in his daily regimen of food. He should grow his food in nature's manner. . . . Man must observe the animal in the field, the bird in the sky and see how they eat. They have set rules in regard to their nutriment, and will not swerve from them.[40]

Sometimes the "nature" premise is tied to religious assumptions, and dietary recommendations are not infrequently linked to biblical quota-

[38] Lansing (Michigan) *State Journal* (March 7, 1963).

[39] A. D. Morse, "Don't Fall for Food Fads," *Woman's Home Companion* (December 1951), p. 33.

[40] J. I. Rodale, "What Does Organic Gardening Mean?" *Organic Gardening* (December 1958), p. 13.

tions.[41] Most often, however, health food promoters use medical literature and government statistics as their source material. Despite a real mistrust of organized medicine and of public agencies, they invest considerable effort in tracking down data which can be used to document health food claims. Wherever possible, they also quote information from unorthodox sources— such as medical authorities or nutritionists who are rejected by the "respectable" profession. The following comment is typical of this admiration for rejected medical innovators:

> Yet in spite of the fact that the FDA is so underfinanced and understaffed, they have plenty of men and money available to "defend the public" against a man who claims to cure cancer and whose claim has never been refuted by a fair and impartial judgment of unbiased cancer experts.[42]

Advertising for health foods is not only documented with material from scientific literature (of all kinds), but also with detailed explanations of physiological mechanisms. The language oscillates uniquely between Madison Avenue superlatives and medical journalese. The reader may thus be enjoined to try a "new, delightful, nourishing treat," because of the fact that "without a sufficiently high tocopherol level, unsaturated fatty acids may consume the body reserves of tocopherols and deplete Vitamin E reserves." Or he may consider an "exclusive" B-12 formula which is "standardized in biofermentation solubles, not in over-refined crystalline form!"[43]

The consumer of health foods is given *authoritative sanction for his hopes.* He derives confirmation for his unhappiness with the pessimistic prognoses of conventional medicine, while he simultaneously gets the benefit of professional backing for a more congenial view. He can dismiss his family physician's cautious appraisals as proof of medicine's susceptibility to the profit-inspired propaganda of chemical firms; but he can also bask in his own familiarity with quotations from recent medical literature.

Especially appealing to older persons is the *combination of science and tradition* implicit in the emphasis on "natural" products. Every jar of vitamins purchased in the nutrition store carries the stamp of laboratory science and the sanction of the ages. It is described as a derivative of the barnyard or the field, transmuted in uncontaminated machinery by altruistic experts

---

[41] Typical of these quotations is Genesis 1:29, "And God said, Behold, I have given you every herb bearing seed, which is upon the face of all the earth, and every tree, in which is the fruit of a tree yielding seed; to you it shall be for meat."

[42] J. I. Rodale, Editor's Note, *Prevention* (September 1958), p. 51.

[43] *Nutrition Digest*, Vol. 5, No. 3 (undated). Items quoted are from two unrelated advertisements.

who have resisted the prostituting efforts of vested interests. Although the processing steps sound complex, the ingredients have the reassuring aura of household remedies, and are suffused with old-fashioned candor. Instead of uninformative polysyllabic formulas (furtively deleted by the druggist), the labels carry references to cereal germ oils, rose hips, black currants, kelp, intestines, alfalfa, brewer's yeast, bone marrow, soy beans, egg shells, safflower oil, garlic, honey, carrots, fish liver, and other familiar (and yet unfamiliar) items, whose therapeutic properties are almost implicit. In addition to this, scientific descriptions are also provided, but they now acquire a familiar, reassuring connotation. Moreover, the manufacturer—in other contexts an impersonal corporate giant—in this case takes the form of a health-minded individual who shows that he is intimately concerned about *precisely* the problems faced by his clients.

Every health food is *explicitly designed to stave off the physical consequences of aging.* These claims are sometimes reinforced with illustrations featuring the smiling faces of Youthful Old Persons. A Youthful Old Person is an athletic individual with gleaming white hair. He is usually shown working in his garden (among "naturally" grown vegetables) or depicted gazing into the sparkling eyes of a Y. O. P. of the opposite sex. These portraits are reinforced with pointed questions such as

> Do you want to prolong your prime of life? are you envious of the health and robust energy and vigor of your young friends and middle-age neighbors?[44]

> Will you be as "alive" in December as you were in May? Will you be "spry as a lark" like some older people or will you be "spent" before you have reached full maturity? Will your body match the stamina and alertness of your brain?[45]

> What good are the extra years if we spend them suffering from distressing physical or mental conditions aggravated by unsuspected nutritional deficiencies?[46]

The smiling portrait of the Youthful Old Couple asks the reader "Does Youth Begin at 40?" and the confident answer follows:

> The first flush of youth quickly wanes—much too quickly to suit most of us. By the time we reach the proverbial middle mark of 40, there is usually a noticeable slowdown. Inevitably—one cannot stop Father Time.

[44] *Health Saver* (Winter 1959), p. 7.
[45] *Nutrition Digest*, Vol. 5, No. 3 (undated), front cover.
[46] *Preventron* leaflet (undated).

Yet, because some of the decline may be due to causes related to nutrition, there is no reason why intelligent humans cannot help themselves. Scientists and observant people know that men and women in all walks of life can and do prolong vigorous health far beyond what the careless and nutritionally indifferent may expect.[47]

To the extent to which the reader becomes convinced of this assumption, health food catalogues offer him listings of available tools. Even if he does not aspire to becoming a Y. O. P. (there may be too much sag in the abdomen already), he at least gains the feeling that he can take measures to prevent or eliminate specific symptoms.

Moreover, he need not be deceived in this expectation. If for no other reason, improvements are likely because of enhanced self-confidence. And if the person's condition remains unchanged, his loss of health is at least converted from a dispirited defeat into an embattled retreat.

Beyond immediate gains, there are the benefits of membership in the health food *movement*. Among these benefits are the partnership with nature, the support of others in the battle against infirmity, the feeling of increased sophistication, the joy of evading physicians, the adventure of the scientific chase, the satisfaction of preserving tradition, and—most importantly—the profit gained from the belief that preventive action can be taken. This premise converts the maturing individual from a helpless instrument of the aging process into a controlling party.

This change, of course, is not only a gain but also a liability—it entails an act of self-deception. The remedies on the shelves of health food stores cannot prevent, or even retard, the process of aging. The supplier of health foods is in part a purveyor of illusions.

But he is not, by this token, an exploiter, as long as he operates within the "legitimate" health food movement. The manufacturer or promoter who believes and practices what he preaches is conceptually indistinguishable from his clients. To the extent to which he damages others, he also damages himself. And his concerns originate (as we shall see) in the same sources as those of the rank and file of his followers.

Exploitation occurs only in the *ostensible* health-food movement. It is limited to the relationship between the ideologically motivated consumer and the nonbelieving manufacturer. It is a transaction that for one party is a business arrangement, and for the other, an act of faith.

Because the exploiting manufacturer is a nonbeliever, it follows that he views his products as (at best) useless. This brings up the question of how

[47] *Nutrition Digest*, Vol. 5, No. 3 (undated), inside front cover.

he arrives at his manufacturing decision. There seem to be options. One is for the exploiter to replicate commodities already on the market, which he knows are consumed. In this case, the incentive for the choice of product rests with others, and ideology is adopted (as an advertising gimmick) with the product. The exploiter here responds in a somewhat mechanistic way to an existing demand.

The second possibility is for the exploiter to innovate or discover ideology, and then to produce items that seem called for. In the case of health foods, innovation is in practice confined to variations on themes that originated among amateur nutritionists in the nineteenth century.[48] A manufacturer may at times revise existing beliefs to encompass his products, or he may produce new products to fit the old headings. In either case, he is following suit, although he is doing so less slavishly than the imitator.

The exploiter is limited not only by precedent, however, but also by information about his market. Since his exclusive motivation is the desire for profit, *either* trial-and-error production *or* originality would involve him in uncomfortable risk. His mercenary outlook directs his attention to "live lines"—types of products that people seem to buy, or which they seem predisposed to acquire.[49]

This being the case, it is tempting to ascribe exploitation to consumer demand. Unfortunately, this leads to a "chicken and egg" argument, because the consumer cannot consume what has not been presented to him. His role seems limited to rewarding with his patronage the manufacturer who correctly diagnoses his needs.

Where, then, does the process start? One source, obviously, is the problem situation that produces the consumer's predisposition. Another source, however, must be the motivation of the *spontaneous innovator within the movement from whom the exploiter takes his cues*. And to the extent to which this original innovator has formed part of the same problem situation as the consumer, their motives need not differ much.

The problem to which health food ideology can be most plausibly traced is the relative remoteness of medicine from the daily life of the average person. It is reasonable to assume that health food pioneers were concerned with obtaining concrete guides for action in matters of health, and—finding them unavailable in the doctor's office—evolved their own.

[48] See, for instance, M. Gardner, *Fads and Fallacies in the Name of Science* (New York: Dover, 1952); G. Carson, *Cornflakes Crusade* (London: Lowe and Brydone, 1957).

[49] For an example of the way in which exploitation can be precluded by consumer apathy, see the chapter dealing with the English funeral industry in J. Mitford, *The American Way of Death* (New York: Simon and Schuster, 1963).

Specific needs, such as fear of being "poisoned" by food, the aspiration toward a "rational" system of nutrition, the desire to utilize the resources of nature, and the wish for concrete rules stemming from simple premises, can all be subsumed under this heading, because the institutionally designated respondent to these concerns was the medical profession. Moreover, several features of institutionalized medical practice—such as the passivity assigned to the patient's role—could have contributed to promoting resentment and a "do it yourself" outlook on medical problems.

The health food *consumer's* interest in health foods would be awakened by a parallel concern. We have noted that in the case of older persons, the inspiration would stem from the intersection of infirmity and medical practice. It would arise because some physicians respond to some maturing patients in a manner that is medically correct but psychologically unacceptable to the patient. At such junctures, particularly susceptible individuals begin to inquire into solutions that are less rational but more pleasing. As it happens, these solutions have been provided by articulate and inventive fellow-sufferers. *The transaction that results can be diagnosed and used by the profit-seeking nonbeliever.*

This kind of brokerage lives and dies with the social movement to which it attaches itself. To preclude exploitation in the area of health, the health food movement would have to be undermined at its source, which would ideally entail reforming medical practice. If exploitation consists of dispensing hope without absolute justification, preaching resignation is not an effective reply. And if patients experience the need for active participation in treatment, one can no longer supply them with prescriptions they must accept on faith.

In other words, the attractiveness of health foods for the aging person might diminish if and only if he received concrete assurance from his physician that they could jointly take every possible measure to furnish him with a happier and a more productive existence.[50]

The exploiter as a middleman

The role of the exploiter, as it emerges from our discussion, is a parasitic one. Exploitation comes about when neither institutions nor "legitimate" social movements have fully countered an existing social problem. An ex-

---

[50] Jarvis, an advocate of home remedies, has thus prognosticated that "the doctor of the future will be a teacher as well as a physician. His real job will be to teach people how to be healthy." (D. C. Jarvis, *Folk Medicine* [New York: Holt, Rinehart & Winston, 1958], p. vi.)

ploiter comes into being when an individual in search of profit discovers unsatisfied persons who are willing to pay for substitute goals. Exploitation is symptomatic of exploitable needs. It is reduced only when needs are less circuitously satisfied.

In the case of latent social movements, the unavailability of susceptible persons would force business enterprises to "sell themselves" on the basis of the overt services they provide. Dance studios would have to make do with short-term clients whose exclusive wish consisted of the desire to waltz. "Sociability" would be a surplus commodity if society provided adequate social outlets. Marriage brokers and correspondence services could not function as lonely hearts clubs in a world which contained no lonely hearts. They would have to confine their activities to providing limited, specialized services, such as brides for remote plantation workers and pen pals for internationally minded children.

Ostensible social movements, under ideal conditions, would merge with institutions. They would be deprived of pretense, and would continue either as business enterprises or at their face value. For instance, fans could be compensated for publicity work; alternately, they could operate as fan clubs, and could establish direct lines of communication with flesh-and-blood idols. Health foods could be dispensed by members of a licensed profession, with the fraternal blessing of physicians and dieticians.

Such changes, however, presuppose that institutions and social movements can keep pace with human needs, thus eliminating the demand for commercial supplements to their services. The prevalence of exploitation is a function of exploitability, and provides an index to the gap between social need and social change. This fact neither condemns nor legitimizes exploiters. It merely places them in context.

Our discussion has suggested that exploitation is not usually the *root* of social movements. Instead, it is merely a *grafted limb*, which acquires life and meaning through the transaction between a nurturing problem situation and the solution it evokes.

two

The career of members

A N advertisement for a well-known bourbon has posed the following question: "How do people *become* drinkers of bourbon—as against imported whiskies, for example?" The advertisement went on to say:

There seem to be various ways:

1. *They're born lucky.* They are reared in a section of the country where, when a man comes of age he *starts* with straight Kentucky bourbon. These people, you might say, are born with an amber spoon in their mouths.

2. *They work their way up.* This is a development similar to that of food tastes—or from pablum to pâté. When such men and women begin to drink socially, they start with blandness. Then as they and their tastes mature—it's straight bourbon for them.

3. *They see the light.* They see their friends taking to bourbon. They discover that it tastes better—and that it tastes *best* undisguised, unchanged, with what country folk call "branch"—plain, pure water. This is the fashionable course to bourbon.[1]

These three ways of becoming a bourbon fancier correspond to ways in which one can become a member of a social movement. The third alternative, "seeing the light," is the road to membership most peculiar to social movements—the one least shared with other types of groups. This

[1] Old Crow Kentucky Bourbon advertisement, *The New York Times*, October 17, 1961.

chapter will focus on this process, which some people have called "conversion." The other two roads to membership, early indoctrination ("being born lucky") and socialization ("working one's way up") will be briefly reviewed by way of introduction.

Indoctrination in childhood

Social movements that last over two or more generations share with other continuing groups the opportunity of transmitting membership from parents to children. Many sons "inherit" membership in the same sense in which certain English infants acquire schools—by being "enrolled" on the day the birth announcement arrives in the maternity ward waiting room. In other words, it is frequently taken for granted that the child will follow in his father's ideological footsteps. Such explicit or implicit infant baptisms do not, of course, predetermine membership, but they do predict it with conviction—they suggest that recruitment will not be left to chance.

The most obvious way in which parents can insure the outcome they expect is by deliberately promoting their beliefs in the home. They can express their own preferences in direct and indirect fashion, and communicate their expectation that these preferences are to be shared. They need not preface their editorials with reservations emphasizing that alternatives are available or legitimate. By the time children discover that beliefs are not facts, the distinction may have become academic for an astronomical number of propositions.

It must be added that even in those rare instances in which every effort is made to convince the growing youngster that he is to regard the political or religious spectrum with an open mind, the child is thus inculcated with a definite ideological position that happens to be markedly at variance with that of most people.

But indoctrination takes place, *whether it is intended or not*. It occurs as a by-product of the child's role, which is a highly vulnerable one on several counts. The first reason for this vulnerability is *perceptual*. The child's early view of society is one in which the godlike figures of his father and mother tend to loom immensely large, with the remainder of the universe revolving around this constellation. The most casual remarks of parents in this context can easily acquire the weight of infallibility.

Second, *dependence* plays a part. A person whose welfare depends entirely on another cannot help but assume that his fate is partly contingent on conformity. This is especially the case, of course, when expressions of like-mindedness are rewarded, as they frequently are in children, as evidence of precocity and genius.

A third corollary of the home is the *restricted nature of its sources of information*. Even if the budding young man or woman were endowed with an inhumanly sceptical outlook on matters of doctrine, there would be no means of securing counterbalancing facts. Adults in comparable situations (such as American GI's in Chinese prisoner-of-war camps during the Korean conflict of the 1950's) frequently conform, even to the point of rejecting some of their basic premises and assumptions. The infant, who operates with a much more limited storehouse of resources, is completely helpless.

A final factor favoring the indoctrination of children is a mechanism that psychoanalysts have called *identification*. The relationship between parents and children is such that at a given age (variously estimated as between the third and seventh year) the need to emulate the parent arises. The child, in an effort to mold his own identity and to give preliminary direction to his life, uses his father or mother as a model. This process is far from limited to surface mannerisms (such as little Beauregard affecting his father's pipe, or Penelope shuffling around in mother's slippers). The growing person must be on the lookout for clues as to his status in the world, his role in relation to other people, and basic "how to's" in the area of human relations. The child is thus prone to build into his repertoire any consistencies he picks up in parental social conduct. He is especially likely to note and assimilate the way in which he is treated by his parents, because this information is most immediately, dramatically (and sometimes painfully) available. It is for this reason, for instance, that a good case can be made for the likelihood that parents who treat their children in a despotic fashion contribute toward the formation of bigotry, as among the children of authoritarian parents (see Chapter 3).

The converse also holds. A pacifist father, in an article entitled "Pacifism for Children," asks the following questions:

> How should pacifists bring up their children? Are they to give them guns to play with, and "horror comics" to read, in the hope that they will "get it out of their system"? Are they to encourage them to hit back when they are attacked, or are they to teach them to turn the other cheek? What can parents do to help their children to grow up strong and secure, and yet ready to stand out against the common acceptance of war?[2]

[2] H. Loukes, "Pacifism for Children," *Fellowship* Magazine (April 1957), published by the Fellowship of Reconciliation, Nyack, New York, p. 10.

In reviewing the alternatives, it soon becomes obvious that no specific actions are called for. Explicit indoctrination can easily boomerang. Instructing the child to turn the other cheek, for example, can make it an outcast among its peers; "children's republics" in the home can develop into frustrating chaos. As another pacifist parent notes:

> Pacifism may be encouraged in children but it does not seem wise to encourage it directly. Shutting off "The Untouchables," barring guns from the house, prohibiting sibling violence, will not of themselves insure a passion in children for peace. These may encourage instead a lust for "The Untouchables."[3]

The remaining option is to *create an atmosphere that contains the premises* for pacifism. This can become effective indoctrination because

> ... our children live in the mental and spiritual life that we live in. This happens whether we like it or not, whether we instruct them or not: The ideals by which we sincerely live are their ideals for a time, without their knowing why ... we can be certain that the life they live on their own will always be affected by the life they shared with us. It is a sobering thought, that our children are thus deeply marked by our deficiencies, but it is a comforting thought that they are equally deeply and silently marked by our faith.[4]

Thus, children

> ... seem to thrive on the contagion of marital affection, infectious good will, and on the feverish ups and downs of their own upbringing.
>
> How do they learn?
>
> From a mother tending to her child, its brothers and sisters discover that love is bestowed without thanks, not for its merit but in answer to a need.
>
> From the care lavished on that mound of mother-flesh wherein the growing foetus sleeps, the child learns that there is love enough for even those who have not yet been born.[5]

The salience of the parents in the world of the infant, the parents' monopoly on sources of welfare and of information, and the child's tendency to emulate his parents in forming his own personality, are all potent instruments of indoctrination during the formative years. With or without de-

[3] K. Lukens, "Good Child, Bad Child," *Fellowship* (January 1965), p. 6.
[4] Loukes, "Pacifism," p. 12.
[5] Lukens, "Good Child," p. 7.

liberate intent, they permit parents to inculcate in their children an infinite number of perceptions, attitudes, and beliefs. These—taken together—*may predetermine memberships*. Where they don't, they at least help create candidates for a restricted universe of social movements.

Subsequent socialization

Early indoctrination would be ineffectual if it were subsequently neutralized. Neutralization, however, is rare, because our society is constructed so as to provide every person with consecutive waves of relatively like-minded associates.

This is partly because members of our society tend to group themselves in more or less uniform layers. Upper-middle-class people, for example, tend to live in the "better" parts of town, attend private schools, and associate together at work and at play. This does not happen invariably, of course, but often enough so that *any given person encounters people similar to himself more frequently than chance*—"chance" being a situation in which you immerse everybody in a giant pot, stir, and extract your acquaintances.

This bias would be irrelevant if it were not that similar kinds of people tend to hold similar views. Two upper-middle-class persons discussing politics, for instance, are apt to find that they are both members of the Republican Party, and that they share comparable attitudes and beliefs about such diverse topics as labor unions, Communism, and civil rights. Their conversation, more often than not, may be mutually reinforcing.

Given this situation, a young boy or girl leaving the sheltered atmosphere of the home is apt to step into the sheltered atmosphere of the group to which his family belongs. Rather than choosing from a cafeteria of diverse views, he or she selects ideological intake from a redundant menu. The child plays in a neighborhood in which he overhears remarks, but since he plays in *his* kind of neighborhood, he is likely to hear congenial remarks. Other children and teachers do exert influence in school, but schools correspond to neighborhoods and income brackets—and so it goes.

Infantile indoctrination forms part of a process of socialization that in many ways support it. The sequence of influences impinging on the growing youngster tend not to be very discrepant from the direction set by his inheritance. Thus, although children do typically grow away from the views and attitudes of their progenitors, the deviations usually represent variations on preexisting themes, rather than the elaboration of new ones. Even in adolescence, outward manifestations of emancipation and rebellion tend to disguise relatively minor changes.[6]

"Working one's way up" is typically a sequence in which the heritage of the past is somewhat modernized to meet the demands of a new generation, and somewhat adjusted to compensate for temperamental variations, differences in intelligence, and unique experiences. There is no *revolution* in this process. Conventional society by and large produces conventional people with conventional views.

Since social movements are usually departures from convention, a conversion to a social movement represents a more or less drastic departure from the socialization process. It represents the emergence of beliefs, attitudes, and feelings that are different from those inculcated in the child. This is not to say, however, that they are divorced from their source. *Basically, socialization lays the groundwork not only for its direct products, but also for its by-products.*[7]

The need for absolutes

Most departures from socialization arise when the process creates demands which it does not satisfy. Such failures, however, are grudgingly registered and cautiously responded to. A person who has been taught from childhood to expect simple, plausible, and unqualified explanations continues to require them. When his childhood assumptions no longer provide assistance, he must nevertheless retain them until he finds others, *similar in kind*, to take their place.

The typical product of socialization is a person who has become incapable of accepting with equanimity the uncertainties and complexities of life. Instead, he has learned to impose the beliefs of his parents on his encounters with the world. These beliefs provide structure where there frequently is none, offer certainty where there is ambiguity, and predict events which are indeterminable. In the words of the playwright Pirandello,

> Don't you see what they are after? They all want the truth—a truth that is: Something specific; something concrete! They don't care what it is. All

[6] In the case of religious beliefs, for instance, see D. Katz and F. H. Allport, *Student Attitudes* (Syracuse, N. Y.: Craftsman Press, 1931); P. E. Jacob, *Changing Values in College* (New York: Harper & Brothers, 1957); and R. V. McCann, "Developmental Factors in the Growth of Mature Faith," *Relig. Educ.*) 50 (May–June 1955), pp. 147–155.

[7] R. K. Merton, "Social Structure and Anomie," in his *Social Theory and Social Structure* (Glencoe, Ill.: Free Press, 1957), pp. 131–194.

they want is something categorical, something that speaks plainly! Then they'll quiet down.[8]

One consequence of our acquired predilection for absolutes is that it creates discontinuity in the way our beliefs change. We are forced to live with unrecognized doubts and hidden inconsistencies; we strain to preserve constancy; we assert convictions that we no longer unambiguously believe. Ultimately, when our reservations and hidden adjustments reach a bursting point, we merely substitute a new set of absolutes for the old. We experience the culmination of changes as a "switch," and we boast of a *conversion*.

Since conversions are merely the surface peaks of the icebergs of change, they can easily seem inexplicable. "We find ourselves believing," wrote William James; "we hardly know how and why."[9] Arthur Koestler speaks of a process of "computation," which is "carried out by an erratic, partially unconscious, piecemeal kind of reasoning," with the "conclusion" coming into awareness "like the result which appears on the dial of electronic calculators."[10] Because such computation remains unconscious until it achieves its results, the believer can uninterruptedly continue to retain whatever beliefs he holds. Moreover, because the result on the "dial" feels relatively spontaneous, it gives new beliefs the appearance of being self-evident.

But conversions are neither sudden nor spontaneous. They merely represent the juncture at which a believer becomes aware that he has been *forced* to discard old assumptions and to try a set of new ones.

Disillusionment

The beliefs a person has acquired are safe as long as they are not put to the test. A person can live with inconsistencies as long as these do not confront each other, and he can operate on the basis of invalid assumptions if these are not directly matched against experience.

An adult is most secure against change if as a child he has been indoctrinated with consistent beliefs, and if these beliefs are also plausible interpretations of experiences that he is likely to encounter.[11] Socialization

[8] L. Pirandello, "It *Is* So! (If You Think So)," in *Three Plays* (New York: Dutton, 1922) p. 210.

[9] W. James "The Will To Believe," reprinted in W. Barrett and H. D. Aiken, eds., *Philosophy in the Twentieth Century*, Vol. 1 (New York: Random House, 1962), pp. 245–246.

[10] A. Koestler, *Arrow in the Blue: An Autobiography* (London: Collins, 1952), p. 239.

[11] H. Toch, R. T. Anderson, J. A. Clark, and J. J. Mullin, " 'Secularization' in College: An Exploratory Study," *Relig. Educ.* (November–December 1964), pp. 490–504.

that transmits anachronisms in a rapidly changing world invites disillusionment, as does the transmission of beliefs which run counter to the person's
needs. Santayana makes the latter point with the following story:

> In the gardens of Seville I once heard, coming through the tangle of palms
> and orange trees, the treble voice of a pupil in a theological seminary, crying
> to his playmate: "You booby! of course angels have a more perfect nature
> than men." With his black and red cassock that child had put on dialectic;
> he was playing the game of dogma and dreaming in words, and was insen-
> sible to the scent of violets that filled the air. How long would that last?
> Hardly, I suspect, until the next spring; and the troubled awakening which
> puberty would presently bring to that little dogmatist, sooner or later over-
> takes all elder dogmatists in the press of the world."[12]

Since beliefs generally differ *to some degree* from experience, are usually
of *limited* flexibility, and are never *completely* consistent or *entirely* functional, they exist undisturbed only as long as they are not confronted with
reality. This requirement is generally met by people who live relatively
passive lives, or who hold their beliefs fairly lightly. On the other hand,
strong and active concern with conventional beliefs can create the opportunities for disillusionment, and fanaticism is almost certain to do so.

One of Martin Luther's biographers observes that Luther's "revolt
against the medieval Church arose from a desperate effort to follow the way
by her prescribed."[13] Luther responded to his Catholic upbringing so intensely that he became permeated with a sense of deep unworthiness and
with intolerable feelings of guilt. The Church offered the means of restoring
self-confidence and reducing guilt (through confession and communion),
but Luther's condition had become so acute that these recourses were inadequate for him. Luther himself wrote:

> My situation was that, although an impeccable monk, I stood before God
> as a sinner troubled in conscience, and I had no confidence that my merit
> would assuage him. Therefore I did not love a just and angry God, but
> rather hated and murmured against him.[14]

In an effort to deal with this predicament, Luther worked out a resolution
which came to represent a significant departure from conventional Catholicism:

---

[12] G. Santayana, "Scepticism and Animal Faith," reprinted in Barrett and Aiken,
Philosophy, pp. 384–385.
[13] R. H. Bainton, *Here I Stand. A Life of Martin Luther* (New York: Mentor,
1955), p. 27.
[14] *Ibid.*, p. 49.

Night and day I pondered until I saw the connection between the justice of God and the statement that "the just shall live by his faith." Then I grasped that the justice of God is that righteousness by which through grace and sheer mercy God justifies us *through faith*. Thereupon I felt myself to be reborn and to have gone through open doors into paradise.[15]

A devout believer may, of course, detect flaws in generally accepted beliefs, but still dismiss his discovery as irrelevant. This does not mean that the experience leaves no impact. Eventually an ideological transmutation may occur, in which "conquered" disillusionments can be presumed to have played a role. An illustration is provided by a story concerning Annie Besant, who *several years after* the following incident rejected Christianity, and become a prominent member of various radical movements:

> She sat down by her table with Bible, pencil, and paper. She would follow step by step through Christ's last days on earth as recounted by each of the four apostles. Innocently she drew four accounts. To her horror she discovered, as so many have done before and since, that the four stories do not agree. When she reached the contradictions of the Friday of the crucifixion, she gave up her attempt in an agony of distress.
>
> Her world of religious fantasy reeled about her. But only for a moment. Remembering the temptations of Augustine and other saints, she recognized this as crude temptation of the devil, a test of her faith. She flushed that she should have been momentarily shaken, and murmuring Tertullian's "credo quia impossibile" ("I believe because it is impossible") she fell to her knees in an extasis of prayer.[16]

A façade of continued conviction may hide a cumulation of disillusioning experiences until a final enforced confrontation brings them to the fore. The end of such a sequence is exemplified by an eminent Democratic politician, who had been brought up as a staunch Republican:

> His transfer of party allegiance was a direct result of an attempt by his father-in-law, a prominent local Republican, to whip up his interest in politics.
>
> It never occurred to [the father-in-law] ... that his mild-mannered son-in-law might, under the stimulus, become an ardent adherent of the New Deal–Fair Deal political philosophy. After all, his forebears had been staunch Republicans for over half a century.
>
> Thus, he invited Charley ... to join a small group of fellow Republicans who met periodically in nearby Pennington to discuss the Republican viewpoint.

15 *Ibid.* (italics added).
16 From *The Passionate Pilgrim: A Life of Annie Besant* by Gertrude Marvin Williams, © 1931, pp. 18–19. Reprinted by permission of Coward-McCann.

Reminiscently, Charley recalls that he felt political apostasy essential if he were to continue to live with himself.[17]

The beliefs Charley had acquired from his family survived until he was forced into a comparison between the Republican position and the problems of the depression. Since he *had already adopted* liberal and humanitarian premises, his "conversion" was immediate. Whereas Mrs. Besant's discovery of unreliable biblical accounts and Martin Luther's inability to assuage his guilt were merely *disillusioning,* Charley's exploration of Republican beliefs was able to *precipitate* conversion.

The role of precipitating experiences

Disillusioning encounters are experiences that weaken the structure of a person's beliefs. *Precipitating experiences are final disillusioning experiences.* They have sufficient persuasiveness to cause the belief structure to finally collapse. Their potency is a product of their dramatic import and of the believer's susceptibility to subversion.

Timing here is crucial. Probably the most dramatic of all precipitating experiences is the expectation of death, which carries a "now or never" connotation. Typically, the assumption that one is going to die precipitates adherence to social movements that center around supernatural beliefs. Martin Luther's religious career began with a menacing bolt of lightning. The adventist William Miller became converted on the battlefield of Plattsburg. Voltaire and Heine adopted religion on their death-beds, after many years of antitheistic crusading. Life rafts and trenches frequently initiate active religious concern. *The New York Times,* under the headline "Korea Horror Turns Him to Religion," provides an illustration involving a twenty-two-year-old veteran who had decided to enter the ministry of a fundamentalist sect:

> It began Nov. 30, 1950, in the grim days of the war, when Mr. Inman and about 230 other soldiers were ambushed. He said that he was the only survivor.
>
> Surrounded, he got down on his knees and prayed. Mr. Inman said that "I was afraid, but suddenly I felt something like a hand on my shoulder and I wasn't afraid any more."[18]

In other cases, the relationship between the precipitating experience and the resulting conversion is more indirect. For instance, *Life* magazine

[17] *The New York Times* (October 29, 1954).
[18] *The New York Times* (December 23, 1953).

reports the story of a wealthy young Bostonian who reacted to the death of his father by settling on an island in an Indian religious community.[19] Archbishop Avvakum claims that he became converted by the sight of a dead ox.[20]

The precipitating experience itself tells us little about its precipitating potential. The key to the effectiveness of these experiences lies in the connotations they carry for the predisposed believer. Thus a person already attracted to religiosity may seize upon any contact with death to justify a step he may have covertly considered for some time. A person with doubts about the social order may be sensitive to experiences suggesting evidence of social injustice. This is illustrated by the "awakening" experience of Charles Bradlaugh (the nineteenth-century English freethinker) who as a young man participated in the eviction of a poverty-stricken Irish family:

> That man was carried out while we were there—in front of us, while the sleet was coming down . . . and he died there while we were there; and three nights afterwards, while I was sentry on the front gate at Ballincollig Barracks, we heard a cry . . . we found this poor woman there a raving maniac, with one dead babe in one arm and another in the other, clinging to the cold nipple of her lifeless breast . . . would not rebellion have seemed the holiest gospel you could have preached?[21]

The answer to Bradlaugh's rhetorical question is that "it depends." It is doubtful, for instance, that every soldier in Ballincollig Barracks reacted to this Irish tragedy by becoming a freethinker. Bradlaugh's response—plausible though it was—was made possible because his adherence to the dominant social institutions of his time had already become tenuous and riddled with doubt.

The precipitating transaction

The stereotyped trappings of conversion—the culminating insight, the flash of intuition, the emotional upheaval, the "death and transfiguration" —are probably dramatic exceptions to a more prosaic rule. Even specifiable precipitating experiences are no doubt comparatively rare. The typical de-

---

[19] "Boston Hindu: In India a U. S. Mystic Seeks Peace of Mind," *Life* (December 23, 1957), pp. 98–99.

[20] Avvakum, *The Life of Archpriest Avvakum, by Himself* (London: Hogarth, 1924), p. 42.

[21] J. E. Courtney, *Freethinkers of the Nineteenth Century* (London: Chapman & Hall, 1920), p. 110.

parture from conventional belief tends to occur when a person whose adherence to the *status quo* has been weakened encounters a plausible solution, at a point of high susceptibility.

Immediate wholehearted commitment to new beliefs is probably unusual. More typically, tentative inquiry into available alternatives eventually culminates in full dedication. We shall examine this sequence in the next chapter. At the moment, it may suffice to illustrate the role of conversion in this context.

For a person who is "shopping" for beliefs, the closest thing to a conversion is the discovery of an attractive item on the ideological counter. It is *the experience of considering an appealing set of beliefs, and the decision to adopt it.*

An example is the reaction of an American physicist, Rodney Satory, to the "Peace Hostage" proposal originated by Stephen James, a New York advertising copywriter. James had suggested that prominent Americans might volunteer to participate in a mass exchange program with Russian colleagues, since "The Russians wouldn't be very likely to bomb this country if hundreds—perhaps thousands—of their citizens were living here."

The proposal reached Satory in transit to New Zealand, where he hoped to "escape a nuclear war." Satory reacted to the document as follows:

> Your organization's proposal towards a war deterrent is so logical and practical that I have no choice but to sign my peace hostage volunteer pledge.
>
> I believe that if the program can be consummated, my chances of survival in Russia as a member of the group would be better than the survival chances without the plan in New Zealand.
>
> Here's hoping to meet you as a fellow pledge in Moscow or Peking. Here's to a better world.[22]

Satory's reaction to the James proposal was conditioned by his obvious disillusionment with American foreign policy, his fear of war, his desire to maximize the chances of survival, and his ambition to contribute to a reduction of international tension. His signature on the pledge is equivalent to the statement, "I feel that your proposal represents a fitting resolution to my own accumulating doubts." That other solutions (such as migration to New Zealand) had previously evoked the same response is a consequence of past intersections between Satory's predisposition and the appeals presented to him.

[22] Detroit *News* (November 24, 1962).

The true believer

Many persons have sufficiently ubiquitous predispositions to experience conversions on various occasions. Some persons even manifest the extreme pattern of the true believer, who joins one social movement after another with apparent disregard for continuity and consistency.[23] Annie Besant, for instance, turned from self-flagellation to organized atheism, and migrated through Malthusianism, feminism, socialism, and theosophy. Her writings include "On the Deity of Jesus of Nazareth," "My Path to Atheism," "Why I am a Socialist," "Why I Became a Theosophist," "Occult Chemistry," and "Self-Government for India."

Another true believer was Orestes A. Brownson, who once remarked, "I deny that I have *changed*, though I own that I seem to myself to have advanced." Brownson's biographer says of him that

> He developed a dozen schemes which promised hope and salvation, but each crumbled under him, in part from the destructive force of his own intellect. *He had not been trained by education to accept skepticism and live in uncertainty.* Doubt bred torment. With heartbreaking intensity *he longed to reach the ultimate certainty.*[24]

Frequent conversions come about in people whose socialization has led them to develop a strong need for comprehensive absolutes, such that when their beliefs are brought into question, a complete new set must be immediately substituted. In each case, the person must feel that "this time, the answer to all the problems of the universe is at hand." He cannot accept less, because his specifications have always included *complete certainty* and *complete coverage.*

The childhood of the true believer typically features an environment in which beliefs play an important role, and shows evidence of strong concern with ideological matters. H. T. Dohrman, a student of California cults, characterizes the "cultist" as a person who "often spent his early life in an oppressive religious atmosphere" and who remembers " 'doing a lot of thinking' about religion during his youth." The career of this type of person may be characterized as follows:

---

[23] The term "true believer" was popularized by Eric Hoffer and his book *The True Believer* (New York: Harper & Brothers, 1951). Hoffer feels that the core of the membership of every social movement is made up of fanatics who are basically unconcerned with the movement's ideology.

[24] A. M. Schlesinger, Jr., *Orestes A. Brownson: A Pilgrim's Progress* (New York: Little, Brown, 1939), p. 282 (italics added).

As the cult individual grew older, he wanted affirmation and hope from his religion: orthodoxy could give him none. Eventually he contacted Christian Science, Unity, or some other realm of metaphysics, and they released him from his sense of sin, deleted Hell and the Devil from his life, and provided him with a positive, healthy-minded system of thought. Thenceforth he progressed onward and upward, ever searching, far into the stratosphere of the cult and the occult—to pyramidology, astrology, hermetics, spiritualism, faith-healing, Yoga, Lemuria, cabalistic prophecy, or a myriad of others, but not until he happened upon ———— did the vision of his cultic dreams come true. There he found satisfactions that no other group had ever given him.[25]

Unlike cultists and other types of true believers, the typical convert is less diffusely motivated, and less ambitious in his demands. He does not pursue affirmation and hope, but rather seeks to resolve a particular set of difficulties with the social order. And he experiences a conversion, *if he encounters the right appeal at the right time.*

Types of conversions

The transaction of predisposition and appeal can occur with varying degrees of *urgency* and *specificity*. One extreme of these dimensions is illustrated in the following letter:

> One day I was sitting in my home and the thought came to me, "Why don't you put your head in the oven, turn on the gas, and end it all?" Just then a knock came on the door. I answered, and saw a tall woman. I said, "The Lord sent you here." She asked why. I told her. She asked me if she could have a prayer. I said Yes, so we knelt in prayer. In her prayer she asked God never to let me think this thought again, and I never have since that time. She asked if she could give me Bible studies. I said Yes. She came for one year every Tuesday—rain, snow hail or blow. She never missed.
>
> I was invited to attend some Adventist evangelistic meetings. Later I was baptized. For me the Adventist faith is all that I need. It provides an inner peace that passes all understanding.[26]

For this woman, the appearance of an Adventist colporteur at her door could not have been better timed. The urgency of her problem is obvious from the fact that she had contemplated a final solution to it. The specificity of her predisposition is implied in her compliance with the request

---

[25] H. T. Dohrman, *California Cult* (Boston: Beacon, 1958), p. 117.
[26] "Why I Became an Adventist," *Review and Herald, 138* No. 1 (1961), p. 12.

for a prayer. Here, the conversion almost follows from the circumstances of the encounter.

In most instances, however, predispositions persist over time and are not completely specific. Available appeals can be more calmly and leisurely considered. A conversion becomes more a lazy step than a plunge into a life-saving breach.

An illustration of the more casual road to commitment is contained in the autobiographical reflections of Ezell Blair, Jr., leader of the student civil-rights group that originated sit-down demonstrations. Blair recalled that the entire demonstration movement originated in a dormitory conversation: "One Sunday night—it was the last day of January—we were talking and Joe said, 'Well, we've talked about it long enough. Let's do something.' "[27] The conversion experience *as such* here is almost inconsequential. It nevertheless represents the adoption of a new set of beliefs, and thereby has inescapable and far-reaching consequences.

The effects of conversion

If a conversion is consummated—if new beliefs are incorporated by the believer—a psychological reorganization tends to follow. The first indication is usually a feeling of relief, which signals the emergence of accumulated reservations. Next, as the convert's perceptions become subservient to new beliefs, he may report that things look different. Not infrequently he claims that confusions have been dispelled and that he now perceives things "as they really are." Koestler reports that

> To say that one had "seen the light" is a poor description of the mental rapture which only the convert knows (regardless of what faith he has been converted to). The new light seems to pour from all directions across the skull; the whole universe falls into pattern like the stray pieces of a jigsaw puzzle assembled by magic at one stroke. There is now an answer to every question, doubts and conflicts are a matter of the tortured past.[28]

Ingersoll describes his feelings as follows:

> When I became convinced that the universe is natural—that all the ghosts and gods are myths, there entered into my brain, into my soul, into every drop of my blood, the sense, the feeling, the joy of freedom. The walls of my

[27] *The New York Times* (March 26, 1960).
[28] A. Koestler, in R. Crossman, ed., *The God That Failed* (New York: Bantam, 1952), p. 22.

prison crumbled and fell, the dungeon was flooded with light, and all the bolts, and bars, and manacles became dust.[29]

Martin Luther, after his break from Catholicism, wrote that "I feel much freer now that I am certain the pope is Antichrist."[30]

These kinds of statements suggest that conversions permit a perceptual reorganization such that what the person sees corresponds to what he feels he ought to see. Whereas his loyalty to conventional society had previously prevented him from reaching unconventional but plausible conclusions, he can now reconstruct his experiences to yield veridicality.

However, the convert's view of the world not only becomes more compatible with his personal experiences; it also becomes more congenial. This follows from the fact that conversion leads to the adoption of beliefs that solve the believer's problems.

As "solutions" begin to take place, the convert may seem to become happier and may appear more at ease. Sara Harris writes of one of Father Divine's followers: "She was never so fortunate as she was on the day she recognized Divine's divinity. For that was the day on which she attained her own security."[31] In the case of George Fox, the founder of the Quaker movement, it was observed that

> . . . as soon as he began to think of himself as a minister of Christ and a new set of beliefs took shape around that role, his personality was reorganized. From confusion and uncertainty and despair, he became a stable, self-assured, and socially effective man who was able to sway others with his deep convictions.[32]

A convert to Elijah Muhammad's Black Muslims declares:

> I find that Islam provides conditions of peace and comfort for me and for all those who may wish to tread the path prescribed by it, whoever they may be, whatever they may be and wherever they may be.[33]

As suggested in this last quotation, the convert may feel that his satisfactions can be widely shared. More often than not, he ignores his own role

[29] R. G. Ingersoll, "Why I Am an Agnostic," *Works*, Vol. 2 (New York: C. P. Farrell, 1907), p. 65.

[30] Bainton, *Here I Stand*, p. 124.

[31] S. Harris, *Father Divine, Holy Husband* (New York: Doubleday, 1953), p. 319.

[32] A. T. Boisen, "The Development and Validation of Religious Faith," *Psychiatry*, 14 (November 1951), p. 460.

[33] L. X, "Why I Believe in Islam," *Salaam* (July 1960), p. 29.

in the conversion transaction, and attributes his contentment to his beliefs. Since, moreover, he also experiences the need to justify his conversion, he may develop a strong urge to prescribe his beliefs for others.

If a movement is obviously unpopular, and it therefore becomes difficult for the convert to see himself surrounded by potential fellow-members, he may resort to another stratagem. This is illustrated in the following excerpts from proceedings of the Third Annual Spacecraft Convention—a meeting of Flying Saucer enthusiats—in Yucca Valley, California:

> The Reverend Morris Ludwig of Portland, Oreg. set the tone for the convention, when, in his invocation he expressed thanks to God for being part of a group interested in searching for the higher purposes of life. "Help us not to force our opinions on others," he said, "but only to point the way to right living and understanding."
>
> First speaker was Mrs. Dana Howard of Palm Springs. She stated, "A large percentage of the world's people live in a shell, and like turtles, are afraid to stick out their necks! We know that we saucer enthusiasts are the laughing stock of the world, but we take it in good grace, knowing that the picture will soon be far different. . . . We are seeking peace and contentment for the entire world! We are trying to open the avenues of space, to build a bridge across eternity!"
>
> .   .   .   .
>
> Frank Scully, "Dean of Saucer Writers," said, "Knowing the truth about saucers is like being too far ahead of a parade—nobody sees you or knows that you are there. If you're ahead in this world, you are out of step with the parade. So it is with the flying saucer information."[34]

The premise here still is that beliefs have intrinsic merit, but this does not lead to the inference that they must have general appeal. On the contrary, the believer argues that it is precisely the validity of his beliefs which makes them unpopular. He thus becomes one of a select few who can benefit mankind by recognizing meritorious solutions to universal problems.

The changes that follow the act of conversion are directed at the task of consolidating psychological gains. As soon as new beliefs are adopted, a stock-taking follows, which records the advantages of the new beliefs over the old. Simultaneously, the reinterpretation of reality begins. Old facts are given new meanings. Premises sprout conclusions and then proliferate into systems. The convert embarks on the sequence to commitment, which we shall examine in the next chapter.

[34] U-Forum, Grand Rapids, Mich. (July 1957), pp. 12, 14.

Conversion in perspective

In the elliptical process that begins with the induction of the growing child into conventional society and culminates with his membership in a group seeking to modify society, conversion represents the apparent turning point. In the foregoing pages, we have tried to show that it is—more modestly—a point of *transition*.

The convert is a *disillusioned* person, and disillusionment is a slow, surreptitious type of change. It begins with undercover reservations to the effort of remaining loyal. It represents a cumulative record of the costs of adaptation. Whether it dies in its suppressed state or becomes publicized in awareness depends on the number and the import of disillusioning experiences that are encountered.

A disillusioning experience is the perception of a discrepancy between conventional beliefs and psychological or physical realities. More accurately, *it represents a perception of a discrepancy between two perceptions*, one of which shows the consequences of belief, and the second of which reveals the import of facts or the demand of needs. These perceived discrepancies are most likely to occur:

(1) with *beliefs* that are
    (a) premised on distortions of social reality,
    (b) nonresponsive to personal needs,
    (c) insufficiently flexible to accommodate emergent events, or
    (d) mutually inconsistent, if matched;
(2) in *situations* which
    (a) challenge existing interpretations of society,
    (b) frustrate existing personal needs, or
    (c) create new needs; and
(3) for *persons*
    (a) whose problems differ from conventional ones,
    (b) who are intensely concerned with applying their beliefs, or
    (c) who have experienced disillusionments in the past.

This listing may be reduced to the statement that *a person will tend to become disillusioned if he becomes actively involved in life situations for which he has been ill-prepared by socialization.*

Although there are many deficits in the socialization process, its most general defect is overambitiousness. Persons who have been oversocialized, in the sense that too many absolutes have been too deeply inculcated in them, are most likely to experience subsequent clashes with reality. The extreme instance of this rule is the true believer, for whom life becomes a constant struggle to impose shaky dogmas on slippery facts. In general, a person who demands that conventional society conform to his mold soon finds that he must either revise his expectations or transform the social order. He may try both.

Oversocialization, however, is only one source of difficulty. A *person may encounter problems because his parents have taught him to expect too much, or because society fails to meet fair minimum demands.* In the case of many underprivileged persons, oversocialization can consist of expecting means of subsistence, or hoping for justice from authorities. Some persons would escape conversions only if they had no expectations and no demands at all.

7 ▷ THE CONSEQUENCES OF BEING A MEMBER

IT may be useful to spell out some of the consequences of a person's becoming a member. What happens to a man who has affiliated himself with a collective enterprise? How is he changed?

At first glance, this question looks nonsensical. After all, the demands of one group often are trivial compared to the sacrifices required by another. Some people have their lives completely changed by joining, whereas others move among affiliations like fish through water. And in any meeting hall, the firm believer sits side by side with the casual sympathizer. Obviously, different groups affect different people in different ways.

But, although membership effects differ, they differ in systematic fashion. Certain effects of membership seem to occur in sequence. As in the progression of a disease or the growth of a plant or the unfolding of affection, we seem able to chart the position of a member along the road of membership. When we confine our attention to large, ideologically oriented groups, we can trace these steps on a continuum from faith to fanaticism. It is especially important to describe this career, because most of us underestimate the extent to which "extreme" personalities can be the products of personal commitment.

Moreover, even though the effects of membership are most often relatively moderate, we must be able to distinguish various degrees of personality change, so as to be able to define the particular fate of individual members.[1]

Commitment

There may be nothing monumental about the transfer of a membership card, which often involves little more than a moderate payment to satisfy a treasurer. In some instances, the new member is one of a limited number who share the privilege of certification. To join a group called "Mensa," for instance, a candidate must score a minimum of 136 on the Cattell III IQ Test. A woman wishing to become a Daughter of the American Revolution has to demonstrate her descent from a "participant," liberally defined as including patriotic ministers and businessmen.

But most collective enterprises do not specify personal qualifications for eligibility. Instead, they generally suppose that every prospective member is in the position to express agreement with at least part of the group's belief system. Another requirement may be attendance at meetings.

In a group having even these minimal membership requirements, some persons may discharge them more assiduously than others. Some may study the movement's ideology painstakingly, for instance, while others may express surface agreement with limited aspects of it. Gabriel Almond, who interviewed members of Communist Parties in four countries, reported that "only 27 per cent of the respondents had been exposed to the classical writings of Communism before or at the time of joining." Almond cites the following as a sample experience:

> While I was trying to get in . . . the members were looking me over. Finally X started giving me pamphlets to read. The first was against Trotsky, of whom I had never heard. It was eighty pages long. The most dreary thing; I couldn't understand it. Later they gave me Stalin's *Foundations of Leninism*, and some Marx.[2]

How far the consequences of membership assert themselves *depends on the degree to which a person commits himself to membership.* Membership is not an all-or-none proposition. Some people are more members than

[1] It must be added that although some social movements routinely affect the personality of their members, others practically never do. This chapter applies primarily to the former type of movement.

[2] Reprinted from *The Appeals of Communism* by Gabriel Almond by permission of Princeton University Press, copyright 1954 by the Princeton University Press, p. 101.

others, and the extent to which a person is a member depends on how much of himself he gives to his group. Different persons feel called upon to make different contributions. A housewife may spend one evening a week typing mailing lists; a college student may invite imprisonment by participating in civil rights actions; a Latin American congressman may resign to become a guerrilla, offering "to exchange a soft and safe life for one of wandering, persecution, hunger, wounds, sickness and nakedness."[3]

Social movements may make provisions for many kinds and degrees of commitment. A sample issue of a pacifist publication, for instance, advertises options such as placing a peace bumper sticker on one's car, writing poems for peace, fasting, or participating as a volunteer in an expedition proposing to take medicines to Cuba.[4]

Individual differences in degree of commitment may be dramatic, and may require several categories of membership. Jehovah's Witnesses, for instance, distinguish between "pioneers" and "publishers." A "pioneer" is a member who accumulates a minimum of 100 hours monthly of doorbell-ringing and salesmanship. "Publishers" work on a more relaxed schedule. Similarly, the inner core of the "I Am" Sect are required to abstain from sexual relations, whereas fringe members are permitted a full family life.

Whether a member shows the effects of membership, and the extent to which he does, is related to gradations such as these. Although there are other factors involved, the progression is somewhat like the path from the first martini to confirmed alcoholism. While personal immunities and predispositions may play a role, no one is completely immune or completely predisposed. Beyond a certain point, the consequences of involvement are inescapable.

Sacrifice of autonomy

Some social movements require close to total commitment of their members. A person belonging to such a movement is expected to dedicate his life almost completely to the movement, and cannot be said to have private concerns of his own. The process in its extreme form is illustrated by the Trappist monks, one of the strictest religious orders in the world. The Trappist spends twelve hours a day in prayer and meditation. He is permitted to communicate with other Trappists only by sign language, and not at all with persons in the outside world. He scarcely sleeps, and retires fully clothed, sometimes to be awakened several times during the night.

[3] *The New York Times* (October 24, 1962).
[4] *Fellowship* (December 15, 1962).

He submits to seven months of fasting every year, in addition to the regular fasts proclaimed by the Catholic Church. Lastly, he is subject to public confession and penance. None of these sacrifices, however, are as painful as that of giving up his individual existence, to merge completely in the group:

> The long hours of prayer, hard work and frugal nourishment, perpetual silence, the vow of stability—living and dying in the same monastery— the interrupted sleep—all of these are considered light by the monks compared with the greatest trial of their existence, communal life twenty-four hours a day until death.
>
> The natural inclinations for privacy or to follow an intellectual or physical task of his own choosing is never permitted a Trappist. His personality must become completely submerged in the community. This the monk considers his greatest cross.[5]

Every act of membership involves a sacrifice of privacy and autonomy, at least in the sense that the member must accomplish some of his objectives as part of a group, rather than as an individual. There are students of social movements who feel that this, in and of itself, appeals to people. Eric Hoffer, for instance, writes that "A rising mass movement attracts and holds a following not by its doctrines and promises, but by the refuge it offers from the anxieties, barrenness and meaninglessness of an individual existence."[6]

Although there unquestionably are *some* persons in *some* social movements whose main concern is to lose themselves in a collective enterprise, most members view their group commitments—including their sacrifice of individuality—as necessary attributes of their brand of life, rather than as ends in themselves. The leader of the Catholic Worker movement, Dorothy Day, who shares an unheated cold-water flat with five other women, explains her living conditions with the phrase "while there are poor here we must be with them."[7] Commitments must be made in order to reach one's objectives.

Not infrequently, the commitment demanded of a member places him in a position of actively suppressing some of his personal proclivities. In theory, the fully committed member invariably makes this sacrifice. Thus the ideal "Communist Party Member" is described by Ch'en Yun as a man who always puts the Party first:

[5] *The New York Times* (August 12, 1958).

[6] Hoffer, *True Believer* p. 39. Also see E. Fromm, *Escape from Freedom* (New York: Farrar & Rinehart, 1941).

[7] D. Day, Circular letter, *"Dear fellow workers in Christ"* (multilith, November 1962).

... in the course of revolutionary work as well as Party work, the individual interests of Party members may come into conflict with those of the Party. At such a time, every Party member should fall back on his unlimited devotion to the revolution and the Party, sacrifice unhesitatingly his individual interests and bow to the over-all interests of the revolution and the Party. ... [He must] put the interests of the revolution and the Party first and deal with all individual issues on the principle that revolutionary and Party interests stand above all others. He must not place individual interests above those of the revolution and the Party.[8]

To the extent to which a person is less than fully committed, we would expect him to depart from this model. For instance, there are persons in the nonviolent resistance movement of the American civil rights struggle who have continuous difficulty with the requirement of remaining nonviolent. Attempts at self-suppression produce the following kinds of compromise resolutions:

After picketers had succeeded in keeping all customers out of a segregated restaurant except one man, each time the picketers walked past the window behind which he was sitting, some of them glared at him. ... During sit-ins, when waitresses stumbled in reading the complicated language of the Maryland trespass law, which they must read aloud as part of the legal process of requesting a sitter to leave a restaurant, some of the sitters unnecessarily corrected the waitresses' English. To do so "makes you feel good," one of the Negro student leaders explained to me.

When a policeman asked a group of picketers to walk outside a certain line on the concrete sidewalk so as not to block a door, two of the picketers taunted the policeman by placing their feet as close to the line as possible, watching their feet with exaggerated care, and occasionally grinning at him.[9]

In the vast majority of situations, however, there simply are no conflicts between personal interests and group demands. Thus, most members of the nonviolent resistance movement are convinced that the return of love for hate is a powerful force for change. Many even feel that this type of activity uniquely expresses their personal values:

Bertha Gerber tried to buy a bus ticket at a white ticket window, and for doing so was suspended from State College, Albany, Georgia, and jailed. But afterwards she said: "I have gained a feeling of decency and self-respect,

---

[8] Ch'en Yun, "How to be a Communist Party member," in B. Compton, ed., *Mao's China: Party Reform Documents 1942–1944* (Seattle: Univ. of Washington Press, 1952), p. 101.

[9] C. Mabee, "Will Commitment to Nonviolence Last?" *Liberation* (April 1963), p. 15.

a feeling of cleanliness, that neither the dirtiest walls of Albany's jail nor the actions of any institution can take away from me."[10]

Most members, in other words, either feel that the sacrifice involved in commitment is worth it, or else they don't experience it as a sacrifice. They *want* to make the commitments demanded by their goals. Where this desire is not a factor in joining, it tends to develop during membership.

Authority

Members tend to be like-minded. This is true not only because similar concerns have brought them together, but also because they share the same *authorities*.

An authority is anything which serves as a source of beliefs. It can be a book or a pamphlet, a person or a group of persons. Whatever its nature, it derives its authoritative quality from the fact that people use it to help them decide what they should believe. Authorities are sources of premises, of assertions which are taken on faith. To the extent to which a person accepts authorities, he relinquishes the opportunity of arriving at his beliefs independently.[11]

By the same token, the only way a piece of literature can become authoritative, or a person can become an authority, is by being accepted as such. Wisdom, perceptiveness, or face validity do not create authority.

[10] *Ibid.*, p. 17.

[11] The concept of authority used in this chapter combines elements from standard dictionary definitions, such as the following, extracted from *The Universal English Dictionary*: "3. Moral, intellectual weight, influence, power, derived from a person's character, knowledge, rank, position, etc., and the esteem and prestige which these carry. . . . 4. *a*. Person who is relied upon, by reason of his special knowledge, experience, study, to give trustworthy testimony or a weighty and credible opinion on particular facts and events. . . *b*. books or documents in which such knowledge, experience and opinions are embodied. . . . *c*. weight of opinion, bulk of testimony." Connotations that relate authority to legal power or to intrinsic superiority are not relevant here.

This use of the concept is similar to that of Rokeach, who defines authority as "any source to whom we look for information about the universe, or to check information we already possess." (M. Rokeach, *The Open and Closed Mind* [New York: Basic Books, 1960], p. 43). As Rokeach points out, authority in this sense is a concept analogous to that of "reference group (or person)," which is currently popular among social psychologists. (See M. Rokeach, *The Three Christs of Ypsilanti* [New York: Knopf, 1964], p. 24). A standard definition of reference group is "any group with which the individual identifies himself such that he tends to use the group as a standard for self-evaluation and as a source of his personal values and goals" (D. Krech, R. S. Crutchfield, and E. L. Ballachey, *Individual in Society: A Textbook of Social Psychology* [New York: McGraw Hill, 1962], p. 102).

Authority cannot be legislated or endowed. It can arise only from the responsiveness and acceptance of its audience.

There are several reasons why people bring authorities into existence. There is obvious economy in not having to make up one's own mind. There is security in having one's beliefs bolstered by dependable foundations. There is order in a world containing places to which one can turn for answers. And if one feels that an issue has already been effectively explored, it might appear foolhardy and pretentious to try to go over the same ground with one's own feeble resources.

Authorities may be explicitly resorted to in the process of trying to arrive at a conclusion, as in the case of Communist Party members asking for directives on an unsettled issue. They may, on the other hand, be used under the guise of truly independent reasoning, as in "discussions" taking forms such as

> In saying "This is my body" what was Jesus referring to?
> ... It is evident that Jesus was referring to his own fleshly body.
> What was indicated by the setting of the Lord's evening meal?
> The very setting under which the words were spoken when Jesus invited his eleven faithful disciples to eat the loaf and drink the cup ... indicated a friendly and intimate relationship.[12]

Here one authority (the Bible) is authoritatively interpreted by another. The reverse can also hold. People may arrive at their beliefs independently, but may invoke authorities to provide them with respectability. In one Gallup survey, for instance, 30 per cent of Southern whites expressed the opinion that the Bible supports racial segregation. Most references were to the Old Testament, which was generally discussed in fairly vague terms.[13]

Social movements as authorities

A social movement or an institution may be used as an authority. A letter to a college newspaper in the context of a debate on pornography, for instance, delegated this function as follows:

> In the name of Pope John XXIII, 11 patriarchs, 85 cardinals, 355 archbishops, 1,841 bishops, 405,989 priests, 94,344 seminarians, 183,956 monks and brothers, 1,002,918 nuns and 527,643,000 Catholic lay people through-

[12] *The Watchtower* (March 1, 1962), p. 142.
[13] American Institute of Public Opinion, *Public Opinion News Service* (June 6, 1962).

out the world, we, the undersigned, humbly offer our apologies for our offense against the superior logic and intellect of . . . .[14]

The obvious implication of this message is that the writers' views must be valid because they coincide with those of other Catholics. Similar implications are involved in the role of political consensus, scientific community, and religious missionary work. This point is made in *The Brothers Karamazov* by the Grand Inquisitor, in the context of his pre-execution lecture to Christ:

> But man seeks to worship what is beyond dispute, so that all men would agree at once to worship it. For these pitiful creatures are concerned not only to find what one or the other can worship, but to find something that all would believe in and worship; what is essential is that all may be *together* in it. This craving for *community* of worship is the chief misery of every man individually and of all humanity from the beginning of time. For the sake of common worship they've slain each other with the sword. They have set up gods and challenged one another, "Put away your gods and come and worship ours, or we will kill you and your gods!" And so it will be to the end of the world, even when gods disappear from the earth; they will fall down before idols just the same.[15]

Dostoevsky here describes one way in which every social movement serves its members. By providing them with like-minded fellow members, it converts their unstable individual beliefs into solid, authoritative norms. In turn, like-mindedness comes about because the members of the movement tend to acknowledge the authority of their ideology, their leaders, and their sacred literature. By holding these authorities in common, members come to hold beliefs in common. And their unanimity then becomes authoritative in its own right. This kind of circle creates a situation from which it is difficult to escape.

Submission to authority

In September 1963, the Rev. Felix J. McGowan, a priest belonging to the Maryknoll Society, was suspended by his bishop for traveling to Cuba against explicit orders. Several weeks later, Father McGowan availed himself of the opportunity to return to the Society in exchange for a promise to refrain from continued political activity. In explaining his action, Father

[14] East Lansing (Michigan) *Michigan State News* (January 23, 1961).
[15] F. Dostoevsky, *The Brothers Karamazov*, Vol. 1, (London: J. M. Dent, 1927), p. 260.

McGowan said that Dorothy Day of the Catholic Worker movement had convinced him that he "could do more good in the long run by remaining in the Society." He further declared, "I have faith that the Church and Maryknoll are dedicated to the goal of relating religion to the necessary social changes facing us today."[16]

This statement represents no modification of Father McGowan's pro-Castro views. What it does reflect is confidence in a group that is presumed to share the philosophy underlying these views. It also expresses the conviction that working within the movement is more effective than operating apart from it. In other words, Father McGowan indicated his acceptance of authority, because he felt that he could in this fashion secure the backing of authority.

The Communist leader Georgi Pyatakov delivered the following statement in the 1937 Anti-Trotskyite trials that condemned him to death:

> In a few hours you will pass your sentence. And here I stand before you in filth, crushed by my own crime, bereft of everything through my own fault, a man who has lost his Party, who has no friends, who has lost his family, who has lost his very self.[17]

This poignant speech is the lament of a member who has been abandoned by his group. It expresses despair and resignation—not because of a feeling of having been unjustly accused, or because of impending death—but because of being left completely without support. The statement "who has lost his very self" implies that a person whose life has been given meaning *only* by participation in a collective enterprise may begin to see himself from the viewpoint of authorities, even where he is the object of condemnation. It is as if he were saying, "if you find me guilty, I must be guilty, even if I have not committed the specific acts with which I stand accused. This is the case because, as you withdraw your support from me, I find that I have nothing left." Richard Wright captures this premise beautifully in his description of the Party trial of Ross, a member of the Communist Party on the South Side of Chicago:

> The moment came for Ross to defend himself. I had been told that he had arranged for friends to testify in his behalf, but he called upon no one. He stood, trembling; he tried to talk and his words would not come. The hall was as still as death. Guilt was written in every pore of his black skin. His hands shook. He held on to the edge of the table to keep on his feet. His

16 *The New York Times* (September 17, 1963).

17 People's Comissariat of Justice, U.S.S.R.,*Verbatim Proceedings, Case of the Anti-Soviet Trotskyite Center, January 23–30* (Moscow: 1937), p. 54.

personality, his sense of himself, had been obliterated. Yet *he could not have been so humbled unless he had shared and accepted the vision that had crushed him,* the common vision that bound us all together.

"Comrades," he said in a low, charged voice, "I'm guilty of all the charges, all of them."

His voice broke in a sob. *No one prodded him. No one tortured him. No one threatened him. He was free to go out of the hall and never see another Communist. But he did not want to. He could not. The vision of a Communal world had sunk down into his soul and it would never leave him until life left him.*[18]

The mechanism inferred by Wright is dramatized on a larger scale by Bukharin, who, in his famous Last Plea to the Anti-Trotskyite tribunal, introspected as follows:

For three months I refused to say anything. Then I began to testify. Why? Because while in prison I made a revaluation of my entire past. For when you ask yourself: "If you must die, what are you dying for?"—an absolutely black vacuity suddenly rises before you with startling vividness. There was nothing to die for, if one wanted to die unrepented. And, on the contrary, everything positive that glistens in the Soviet Union acquires new dimensions in a man's mind. This in the end disarmed me completely, and led me to bend my knees before the Party and the country.[19]

The personal crisis reported by Bukharin is produced by the fact that he had learned to accept authority to the point where the world of the movement was the only world he knew. "In our country," he says in the same speech, "the antagonist, the enemy has at the same time a divided, dual mind." The movement's authority remains with him, presumably, even in his opposing role. Thus, when the deviant can no longer follow his deviant course, he has to return to the group on its own terms, even though this means confessing to spurious crimes. By confessing, he can at least give himself the feeling that his role is a meaningful one.

The same kind of pattern emerges in pre-execution self-reproaches of persons condemned in the Tudor treason trials. These victims of tyranny, having been found guilty, meditated on this fact at length, and deduced that they must deserve death. Their speeches to the multitude assembled

[18] R. Wright, in R. Crossman, ed., *The God That Failed* (New York: Bantam, 1952), p. 158 (italics added).

[19] People's Comissariat of Justice, U.S.S.R., *Report of the Court Proceedings in the Case of the Anti-Soviet Bloc of Rights and Trotskyites, March 2–13* (Moscow: 1938), p. 777. The same point is made by Koestler in his play *Darkness at Noon,* which seems heavily based on Bukharin's last plea.

around the execution block enabled them to end their lives within the six-teenth-century conception of the social order. Lacey Smith discusses this apparent paradox, and concludes that

> There is obedience to the law, to the desire of the king and to the mandate of the nation which had willed his death. The victims of Tudor tyranny may have felt themselves innocent of the crimes immediately ascribed to them, but if the law, administered as the will of the king, deemed them worthy to die, then the prisoners considered themselves guilty, deserving death as men no longer useful to society. Fully to comprehend this alien attitude, it is necessary to appreciate sixteenth century mores which demanded absolute obedience to King, to law and to society. These three are a veritable trinity, being both separate and indivisible, representing the highest and most esteemed faith of the realm and closely associated with the religious ideal of the day.[20]

Full submission to authority thus produces a situation in which the individual accepts its conclusions even at the expense of his most cherished goals, when these fall outside the pale. And in the extreme case, where his entire person stands condemned, he must share this condemnation.

Most members, however, submit to authority with varying degrees of latent reservation. "I should like to comply," they implicitly declare, "but I do hold convictions which I propose to retain, no matter what."

The limits to authority

On May 23, 1432, the Inquisition of Paris submitted to Joan of Arc the Articles of Accusation they had drawn up in her case. The document accused her of a variety of offenses, including the misrepresentation of saints and angels (Joan claimed that the saints spoke only French), superstition and divination, wearing men's clothes, attempting suicide, disobeying her parents, using the Trinity as a letterhead for instructions to the troops, and taking an unjustified oath of virginity. By far the most important accusations, however, were those contained in Articles XI and XII, which read in part as follows:

> XI. Reverencing the celestial visitants and believing them to come from God without consulting any churchman, feeling as certain of it as of Christ and the Passion . . .

[20] L. B. Smith, "English Treason Trials and Confessions in the Sixteenth Century" (MS, Massachusetts Institute of Technology), p. 35.

XII. Refusing to obey the mandate of the Church if contrary to the pretended command of God, and rejecting the judgment of the Church on earth—"Thou art schismatic, believing wrongly as to the truth and authority of the Church, and up to the present time thou errest perniciously in the faith of God."[21]

The key provision of the indictment, in other words, was the charge that Joan had by-passed the Church, and was substituting her own authority for that of her superiors. This charge was not at all unusual. Father Knox, a student of the Inquisition, explicitly pointed out that "the head and chief of the offence, in their eyes, was the defiance of spiritual authority of which their other doctrines were merely the corollaries."[22] The theologian Harnack has written about heresy that "something self-chosen is maintained here, in contradistinction to the acceptance of something objectively inherited."[23] Christ himself is quoted by Matthew (12:30) as declaring, "He that gathereth not with me scattereth abroad."

Thus Joan had to contend with the premise that her membership in the Church was contingent on the acceptance of authority. She wanted to remain a member, but she was also unwilling to deny the validity of her visions, and the direct authority of God under which she felt she had embarked on her campaign. Her attempts to reconcile these desires—and the impossibility of accomplishing this reconciliation—are obvious in her behavior during her trial. The following marks the climax of these proceedings:

Q: *Will you refer yourself to the decision of the Church?*
A: I refer myself to God Who sent me, to Our Lady, and to all the Saints in Paradise. And *in my opinion it is all one, God and the Church; and one should make no difficulty about it. Why do you make a difficulty?*
Q: There is a Church Triumphant in which are God and the Saints, the Angels, and the Souls of the Saved. There is another Church, the Church Militant, in which are the Pope, the Vicar of God on earth, the Cardinals, Prelates of the Church, the Clergy and all good Christians and Catholics: this Church, regularly assembled, cannot err, being ruled by the Holy Spirit. *Will you refer yourself to this Church which we have thus just defined to you?*

[21] H. C. Lea, *History of the Inquisition*, Vol. 3 (New York: Macmillan, 1922), p. 369.
[22] R. Knox, Introduction to A. L. Maycock, *The Inquisition* (London: Constable, 1926), p. xiv.
[23] A. Harnack in J. Brosch, *Das Wesen der Heresie* (Bonn: Hanstein, 1936), p. 113.

A: I came to the King of France *from God, from the Blessed Virgin Mary, from all the Saints of Paradise, and the Church Victorious above, and by their command.* To this Church I submit all my good deeds, all that I have done or will do. *As to saying whether I will submit myself to the Church Militant, I will not now answer anything more.*

Q: Will you refer yourself to the judgment of the Church on earth for all you have said or done, be it good or bad? Especially will you refer to the Church the cases, crimes, and offenses which are imputed to you everything which touches on this Trial?

A: *On all that I am asked I will refer to the Church Militant, provided they do not command anything impossible. And I hold as a thing impossible to declare that my actions and my words and all that I have answered on the subject of my visions and revelations I have not done and said by the order of God: This, I will not declare for anything in in the world.* And that which God hath made me do, hath commanded or shall command, I will not fail to do for any man alive. It would be impossible for me to revoke it. *And in case the Church should wish me to do anything contrary to the command which has been given me of God, I will not consent to it, whatever it may be.*

Q: *If the Church Militant tells you that your revelations are illusions, or diabolical things, will you defer to the Church?*

A: *I will defer to God, Whose Commandment I always do . . . In case the Church should prescribe the contrary, I should not refer to any one in the world, but to God alone, Whose Commandment I always follow.*

Q: Do you not then believe you are subject to the Church of God which is on earth, that is to say to our Lord the Pope, to the Cardinals, the Archbishops, Bishops, and other prelates of the Church?

A: Yes, *I believe myself to be subject to them; but God must be served first.*

Q: Have you then command from your Voices not to submit yourself to the Church Militant, which is on earth, not to its decision?

A: I answer nothing from my own head; *what I answer is by command of my Voices; they do not order me to disobey the Church, but God must be served first.*[24]

Under relentless examination by the tribunal, Joan had admitted that for her, ultimate authority was contained in her hallucinations, and did not rest with the Church. She knew that this admission would cost her not only her life, but her membership in the religious community in which she had been raised and which represented the institutional link to the

[24] E. London, ed., *The World of Law*, Vol. 2, *The Law as Literature* (New York: Simon and Schuster, 1960), pp. 343–344 (italics added). By permission of The Folio Society.

supernatural universally accepted by the people she knew. Hers was by no means an easy decision to make. Assigning priority to her "voices" completely invalidated the theological framework of the times. To have accepted the alternative conclusion, however, would have denied validity to Joan's guiding principles, which gave meaning to her undertakings. She had to select the lonely rejection of authority to preserve her identity and to make consistent sense out of her world.

A more contemporary illustration, also involving the Catholic Church, is the excommunication of three segregationist leaders by the Archbishop of New Orleans. In a letter warning of this impending move, the Archbishop charged each that

> While avowing that you are a dutiful member of Holy Mother Church, you have nevertheless promoted flagrant disobedience to the decision to open our schools to *all* our Catholic children and have even threatened and incited others to take reprisals, legal and otherwise, against our actions.

The letter went on to refer to Canon 2331, 2, of the Code of Canon Law of the Church, which provides for restraints of "those who conspire against the authority of the Roman Pontiff or his legates or against their own proper ordinary," or who promote disobedience in others. The Archbishop's letter closed with the hope that "it please God that your faith inspire you to render humble obedience to the teachings and discipline of Holy Mother Church."[25]

One of the segregationist leaders who had received this letter replied that he saw the charge motivated by the fact that "I am fighting a forced racial, political and revolutionary movement instigated and supported by the Communist Party, arch-enemy of all Christendom."

In discussing the Archbishop's prerogatives, the segregationist official commented:

> I think it is my duty to state that if your excellency has found fault with my conduct it is because your excellency has gone beyond the boundaries of your ecclesiastical regimen and has engaged in anthropological aberrations with the support of a number of theologians.

But the reply not only questioned the Archbishop's authority. It advanced authorities of its own:

> I base my support of racial integrity on the Constitution of the United States, the greatest document of its kind ever conceived in the mind of man, and the fulfillment of 4,000 years of Caucasian manhood!

25 *The New York Times* (April 7, 1962).

"The forced mixing program," the letter continued, "lacks scriptural approbation and the clergy is hopelessly divided on the issue."

In a statement reminiscent of Joan of Arc, another of the three segregationist leaders, the female head of an organization called Save Our Nation, declared, "the Bible says we must obey God rather than man." "Better excommunication than integration!" was a slogan coined by the third addressee, a prominent Citizen Council official. "Excommunication," he told a rally, "might send you to hell, but integration would condemn your children to hell on earth!"[26]

Here, as in all other cases in which a person rejects the authority of a group to which he belongs, he in fact resolves an internal tug of war. In Joan's case, she had to live by her voices, or sacrifice this important source of inspiration to become an obedient Catholic. In the case of the Louisiana segregationists, the conflict was between strongly held segregationist views (reinforced by membership in racist social movements) and the restraining order of the Church. In both cases, the persons involved had invested too much of themselves—including feelings, logic, and activity—to retreat in the face of other values. Rather than *rejecting* authority, the recalcitrant members were *choosing between authorities*, and were making the choice most in line with their past commitments, their perceptions of the present, and their expectations of the future.

This kind of action is an affirmation of authority as much as it is a rejection of authority. G. K. Chesterton implied this when he wrote that

> The heretic was proud of not being a heretic. It was the kingdoms of the world and the police and the judges who were heretics. He was orthodox. He had no pride in having rebelled against them, they had rebelled against him. . . . If he stood alone in a howling wilderness he was more than a man; he was a church.[27]

Leon Trotsky exemplified this description when he reported that

> From the time that I entered into opposition to the bureaucracy, its courtier theoreticians began to call the revolutionary essence of Marxism "Trotskyism." At the same time, the official conception of Leninism changed from day to day, becoming more and more adapted to the needs of the ruling class.[28]

[26] J. G. Ricau, "Misinformed Help Divide: The revealing story of my excommunication; an act of desperation by the race mixers," *Common Sense* (June 15, 1962), pp. 1–2.

[27] G. K. Chesterton, *Heretics* (London: Dodd Mead, 1923), p. 11.

[28] L. Trotsky, *The Case of Leon Trotsky: Report of the Hearings by the Preliminary Commission of Inquiry* (New York: Harper & Bothers, 1935), p. 581.

Archpriest Avvakum declared, after being expelled from the Russian Orthodox Church:

[The excommunication] came from heretics, and in Christ's name, I trample it underfoot . . . they are God's enemies, and, living in Christ, I do not fear them . . . all we need do is to spit on their doings and their ritual, and on their new-fangled books, and all will be well.[29]

People thus adopt, reject, and select between authorities to arrive at beliefs that represent the most plausible solutions to their problems. Authorities are psychological instruments, used to produce other psychological instruments. *Once they are in operation*, however, authorities tend to make servants of the persons they serve. They do so primarily by causing beliefs to be held more categorically and strongly than they would be in the absence of authoritative backing.

Indirectly, authority influences people through all the consequences of holding beliefs. And it is in this area, in his role as a believer, that each member experiences the most pervasive and subtle repercussions of his membership.

The effects of being a believer

Francis Bacon wrote in his *Novum Organum* that

. . . the human understanding, when any proposition has been once laid down (either from general admission and belief, or from the pleasure it affords), forces everything else to add fresh support and confirmation; and although most cogent and abundant instances may exist to the contrary, yet either does not observe or despises them, or gets rid of and rejects them by some distinction, with violent and injurious prejudice, rather than sacrifice the authority of its first conclusions.[30]

In other words, beliefs, once adopted, become vested interests, and are actively defended. Perceptual and cognitive mechanisms of various kinds "dispose of" facts and logic, so as to insure that the world we encounter corresponds to our conception of it, rather than vice versa. Sebastian Castellio, a Reformation theologian, wrote about his colleagues that "they have been persuaded to shut their eyes and reject the evidence of the senses of the body and the mind, to believe words, though all the senses refute the words." As a result, wrote Castellio, "nothing is so absurd, impossible or

[29] Avvakum, *The Life of Archpriest Avvakum, by Himself* (London: Hogarth Press, 1924), pp. 94–95.

[30] F. Bacon, *Novum Organum* (London: P. F. Collier, 1902), p. 290.

false as not to be accepted. Why not believe that the white which you see is not white?[31] A good illustration of the basis for Castellio's charge could probably be furnished by the indictment of Galileo, in which it was proclaimed

> That the earth is neither the center of the world, nor immovable, but that it possesses a daily motion is likewise an absurd proposition, false in philosophy, and theologically considered, erroneous in point of faith.[32]

A more recent illustration is a 1958 news item informing us that "A canon of the Church of England said today that many of the people in mental hospitals were possessed of demons rather than diseases of the brain."[33]

Castellio's charge, however, applies to members of social movements that are far from religious in orientation. Thus Louis Fischer, a former Communist Party member, tells us that

> One's general alignment with a cause is more compelling than all but the most shocking facts about it. Just as religious conviction is impervious to logical argument, and indeed, does not result from logical processes, just as nationalist devotion or personal affection defies a mountain of evidence, so my pro-Soviet attitude attained complete independence from day-to-day events. Developments which seemed detrimental to Russia were regarded as ephemeral, dishonestly interpreted, or canceled out by more significant and countervailing developments.[34]

As if to provide official confirmation of Fischer's observation, the Central Committee of the Communist Party of the Soviet Union, in a preamble to its *History of the Communist Party of the Soviet Union*, explains that

> The power of the Marxist-Leninist theory lies in the fact that it enables the Party to find the right orientation in any situation, to understand the inner connection of current events, to foresee their course and to perceive not only how but in what direction they are bound to develop in the future.[35]

[31] S. Castellio, "Concerning Doubt and Belief, Ignorance and Knowledge" in R. H. Bainton, ed. *Concerning Heretics* (New York, Columbia, 1935), p. 295.

[32] E. M. MacDonald, *A Short History of the Inquisition* (New York: Truth Seeker, 1907), p. 251.

[33] *The New York Times* (October 1, 1958).

[34] L. Fischer, in Crossman, *The God That Failed*, p. 205.

[35] Central Committee of the Communist Party of the Soviet Union, *History of the Communist Party of the Soviet Union (Bolsheviks)* (Moscow: International Publishers, 1939), p. 355.

Denial

The most obvious way in which a belief system can "process" facts is to induce the believer to deny or reject anything that might undermine the system. This kind of stratagem represents a desperation measure, however, which is rarely resorted to by believers who are not psychotic. When a normal believer does use denial, it usually indicates that his belief system is vitally threatened, as in the following incident concerning one of Father Divine's female followers:

> She was entering one of the cars of Father's caravan . . . when somebody accidentally closed the car door against the palm and fingers of her right hand. The pain was intense. The hand began to bleed.
> A follower who sat beside Miss Sanderson was frightened by the sight of the blood. "Oh, how awful," she whispered tensely, "you'll have to do something."
> Miss Sanderson only smiled at the other woman's concern. "It never happened," she said.
> "But it's bleeding," the woman persisted.
> Miss Sanderson stayed calm. "That is not a fact."
> "It is a fact," the woman argued.
> Miss Sanderson pursed her lips as she does up until today when she is displeased. "There is only one fact in the universe," she told the woman beside her, "and that fact is Father Divine."[36]

To appreciate the significance of this incident, it must be understood that granting the reality of the injury would have entailed casting doubts on Father Divine's willingness or capacity to protect the physical well-being of his followers. Denial is used in relation to facts that, if admitted, might cast doubts on the validity of one's entire ideological structure.

Other extreme processing mechanisms

There is an interesting story concerning a patient who was convinced that he was dead. Neither entreaties nor reasoning could sway the self-styled corpse from this conclusion. As a last resort, it occurred to one of the doctors to ask whether dead men bleed. "Why no," the patient replied, "as a matter of fact, we don't." A jab with a scalpel brought a flow of blood. "By golly," howled the patient, "dead men do bleed!"

[36] From *Father Divine: Holy Husband* by Sara Harris. Copyright 1953 by Sara Drucker Harris and Harriet Crittenden. Reprinted by permission of Doubleday & Company, Inc., pp. 314–315.

The patient in this story could easily be envisaged as a member of a social movement offering an escapist formula for the vicissitudes of life. The ideology of the social movement could say, in effect, "some of us are dead, and therefore nothing can harm us. Nor do we have to expend any effort, or have needless relations with the Living, whose function it is to provide for our wants." Given this system, it would be vital to preserve the belief "I am dead. " In the face of the physician's evidence, the patient could use one of several alternative mechanisms—all relatively extreme—to maintain this belief.

One would have been a denial, consisting of the bland assertion "I see no blood!" Or he could have maintained that a liquid was there, but that it was something other than blood (like ink or rubber cement). This, however, could have subsequently complicated matters. Another alternative would be invalid reasoning: "dead men don't bleed, as I told you. I do bleed, but I am so dead." This, again, could have involved troublesome altercations later. It would probably have been easiest to use a retroactive qualification, such as "*some* dead men may not bleed, but others do." Instead, the patient in the story decided to retract the entire proposition "blood, therefore not dead," which entailed a revision of his ideology, but had the advantage of offering protection against future incursions.

Protection can be a powerful consideration. That it operates in the real world may be seen, for instance, in a 1954 dispatch from the Dachau Concentration Camp near Munich, which is now a museum:

> Relatively few Germans are among the steady flow of visitors to the memorial. One of the caretakers said some of the German guests had said the larger of the two crematoria was built by the Americans after the war for propaganda purposes. Other informants in Munich said this view is still fairly widely held in Bavaria.[37]

The assumption of an American conspiracy to discredit Germany not only fits neatly into a neo-Nazi frame of reference, but also provides a ready interpretation for other war crime data. The same type of mechanism in a similar context was used by some defendants in the Nuremberg Trials. Streicher, for instance, very early in the Trials announced that

> "They are crucifying me now. . . . I can tell. Three of the judges are Jews."
> "How can you tell that?"
> "I can recognize blood. Three of them get uncomfortable when I look at them. I can tell. I've been studying race for twenty years. The body

37 New York *Herald Tribune* (March 8, 1954).

structure shows the character. I'm an authority on that subject. Himmler thought he was, but he didn't know anything about it. He had negro blood himself."

Toward the end of the Trials Streicher seemed to undergo a change of heart, but this was deceptive. He closely maintained his systematic position, and merely switched sides within the system:

"The Democratic world isn't fit to exist! I warned them for 25 years, but now I see that the Jews have determination and spunk—They will still dominate the world, mark my word!—And I would be glad to lead them to victory because they are strong and tenacious, and I know Jewry. . . . If the Jews would be willing to accept me as one of them, I would fight for them . . . !"[38]

Closed systems and sacred cows

The ideologies most prone to demand extreme dispositions of data and contortions of logic are closed systems. A closed system is a set of beliefs that has come to be self-sufficient, in the sense that a person would no longer have to go outside of it for interpretations. Arthur Koestler has defined it as "a universal method of thought which claims to explain all phenomena under the sun." He lists as one of the characteristics of a closed system that it "refuses to be modified by newly observable facts but has sufficiently elastic defenses to neutralize their impact—that is, to make them fit the required pattern by a highly developed degree of casuistry."[39] William James similarly speaks of closed systems as "irreversible."[40]

What this means is that to the extent to which a belief system is closed, it must ensure that all incoming data fit. Everything must be evaluated in terms of how well it can be reconciled with existing beliefs, and how well it can be used to serve the system. This procedure prevents the person from acquiring really new information, but it does provide him with security, and it minimizes the work involved in his efforts to make sense of the world. In that way, a closed system is somewhat like a bird's cage—snug, but a bit confining. Unlike the bird's cage, though, the closed system is not imposed on the believer, but is cumulatively constructed by him as he applies authoritatively sanctioned premises to ever-increasing portions of reality.

[38] G. M. Gilbert, *Nuremberg Diary* (New York: Farrar, Straus, 1947), pp. 41, 419.
[39] A. Koestler, *Arrow in the Blue: An Autobiography* (London: Collins, 1952), pp. 230, 231.
[40] W. James, *The Will to Believe and Other Essays in Popular Philosophy* (New York: Longmans Green, 1902), pp. 12–13.

Besides closed systems, the types of belief that are most likely to be strongly defended are sacred cows—i.e., beliefs that the believer feels are important to him. These beliefs are usually heavily invested with the feelings that in some social movements are contained in testimonials and pledges. A typical illustration is the following declaration by Great Love, one of Father Divine's secretaries:

> "Nothing in the world could make me doubt Father—" she says. "He is my world, all my world. If I didn't have Him, if ever I unconsciously did anything against Father's principle, and Father said, 'Great Love, you can no longer stay with me' I would" her voice trails away. "I would—well, life would be worthless for me that's all, just plain worthless."[41]

One could easily predict that if Great Love were faced with an announcement of Father Divine's death, she would make every effort to deny the possibility, or to explain it away. She might conclude, for instance, that Father had assumed another earthly shape for inscrutable tactical purposes of his own. But she could not afford to sacrifice her belief. This is the case because Great Love's belief in Father Divine, like other sacred cows, *satisfies personal needs.* Any threat to such a belief becomes a threat to the person who holds it, and he will try to prevent such a contingency as best he can.

This is the reason why a believer may react in a very personal fashion when certain of his beliefs are questioned. Attacks on sacred cows are personal attacks, and call up replies in kind. The following excerpt of a "letter to the editor" provides an extreme example:

> Dear contemptible cur:
>   After reading about your sadistic editorial gloating over the passing of that Great Patriot, Robert Edward Edmondson, I hereby nominate you for the award of the "Number One Heel of the Year."
>   You should have no trouble winning as it is doubtful if anyone else can match the perverted verbosity of your depraved editorial. Have you been out to urinate on his grave yet? You are the type!
>   In the future when anyone remarks to me, "How low can a man get?" I can always point to you.[42]

The latent message in this communication is something in the order of: "your negative characterization of one of the leaders of my movement

[41] Harris, *Father Divine*, p. 257.
[42] H. Toch, S. E. Deutsch, and D. M. Wilkins, "The Wrath of the Bigot: An Analysis of Protest Mail," *Journalism Quarterly* (Spring 1960), pp. 173–185, 266.

hurts me deeply, because I had come to rely on this person (and others like him) for security and support. If what you said were true, I would be in a serious predicament. I am therefore constrained to regard you as a very evil person." This reaction can even extend to persons who have not attacked a sacred cow, but who are threatening it by their indifference or lack of support. Thus Gordon Allport points out that religious people for whom religious beliefs satisfy ulterior motives (such as needs for status or security) tend to be prejudiced, while "intrinsically" religious persons are not.[43] Similarly, Rokeach has made the point that one type of prejudice—characteristic of dogmatic persons—consists of having strong negative feelings about people who disagree with one's beliefs.[44] Sacred cows are perpetually in search of consensus.

This is one reason why sacred cows are frequently encountered among fully dedicated members. Another reason is that persons whose problems are acute enough to push them easily into full commitment also grasp at beliefs with equivalent desperation. For such a person, beliefs are akin to neurotic symptoms, in that they resolve internal problems in addition to external ones. Great Love, whom we have quoted above, is a case in point. She was brought to Father Divine because of a psychosomatic skin condition, and her belief in Father simultaneously represented a personal and a theological solution:

> She had tried all sorts of remedies to improve her complexion. She'd gone to doctors. She'd used commercial mixtures. She'd taken exercises and gone to Turkish baths. Nothing had helped her. Then, purely by accident, she'd heard of Father Divine and his miraculous healing. As a last hope, she'd written to Father. Three weeks after, she'd received a letter from him telling her to trust his spirit. She had. The pimples had disappeared. And Great Love had known Father Divine was God.[45]

Another reason why sacred cows are often encountered in advanced stages of membership is that care and maintenance of a belief tend to convert it into a vested interest. Like any other instrument that acquires sentimental value through use, the veteran belief comes to occupy a place among our cherished psychological possessions.

[43] G. W. Allport, *Personality and Social Encounter* (Boston: Beacon, 1960), p. 264.

[44] M. Rokeach, *The Open and Closed Mind* (New York: Basic Books, 1960), pp. 132 ff.

[45] Harris, *Father Divine*, p. 257.

Routine processing

Because sacred cows (and closed systems) can develop from less dramatic and more flexible ways of believing, one would expect that the extreme processing mechanisms used to protect these forms of belief may also evolve. We would expect to encounter more routine "processing" devices at earlier stages of believing. We would expect a person's beliefs to affect to *some* extent the way he perceives, even when the belief is a "let-us-see-whether-this-makes-sense" type. And we would expect that as soon as a person joins a social movement he would begin to see things differently from outsiders, and similarly to the way they are seen by his fellow members.

Although these kinds of routine differences in the way the world is perceived are relatively difficult to spot, they become obvious when contrasting beliefs provide widely different views of the same events.

As a typical example, we may consider the way World War I was viewed by members of the Theosophic Society:

> This world war was inevitable, a final clearing of the ground in preparation for the Coming of their World Teacher and the New Civilization. . . . The supernatural powers of evil had realized that if . . . they could get control of the Theosophic Society they would have a tremendous strategic advantage in the conduct of the war. In short, Great Britain and the Allies, embodying the ideals of freedom were the servants of the Masters of Wisdom. The German autocracy founded on force was under the control of black magic and the Lords of the Dark Face.[46]

By contrast, Jehovah's Witnesses recall the same war as the advent of the Battle of Armageddon, as foretold in Matthew 24:7: "For nation shall rise against nation, and kingdom against kingdom: and there shall be famines, and pestilences, and earthquakes in divers places." Other wars, famines, international crises, earthquakes, train wrecks, plane crashes, and sundry misfortunes occurring in the world since 1914 have "confirmed" this interpretation.

The American Socialist leader Eugene Debs perceived World War I as a blood bath in the service of empire builders. A patriotic reporter arranged for his conviction under the Espionage Act, and Debs told him after the trial:

> You look upon the world and see certain things that you regard as facts and you have come to definite conclusions about them. You are willing to go to

[46] G. M. Williams, *The Passionate Pilgrim: A Life of Annie Besant* (New York: Coward-McCann, 1931), p. 293.

France and risk your life. Well, I look upon the same world and see things that I regard as facts, and I have come to conclusions diametrically opposed to yours. You are going to France and you may never come back. I'm going to Atlanta and I don't know whether I'll live out my sentence.

The reporter experienced the war in France, and subsequently became a pacifist.[47]

Let us take a second illustration: In March 1960, South African police fired on a peaceful demonstration in Sharpeville, massacring 67 and seriously injuring 180 persons. Most civilized humanity deplored this incident. The John Birch Society, however, reported the event as follows:

... at Sharpeville, a company of 137 policemen, isolated by the cutting of their telephone wires and surrounded by 200,000 frenzied savages armed with clubs, knives, revolvers, having used tear gas in vain and being the targets of pistol-fire from the mob, opened fire themselves and killed fifty-eight of the insurgents before the rest ran away. This set off screams of indignation in our Communist-influenced press, and our State Department spat at South Africa in protest at the denial of blacks' civil right to stomp white men to pulp whenever disinclined to eat them.[48]

The same movement has recently interpreted the civil rights campaign in the United States as a Communist plot aimed at creating a "Soviet Negro Republic" with its capital in Atlanta, Georgia.[49] After President Kennedy's assassination, a spokesman for the Society explained that the president had been eliminated "because he was falling behind in the Communist timetable for the take-over of the United States."[50] How do such interpretations come about?

Selective perception

Selective processing starts with selective perception. Belief systems enable their adherents to pay attention to *some* events, and to regard others as unworthy of consideration. A health addict, for instance, may peruse his newspaper constantly alerted to any indications of physical decline among the general public. Such data would "confirm" his view that chemi-

[47] C. R. Miller, "The Man I Sent to Prison," *The Progressive* (October 1963), pp. 33–35.
[48] G. Grove, *Inside the John Birch Society* (Greenwich, Conn.: Fawcett Publications, 1961), p. 143.
[49] *The New York Times* (August 8, 1963).
[50] New York *Herald Tribune* (February 13, 1964).

cals are poisoning the rest of humanity. In a similar fashion, an anti-Semite would go through his newspaper attending to the names of prominent Jews, to document his movement's contention that the world is dominated by non-Christian aliens. Adolf Hitler reported in *Mein Kampf* that

> Since I had begun to think about this question, since my attention was drawn to the Jews, I began to see Vienna in a different light than before. Wherever I went I saw Jews, and the more I saw of them, the sharper I began to distinguish them from other people.[51]

He not only became more aware of differences between Jews and non-Jews, but he found himself suddenly faced with Jewishness wherever he turned: "Now I began to notice thousands of things which previously I had hardly seen, and I began to understand others which had already caused me reflection." In taking a second look at the press, for instance, he discovered that "I could no longer stand its style, I had to reject its contents on account of its shallowness, the 'objectivity' of its presentation seemed untrue rather than honest truth; the authors, however, were—Jews."

Similarly, the novel "now became obscene, and the language contained tones of a foreign race, the general theme was obviously so detrimental to the German nationality that it could only have been intentional."[52]

Such "discoveries," needless to say, are far from coincidental. A person who becomes selectively sensitive (1) perceives certain events as standing out of the total situation that surrounds him, and therefore as having increasing *importance*, and (2) comes to exaggerate their *prevalence*, because he attends to every available instance of them (plus others that can be reinterpreted to join the list). This creates a picture in which everything revolves about whatever is the focus of attention.

The reverse also holds. Selective attention dismisses as unimportant any type of data that are difficult to incorporate into the person's conceptual scheme, and thereby makes them objectively trivial. When Goering responded to a remark made to him at the Nuremberg Trials, "Ach, those mass murders! It is a rotten shame, the whole thing. I'd rather not talk about it, or even think about it. . . . But that conspiracy charge . . ."[53] he rearranged the complexity of the trial into a hierarchy in which the potentially disturbing genocide issue played no particular role.

The believer thus comes to be faced with a stage prominently peopled

[51] A. Hitler *Mein Kampf* (New York: Reynal & Hitchcock, 1941), p. 74.
[52] *Ibid.*, p. 77.
[53] Gilbert, *Nuremberg*, p. 107.

by a cast of his own choosing. He can then proceed to impose his own
script, by viewing the relationship among events in terms of whatever logic
his system dictates. The anti-Semite comes to see not merely Jews, but
strategically positioned evil Jews. The health addict sees not only a general
decline in the nation's health, but perceives this as the outcome of a conspiracy by mercenary industrialists. Even as brilliant and insightful a scientist as Sigmund Freud, whose point of view developed into a social movement during his lifetime, assigned psychoanalytic interpretations to art,
history, current affairs, his own actions, the resistance of his opponents, and
the deviations of his less orthodox followers.

Selective attention, in other words, is the first step in the processing of
information that in itself is neutral, to support and reinforce pre-existing
interpretations. It provides the believer with precisely those ingredients
which can best be incorporated into his ideological recipes. Once these
data are "cooked," the believer's intellectual fare loses its capacity for di-
versification and proliferation. New evidence comes to be evaluated in terms
of its usefulness for whatever is already concocted. And as in the immortal
trial scene in *Alice in Wonderland*, the verdict precedes the consideration
of the facts.

The closing of the mind

What all this suggests is that the effects of being a member are a
cumulative progression from first commitment to dogmatism.[54] The social
movement that presents its inductee with authoritatively reinforced beliefs
responsive to his problems unwittingly initiates a chain of events which
may culminate in the confined, self-contained world of the veteran member.
The first stage in this sequence is the initial commitment to membership, which presupposes an investment of time and effort, as well as the
explicit or implicit adoption of beliefs. This can lead to extensions involving
further sacrifices of autonomy, in which beliefs are accepted on the basis of
authority, rather than through independent verification. Conjointly with
the acceptance of authority, one can expect a transmutation of perception
and cognition from deduction to induction—or rather, from building *on the
basis of* data, to the utilization of data to cement *pre-existing* belief structures.

This enterprise is a never-ending one. Supporting structures come to re-

[54] Studies of some of the end products of this sequence are available in Rokeach,
The Open and Closed Mind.

quire support, and construction efforts become increasingly elaborate. As the believer becomes more intensely dedicated to the repair and buttressing of his current constructs, these come to assume greater personal significance for him. Moreover, supporting efforts tend to systematize beliefs. As a result, it becomes of greater import that new data conform, and extreme pains are soon taken to this end.

At a given point in this process, the believer has walled himself in. Every event he encounters must be processed in terms of his beliefs. Every opportunity must be used to cement his system. At this stage, only authority can produce innovation. Nothing remains of autonomy except the ingenuity exercised in the all-consuming enterprise of ensuring that real autonomy can never be regained.

IN preceding chapters, we have sketchily delineated the road to membership: We have examined the sequence culminating in conversion, and we have gone on to trace progression through various stages of commitment. We have tried to make a case for the postulate that to become a member is a *cumulative* enterprise.

In the present chapter, we shall examine the reverse of the coin. We shall attempt to discover different resolutions of the membership career, and try to show how these are built into various stages of becoming a member. We shall try to isolate the subtle beginnings of *disaffection*, and inquire into the way in which these can result in *defection*.

We assume that although the act of defection is a dramatic event, it is merely a landmark in an unsuccessful membership career. To understand defection correctly we must study the effort to belong that leads up to it. We must understand the changes that occur in the defecting member throughout membership, and even prior to joining.

Gabriel Almond, in his discussion of former Communist Party members, writes that "in some of our cases, dissatisfaction began at the point of affiliation, and even before any involvement in activities." And in the majority of instances, according to Almond, "becoming dissatisfied with the party was cumulative." For example,

An individual may join the party in some doubt as to the wisdom of his decision. He may resent the impact of party activities on his non-party interests and relationships. He may be offended by the process of indoctrination by slogans. But even though dissatisfactions may accumulate at each one of these stages, his original momentum and party pressure keep him in line until some sharp impingement on his interests, feelings or values takes place. Even at this point, inertia may keep him in the party, even though he has already defected in spirit. He may wait until a general party crisis makes it possible for him to withdraw with a minimum of conflict and publicity.[1]

The initial steps in the type of sequence outlined by Almond *usually occur without awareness of their import.* The potential defector tends to feel that he is an unreservedly dedicated member, despite the fact that he has created conditions that make continued membership unlikely.

Setting the stage for dissent

In the period following World War II, a diffusely educated, upper-class Italian woman joined the Communist Party after she had been alienated from her Fascist husband and had experienced the death of her only child. Her misfortunes, she felt, united her with "the masses who were suffering." She perceived the Communist movement as motivated by profound compassion, and as aiming at the promotion of liberty for the poor:

> To belong to a party whose aim it was to give to the people their rights and to combat every form of tyranny which menaced them, I considered a great honor and the reward for all the suffering and delusions of my life. I had the impression of bringing my grain of sand which would contribute to the erection of a new social order.

Intensive reading of party literature reinforced her assumption that Communism was a champion of freedom: "Reading, I fell in love with this grand idea which places individual liberty above everything else, subordinating it to a splendid social equality." Over time, this rarified conception of Communism was further elaborated and intensified:

> As time passed, I became more enthusiastic about the doctrine, so great as to be able to call it a religion. . . . More than once it seemed to me that Marx had borrowed from the doctrine of Christ, to explain it to man in

[1] Reprinted from *The Appeals of Communism* by Gabriel Almond by permission of Princeton University Press, copyright 1954 by the Princeton University Press, p. 299.

more modern terms, such as "historical materialism," "economics," "communism."

I had indeed reached the point in which all the voices of the great philosophers became identified with my belief. I had idealized communism, and attributed to it all the mysticism shut up in my character.

When the woman finally left the Communist Party, she had come to view it as the destruction, through practical application, of the "perfection" of a "really beautiful idea." She was convinced, moreover, that she had "remained profoundly Communistic," although she advised Communist officials, before she defected, "that to give the government into the hands of ignorant and backward people would be the most unpardonable madness."[2]

A member may join a movement fully aware that his frame of reference differs from that of other members, *but expecting this difference to be irrelevant.* A second of Almond's Italian interviewees had become a Communist in the course of a search for "some superior Being" who could serve as his moral guide. Conventional religious belief had seemed "too distant," and so he joined the Party: "I was . . . a communist, but with the expectation that Communism would adapt itself to my ideas, not I to theirs." When this contingency did not materialize, he explained his disaffection as follows:

> Experience has demonstrated to me that it is not on a political plane that the problems of our times will be resolved . . . it is not a political idea of socialism, but rather a moral idea, the same idea that was seen by Plato and Aristotle, which Christ confirmed and Marx explained to people who could not understand, they were so profoundly ignorant.

This, of course, was precisely his point of view in joining the movement. The discovery was potentially available at that time, but was not made because of his desire to sustain the illusion of unconditional membership.

It is only in exceptional instances that the member of a movement recognizes his own contribution to the process of defection. Such was the case with a third member of Almond's Italian sample, a lawyer who had joined the Communist Party during the war. He defined himself as a "lower-middle-class humanist by cultural tradition," and contrasted persons in this category to "born" Communists: "It is much too difficult for one who is accustomed to follow a certain trend of thought to adapt himself to a completely new and different process of reasoning."

---

[2] These and other quotations throughout this chapter are taken from transcripts of interviews conducted under the direction of Gabriel Almond for his study of the appeals of Communism. Quoted by permission.

The lawyer complained of difficulties in communicating with working-class Party members, and in experiencing their concerns:

> They spoke a language which I could not understand: The slogans which, from time to time, the Party created to incite to action the masses of working people (who then and now constitute the foundations of the Party) had no appreciable significance for me: the words "hunger, cold, poverty," which had such effects on the masses . . . had no effect on me. All such problems were extraneous to me.

This type of insight is exceptional, because it requires the ability to transcend one's frame of reference and to recognize its subjectivity. It requires an awareness of self in which the member feels free to admit that he reacts to his unique perception of the movement in line with his own needs, and in a way compatible with his experiences and expectations. This discovery is usually reserved for an outside observer—sometimes an irate spokesman for the social movement.

Latent perceptual discrepancies

There are two types of predispositions to defection. The first of these is the tendency of members to perceive social movements in terms of their own individual concerns. The Chinese Communist ideologist Liu Shao-Ch'i tells us that his movement has attracted many persons for reasons that are secondary to its main objectives. Although many of his fellow-members "enter the Communist Party to attain such great objectives as the realization of Communism and the liberation of the proletariat and mankind," there are others "who enter the Party for other reasons and to attain other objectives." "Other objectives," according to Liu, *are then perceived by Party members to be the aims of the entire Party*:

> For example, we have some former comrades who consider "striking the local bullies and distributing the land," as the meaning of communism. When they enter the Party they do not understand the more advanced true communism. For not a few, the most important reasons for entering the Party today are the National Anti-Japanese United Front and the Communist Party's determination to fight Japan. For others, the most important reason is that they have not found their way in society—they have no profession, no work, no education, or they want to get rid of their families or wives, etc., so they come to the Communist Party to find their way. There are still others who come because they are impressed with the popularity of the Communist Party, or just dimly realize that the Communist Party may save China. And finally, there are even some who came because they

wish to rely on the Party to escape taxation or be certain of "something to eat" in the future, and there are some who are brought in by friends or relatives, etc.[3]

Almond notes this same tendency among his Western Communists:

Almost all the respondents perceived the party at the point of joining in terms of one or a combination of its agitational goals, as a means of combating and destroying Fascism, racial, ethnic and religious discrimination, or imperialism; or positively as a means of attaining trade union objectives, peace, general social improvement, or humanitarian social goals.[4]

Non-Communist movements can make the same kind of observation: Many members join for reasons far removed from the central concerns of the movement; as a consequence, their perceptions of the nature of the enterprise can become rather parochial. For example, among the "anti-Communists" engaged in the Guatemalan civil war of 1954 was Maria Lemos, who testified that "Some time ago a government party contracted a debt of eighty quetzal that was never paid."[5] This fact became her "primary motive in choosing sides." One would expect to find a substantial discrepancy between Señora Lemos' conception of the civil war and the "official" view of its aims.

This discrepancy exists, to some extent, in every member's perception of his social movement. Although a common basis for the perception of social movements is created by the problems that members have in common, and by information about the movement that is available to all, it is still a fact that *each person joins a somewhat different social movement.* Every person's perception of the appeals of his movement is partly a reflection of his private concerns and interests. Every member's views are colored by his unique past experiences. These personal images of social movements can produce differences between conceptions and preconceptions in subsequent perceptual encounters.

Latent reservations

The possibility of disillusionment through the discovery of new features in the movement is not the only type of predisposition to disaffection. In addition to latent perceptual discrepancies, personal and ideological reserva-

[3] Liu Shao-Ch'i, "Training of the Communist Party Member," in B. Compton, ed., *Mao's China: Party Reform Documents, 1942–1944* (Seattle: Univ. of Washington Press, 1952), pp. 117–118.

[4] Reprinted from *The Appeals of Communism* by Gabriel Almond by permission of Princeton University Press, Copyright 1954 by the Princeton University Press, p. 103.

[5] *The New York Times* (June 24, 1954).

tions to full membership can also be potentially available. Liu Shao-Ch'i complains about various kinds of personality traits in Communist Party members which he feels can at times create problems. Opportunists, for instance, are tractable when they meet with personal success, but "when they can't achieve their objectives, when they are attacked or treated coldly by comrades in the Party, there is a danger they will waver."[6]

The objection here is not only to the qualified acceptance of authority we discussed in Chapter 7, but *to any personal values and aims that are at variance with those of the movement.* The need for security, the desire for professional work, a personal antipathy toward other members, pet projects, or doubts about one or more of a movement's premises can make a person susceptible to defection under special circumstances.

From the point of view of a social movement, it is important to diagnose latent reservations, and if possible to deal with them in some fashion. Hopefully, the wrong person can be prevented from joining the wrong movement for the wrong reasons; seeds of doubt can be discussed before they develop into overt conflict; differences in feelings toward particular events can be resolved.

An excellent case in point is provided in the following catalogue of latent reservations among nudists. The list was compiled by an insightful publisher of sunbathing magazines, who was asked to explain the turnover of membership in the American Sunbathing Association:

> Some people feel that they must make a choice between being a social nudist and a social non nudist, i.e., they feel to accept nudism socially automatically means expulsion either of them or by them, from clothed society.
>
> The family group with adolescent children of either or both sexes is sometimes weaned from nudism as they acquiesce to the increased modesty of their teenaged children.
>
> Because of the status of social nudism the organization should be operated in a conservative manner. Many group leaders and influential people in the nudist movement recognize this fact and accordingly provide restrictions within the nudist movement from which many nudists rebel as a result of the predominantly progressive movement in society throughout the nation.
>
> Some groups of individuals endeavor to keep their nudist affiliation a deep, dark secret. The odds are against their success over a prolonged period of time and as the prospects of their being found out become more and more probable they decide to withdraw from the movement.

[6] Liu Shao-Ch'i, "Communist Party Member," p. 122.

Quite to my dismay, I have talked with a number of people who feel that social nudism is good for adults but not too good for children. In the case of childless married couples there is always threat that they will eventually have children and withdraw from the movement at that time because of their conviction.[7]

In addition to this listing, there presumably exists a category of member whose interest in nudism is specialized, such as "the exhibitionist, the 'joiner,' the faddist, perhaps the sexually abnormal, etc." These types of individuals are assumed to be drawn to the movement by inflexible needs that cannot be satisfied through membership. Remedial action would consist of excluding such persons from the movement.

But among less deeply rooted preconceptions, re-educational efforts may conceivably inhibit disaffection in its early stage. For instance, if a member has apprehensions based on untested assumptions, he might be exposed to reassuring experiences. If a self-fulfilling prophecy is operating, the member could possibly be dissuaded from bringing about the crisis he expects. The best time for such educational ventures is the stage at which reservations have not yet consciously qualified commitment.

The manifestation of latent reservations

When latent reservations emerge, they may do so *cumulatively*. The perception of some imperfections or weaknesses may make the member's eye more critical to others and minor quibbles may disguise relatively fundamental doubts, which may emerge more openly later. One of Almond's American Communist interviewees, for instance, describes the sequence of his disaffection as follows:

I had always felt the leadership of the American Party was slipshod— people who found it easier to speak translated Russian or stilted gobbledegook than appeal to American workers. I always felt that I could understand American society better and had made better appeals.

I had never much faith in American leaders or members but as part of a world movement (the party) had tremendous power—and the world movement was stimulated by Russia.

With the Moscow trials the logic went out of it—in addition Russian deals in the League of Nations also seemed unholy. . . . So I was through

---

[7] Letter from the files of the public relations chairman of the American Sunbathing Association. The author is indebted to Paul Arnold for making it possible to secure this material. Quoted by permission.

with Russia and Communism at the time I broke but still felt that socialism was a proper thing. In the years since then I have re-examined my position completely and feel that socialism is a menace and that Russia is an example of its ultimate form.

Here reservations relating to the American Communist Party opened the way to reservations about the international Communist movement, which in turn facilitated reservations of a basic ideological nature. A member whose commitment has been partly weakened is thus susceptible to further disaffection.

In other instances, relatively minor reservations may be diagnostic of fairly fundamental reservations. The following, for instance, was the first manifestation of skepticism in the famous freethinker Charles Bradlaugh: At the age of fourteen, he

> . . . was to be confirmed, and by his vicar's instructions he began to learn the thirty-nine articles and to study the Gospels closely. He took his New Testament seriously and very soon found, like maturer thinkers, that it is no easy matter to harmonise even the Synoptists, and still harder to reconcile them with John.
>
> He wrote to the vicar for help and explanation. The vicar replied by suspending him for three months and informing his father of his 'atheistical' tendencies.[8]

Although it is conceivable that young Charles's analysis of the Bible was a manifestation of faith rather than doubt (and that his atheism dates to his being *labeled* as an atheist, as his biographer assumes), this is unlikely. Checking the reliability of authority, after all, presupposes a questioning attitude. It is thus probable that the vicar overreacted to what was essentially an *accurate* diagnosis. In fact, many years later, Charles Bradlaugh himself drafted the following prescription:

> As it is by Act of Parliament declared to be a criminal offence in this country for any person to deny this book to be God's Holy Word, it is not only a right, but it becomes an unavoidable duty, on the part of a Freethinking critic, to present as plainly as possible to the notice of the people every weakness of the text, however trivial, that may serve to show that the Bible . . . is fallible, that it is imperfect. . . ![9]

Although not every qualification, inquiry, or expression of dissent represents a symptom of deeper disagreement, or marks the beginnings of an

---

[8] J. E. Courtney, *Freethinkers of the Nineteenth Century* (London: Chapman & Hall, 1920), p. 98.

[9] *Ibid.*, p. 136.

ideological landslide, there is sufficient unity in the mind for suspicion to arise in most instances. At the very least, an expressed reservation with respect to some aspect of a movement represents less than full commitment. And reservations tend to point to areas where vulnerability to disaffection is at its maximum.

Conflicting ideologies

Usually, the hold of the movement is thus weakened *gradually*: First a few outposts are sacrificed; doubts about minor matters come to the fore; other "weaknesses" are perceived; and eventually, the bonds linking member to movement become sufficiently tenuous to snap under stress. However, an alternative process may occur, particularly among persons who arrive at membership with a history of prior commitments. Such individuals may find that the ashes of abandoned ideologies are not extinguished. Discarded beliefs and ways of thinking intrude themselves; unorthodox interpretations exert their temptation; voices from the past, long silenced, reassert demands for loyalty. Douglas Hyde, a former seminarian who had become a Communist, reports the following experience, which he entertained as he distributed revolutionary pamphlets in the entrance way of a church:

> It was all utterly alien to me. It represented superstition at its lowest depths. Yet suddenly for one brief moment the craziest and most outrageous of impulses took possession of me. I, too, wanted to go and confess. To say to the priest inside: "Look here, you who live in a world of your own, you are wasting your time. The children whose confessions you have heard have not come within a million miles of sinning. That man and woman still go to church. They live respectable lives. They believe in God. Here's a real job for you. I'm up to my eyes in sin. I sin more in one day than they'll sin in their whole lives. Confess me." The impulse was so mad, so preposterous, yet so strong and urgent that it all but swept me inside. Instead I stuffed a few more Red pamphlets into the rack, went out into the night, and blasphemed all the harder to get myself back to "sanity" again.[10]

Hyde also read the Catholic press, purportedly to sustain a leisure-time interest in medieval art and literature. Soon he discovered "the appeal of a completely opposed philosophy," and even observed "a good deal of sound common sense mixed with what seemed crude and extravagant anti-Communism."[11]

[10] D. Hyde, *I Believed* (London: G. P. Putnam, 1950), pp. 65–66. By permission of the publishers, Copyright © 1950 by Douglas Hyde.

[11] *Ibid.*, p. 230.

Eventually, Hyde began to experience acute conflicts, culminating in a self-styled double personality:

> There were, actively at work, "two Douglas Hydes," one whose spontaneous reactions were what they had been for so long, the other whose reactions were almost the exact opposite. Sometimes one seemed in the ascendancy, sometimes the other. Most often, still, it was the Communist, for, even though I was losing my health because of the accumulating secret doubts and misgivings, I still could not think of myself as anything but a Communist.[12]

The fiction of commitment to Communism became ever more difficult to sustain. The political joke, for instance, a traditional vehicle of cautious opposition, served to express hostility to the movement:

> I had always had the reputation among the staff for a bitter, cynical humour. Now that humour appeared more outrageous than ever. I wisecracked about everything that my colleagues held to be most sacred—the Soviet leaders, our own most revered British Party members, the Party line. And I more than half meant what I said. In those cracks the two watertight compartments came together.[13]

Ultimately, two attacks of illness, both seemingly serious, brought an unambiguous return to religion. The few remaining excuses for continued party membership (such as the desire to "unconvert" other Communists) eventually collapsed, and Hyde defected.

Although victory for the latent ideology is probably the most frequent resolution of ideological conflict, in some instances the result may be complete disillusionment. Dostoevsky makes this point very forcefully in his novel *The Possessed*:

> "Well, everyone seeks to be where he is best off. The fish. . . . that is, everyone seeks his own comfort, that's all. That's been a commonplace for ages and ages."
>
> "Comfort, do you say?"
>
> "Oh, it's not worth while quarreling over words."
>
> "No, you are quite right in what you said; let it be comfort. God is necessary and so must exist."
>
> "Well, that's all right, then."
>
> "But I know He doesn't and can't.'
>
> "That's more likely."

[12] *Ibid.*, p. 226.
[13] *Ibid.*, p. 229.

"Surely you must understand that a man with two such ideas can't go on living?"[14]

In still other instances, the outcome may be the adoption of a third ideology, which supersedes both of the contending systems, or integrates them in some fashion. The need for consistency, present to some degree in all believers, does not necessarily result in logical continuity, but it does tend to produce efforts at bridging discontinuity.

It also produces a tendency to perceive change as taking place in the outside world, to avoid the recognition of internal transmutations. The true believer, in the words of Lowell, frequently

> Shifts quite about, then proceeds to expound
> That 'tis merely the earth, not himself, that turns round,
> And wishes it clearly impressed on your mind
> That the weathercock rules and not follows the wind.[15]

Precipitating events

Almond points out that "movement into and movement out of the various Communist parties increases or decreases with each great change in the party line, each 'zig' or 'zag,' to use the Communist expression." In particular,

> . . . party policies which affect the interests of specific party strata are likely to produce special party crises. The calling of political strikes, for example, may produce defection among workers, while a cultural purge is likely to result in defection among intellectuals. Secondly, any action which has the effect of moving people out of their accustomed milieu, such as a military mobilization, facilitates defection, since party members are withdrawn from the controls of Communist organization and communication.[16]

Since some events affect members more intimately than do others, they are not equally potent in their catalytic role. Some zigs and zags in the Communist party line, for instance, promote more defection than other zigs and zags. The Russian suppression of the Hungarian revolt in 1956 reduced the membership of the British Communist Party by one-fifth, from

[14] F. Dostoevsky, *The Possessed* (New York: Macmillan, 1948), p. 560.

[15] J. R. Lowell, "Fable for Critics," in A. M. Schlesinger, Jr., *Orestes A. Brownson— A Pilgrim's Progress* (New York: Little, Brown, 1939), p. 278.

[16] Reprinted from *The Appeals of Communism* by Gabriel Almond by permission of Princeton University Press, Copyright 1954 by the Princeton University Press, pp. 332–333.

33,381 to 26,741. In 1963, when Party affiliation had risen to 35,000 members, vitriolic disagreements following the Russo-Chinese ideological division were confined to a handful of London intellectuals, and made no dent in membership statistics.[17]

On the other hand, as Almond suggests, the extent to which an event is a precipitating agent depends on its significance to particular members. The same occurrence may induce a crisis for one person, but go almost unnoticed by another. Comparatively trivial actions may, if they strike responsive chords, eventuate in personal explosions. Such is the case, for instance, with the "Pie of Mrs. Petrov," in the following story reported from Melbourne, Australia;

> Vladimir Petrov, former secretary in the Russian Embassy in Canberra, said today that Soviet Ambassador, Nikolai Beneralov, once accused Mrs. Petrov of having thrown a pie at Mrs. Beneralov at a New Year's party.
>
> Mr. Petrov told the commission investigating Red espionage in Australia that the accusation was false, but added, "my wife is a woman who likes the truth." "When the truth is not spoken, she reacts," he added.
>
> Mr. Petrov said this was just one of "truly frightening" reports about him sent to Moscow. It was these reports, he told the commission, that first made him think about defecting to the West.
>
> The Petrovs received asylum in Australia in April.[18]

Types of crisis situations

External events can precipitate disaffection in a variety of ways. One, which is mentioned by Almond, is freeing the person from the physical impact of his movement, thus enabling him to escape the forces that reinforce and mold his beliefs and his perceptions. Permitting incompletely committed members to operate in the outside world is risky, not because it removes physical controls, but because it eliminates the usual ideological restraints on latent reservations. Shifts within the movement may have the same effects, because they represent a reshuffling of sustaining forces. That the person has become a loyal member of some aspect of a social movement does not mean that he will find the remainder equally attractive. The following story illustrates this point:

> Three weeks ago, Karl Mans, Deputy District Chairman of the Communist Party of Tirschenreuth, near here, left for a "political enlightenment and

---

[17] *The Sunday Times* (London, November 17, 1963).
[18] *The New York Times* (July 6, 1954).

training tour" of Soviet-occupied East Germany. He was a guest of the Soviet Zone trade unions. Herr Mans returned and today announced his resignation from the party. "I have been enlightened by the catastrophic conditions in Communist East Germany," he said.[19]

Periods of imprisonment, which often precede defection, clearly remove members from the protective environment of their movement, and allow latent reservations to emerge. Such was the case, for instance, with Imperial Wizard Thomas J. Hamilton of the Ku Klux Klan, who defected in October 1953, while in a North Carolina prison camp. In a letter denouncing the Klan, Hamilton reports that

> . . . coming as close to my Lord as I have in recent months, convinces me that I can no longer have confidence in such an organization.
>
> Because I realize the evils which result from secrecy, I wish to declare publicly that I shall never again join or be active in any movement which is not open to any reputable citizen and whose membership is not available to the forces of law and order.
>
> . . . I have prayed over the matter and I'm sure that God would want me to stay aloof from any organization which presents an opportunity for a person to hide himself behind a mask and commit a crime.[20]

Although Hamilton had organized and presided at many floggings, his scruples and religious convictions had not emerged in this context. His review of the Ku Klux Klan in religious terms required a setting in which the reinforcing pressures of the movement could not operate. It also required a setting conducive to self-examination. "Thinking things over" leads to the consideration of alternatives, whereas the active utilization of beliefs discourages it. This point is made by Ignazio Silone when he writes that

> . . . it may be dangerous for anyone in the thick of the struggle, myself included, to analyze the "whys" and the "wherefores," to look back. At a certain moment the game is set and *rien ne va plus*. You can't leave off dancing in the middle of the dance.[21]

Imprisonment also has a third function, which it shares with some other precipitating situations. The individual in prison can easily come to feel that his movement has abandoned him. He can unconsciously blame

---

[19] *The New York Times* (September 11, 1953).

[20] *The News Reporter* (Whiteville, North Carolina, October 22, 1953).

[21] I. Silone, in R. Crossman, ed., *The God That Failed* (New York: Harper & Brothers, 1950), pp. 80–81.

his group for failing to protect him, and for providing the occasion for his discomfort. "Here," he may say to himself, "is what my membership in the movement gets me." From this hidden premise, more specific doubts and complaints can follow.

But precipitating events may also play a direct role in mobilizing latent reservations. They may be sufficiently nonroutine to prevent people from continuing to act routinely, or sufficiently shocking to provoke a re-examination of values, motives, or premises.

Intimate, unsettling experiences can also dramatize the discrepancies between subjective and objective reality. A case in point is the defection of John Hale, one of the leading figures in the Salem witch hunt. Reverend Hale had participated actively in the persecution of innocent citizens, despite occasional doubts about particular features of the trials. Eventually, the witnesses ranged more widely in their accusations, and several testified against Mrs. Hale:

> Hale, however impassive his ministerial demeanor, felt the ground rock under him when he heard the story. What man would not feel so on getting evidence that his wife had committed a capital crime? Yet that was not the point. Hale knew that his wife had done nothing of the sort; she was flesh of his flesh, and had she been practicing witchcraft he would have known it. . . . Suddenly Hale knew with a conviction beyond logic that spectral evidence was madness. . . . And this being so, how many of the innocent had been hanged at Salem?[22]

Respectable backers of Senator Joseph McCarthy were probably similarly disillusioned after eminent military leaders and other public officials began to be "identified" as Communists.

Alternative resolutions

A young soldier named William Miller saw American forces emerge victorious in the Battle of Plattsburg, and concluded that God had intervened to turn the tides of war. This "discovery" led Miller to peruse his Bible for forecasts of other divinely ordained events. He worked systematically at this task for fourteen years, resolving apparent contradictions and applying various formulas in an effort to decode prophecies. The investigation seemed to yield two conclusions: (1) the Bible revealed that Christ

---

[22] M. L. Starkey, *The Devil in Massachusetts* (New York: Knopf, 1949), p. 218.

would return; and (2) the Bible fixed the date for this second advent at approximately 1843. Later, under public pressure, Miller returned to his calculations and set the date at October 22, 1844.

The consequences of this prediction proved tragic. Thousands of followers—mainly frustrated farmers in the "burned-over district" of western New York—sold their possessions to propagate the message. In the days immediately preceding the fateful October evening, they gathered at appointed meeting places and prayed. Many were penniless at this juncture; having disposed of their farms and other worldly things, they faced immortality with nothing to their names except white ascension robes.

The completeness and irrevocability of this commitment converted the fruitless vigil of October 22 into an event which endangered more than a prediction. It cast doubt on a source of information which had been exclusively and unreservedly relied upon; it brought into question the availability of the only obvious relief for otherwise hopeless lives; it threatened to turn a patterned and understandable world into a bewildering jumble. A crisis of this magnitude could not be tolerated by the more devout adventists. They could not permit this ostensibly invalidating experience to sever their relationship with their movement:

> Faced with an intellectual alternative utterly impossible for minds of their character and training, the more sincere Millerites could only hold to the substance of their faith. There could be no major error, only some slight misinterpretation attributable to still-fallible human judgment. The emotional experience of martyrdom reinforced the same conclusion. Rendered the more peculiar by failure of their expectations, they could only consider themselves even more than formerly, the Lord's chosen people.

The relatively less committed members—those who had joined Miller's church "just in case"—disappointedly packed their camping gear and returned home. However,

> . . . those "who had oil in their vessels" were certainly a respectable number in western New York, and they remained steadfast. Their problem, once they recovered from the first thought-sterilizing dejection, was to discover an adequate explanation for the failure of October 22. Where did the error in reckoning occur?[23]

No one explanation satisfied a substantial number. Sects developed, split into subsects, and in turn were divided into fragments. A more conservative

---

[23] W. R. Cross, *The Burned-over District* (Ithaca, N. Y.: Cornell Univ. Press, 1950), pp. 308–309.

faction, including most of the preachers Miller had converted to his cause, organized the General Conference of the Second Adventist Church of America, which claimed that an error in calculation had been committed. Disagreements then developed concerning alternate dates. Some members felt that no new calculations should be made, but that everyone should remain steadfastly prepared for Christ's Second Coming. Others kept setting new dates. With time, it became more difficult to engender enthusiasm for camp meetings that remained unrewarded.

The second wing of the movement took the more radical position that Christ had in fact appeared on October 22, 1844. Those who interpreted this to imply a change in man's condition sometimes felt entitled to unconventional behavior. Many groups who survived this phase eventually joined the Seventh Day Adventist Church.

Analogous developments have occurred in other movements where "objectively" invalidating events impinged on ideologies to which people were fully committed. When too much was at stake, logically expected defections did not take place. Closely parallel to the Millerite episode, for example, is the career of Shabbethai Zevi, the most famous of the Jewish pseudo-messiahs—whose presence dominated Judaism in the seventeenth century.

Like Miller, Shabbethai catered to a clientele for whom he served as the last resort. During the Middle Ages, Jewish communities in one city after another underwent extermination. Temporary escape elsewhere meant at best a brief respite, with most means of livelihood prohibited, and mobility severely circumscribed. Emotional outlets were few, and conventional religion was demanding, formalized and coldly intellectual. The tall, imposing figure of the messiah emerged into this scene with a message of hope. He preached a doctrine of joy and anticipation. He offered immediate accessibility to the promised land.

The magic of Zevi's message was felt in congregations all over Europe, to the dismay of rabbis and their conservative followers. Entire families disposed of their belongings, and followed Shabbethai to the Middle East.

With salvation ostensibly at hand, the messiah was captured by the Turks, and was persuaded to become a Mohammedan. He made extensive public appearances under Turkish sponsorship in his new role. This development prompted the return to conventional Judaism of European Jews who had been toying relatively lightly with membership in the movement.

The fully dedicated members, however, could not retreat. Some of them viewed Shabbethai's apostasy as symbolic, and underwent "allegorical" conversions. Others declared that the person who represented himself as their messiah was an illusion, or identified him as a fraud. A contemporary history of the Turkish Empire records that

> ... most of them affirm that Shabbethai is not turned Turk, but his shadow only remains on earth, and walks with a white head, and in the habit of a Mohametan; but that his body and soul are taken into heaven, there to reside until the time appointed for accomplishment of these wonders. And this opinion began so commonly to take place, *as if the people [were] resolved never to be undeceived*, using the forms and rules for devotion prescribed them by their Mohametan Messiah.[24]

Festinger, Riecken, and Schachter recently studied a small Midwestern group that predicted the end of the world. They point out that the missionary efforts of this movement increased after its prophecy failed. Members of the group thus showed the need to convince themselves (by convincing others) that their beliefs were valid.[25]

The import is clear. We have seen that precipitating events can act as catalysts to defection, provided membership is sufficiently tenuous to be sacrificed. If a person has latent reservations, these can sometimes be mobilized. If the process of becoming a member is still in its preliminary stages, the sequence may prematurely terminate during times of stress. And although a less than fully committed member (if he has no alternative to his faith) may temporarily patch up his beliefs, the seeds of doubt will tend to germinate: the next juncture at which beliefs are tested may find the same person more vulnerable.

The fully committed member, on the other hand, has a variety of options, each of which helps him to neutralize invalidating experiences. It is only because different members can exercise different options that social movements may be weakened, split, or even destroyed despite the fact that individual members have retained their faith. At best, social movements tend to survive such crisis situations with their ideologies considerably changed.

[24] P. Rycaut, *History of the Turkish Empire*, in J. B. Marcus, *The Jew in the Medieval World: A Source Book* (Cincinnati: Sinai Press, 1938), p. 267 (italics added).

[25] L. Festinger, H. W. Riecken, Jr., and S. Schachter, *When Prophecy Fails* (Minneapolis: Univ. of Minnesota Press, 1956).

The crystallization of defection

When the stage has been set for defection, the culmination of the process may occur either dramatically, or in a relatively subtle fashion. The former is analogous to conversion, and could be labeled "deconversion." It consists of precipitating revelations, discoveries, and other sudden changes in perception and attitude.

The latter is a more gradual change, comprising terminal shifts in the way the movement is perceived. Here, the feeling may be one of having scales removed from one's eyes. As defenses fail and reservations emerge, the movement appears to diminish in appeal. In one of Almond's interviews, for example, an American Communist offered the following recollections of changes that preceded his defection:

> When I came back to St. Louis something happened. Things seemed to go flat. I really began to lose interest and feel critical—and notice the people who were running things—they seemed to be inadequate people. Various little scandals broke out—some ridiculous expulsions which I spoke out against.
>
> I began to feel that my inner assumptions didn't jive . . . I can't say why, but I just began to become more objective and I realized that people were saying things that not only were foolish but untrue. . . . I felt very awkward . . . I felt that times or I had changed.

It is characteristic of gradual defection that the defector himself may not be able to specify a turning point or locate a precipitating experience. At a given stage of the process, the realization simply seems to dawn on him that his membership is a formality, or worse. "Deconversion," on the other hand, occurs rapidly, as conversion does, so that culminating occasions for it tend to stand out in the member's mind. Robert Ingersoll, for instance, reports that he read Darwin, Spencer, and Huxley, and as a consequence "The Garden of Eden faded away, Adam and Eve fell back to dust, the snake crawled into the grass, and Jehovah became a miserable myth."[26]

One of Almond's Italian ex-Communists had no difficulty tracing her disaffection to her husband's expulsion from the Party: "At last, all of the troubles, all of the jealousies, the malignity, the personal grudges existing in the Communist Party were revealed to me in full, as was all of the internal weakness of the Party."

[26] R. G. Ingersoll, "Why I Am an Agnostic," *Works*, Vol. 2 (New York: C. P. Farrell, 1907), p. 508.

In fact, of course, this kind of experience is partly an illusion, because reservations pre-exist their discovery. In the Italian woman's case, for example, the occasion for her husband's expulsion had been his disapproval of the Party's line on Tito, which in turn reflected more general doubts. The expulsion served to precipitate for both husband and wife what otherwise would have occurred anyway, but more slowly.

The difference, in other words, between step-by-step defection and de-conversion is that the latter is more urgent and obvious. A person becomes a defector when the disaffection initiated at some earlier date seems inadequate in the face of new disillusioning experiences. And whereas gradual defection may preserve an impression of ideological constancy, an acceleration of the process dispels this illusion, and makes a person sensitive to changes and to the occasions for them. In other respects, normal and accelerated defections are probably very much alike. The cup "runs over" in both cases, and only the rate of drainage differs.

Impediments to defection

Douglas Hyde reports a conversation with a fellow Communist Party member, during which it developed that his companion disagreed with Communist ideology. He suggested that she resign from the Party, but she refused:

> Her answer startled me. "I will do it if you think I ought. But don't hold me responsible for what happens next, because I may do what poor old Jan Masaryk has just done. You see I am terrified of the vacuum that would be left in my life if I went."[27]

The word "vacuum" is very apt. Defection is an easy process only for members who have been lightly or tangentially committed, and for the very few who have another commitment standing by. In more typical instances, breaking away from a social movement can be hard and painful. Almond tells us, for example, that defectors from Communism typically

> . . . go through a period of doubt and conflict some time before leaving the party. Thus 10 per cent of our respondents reported having spent their entire membership in doubt as to the wisdom of their decision, 10 per cent reported more than half their membership, and 36 per cent reported somewhere between one-fourth to one-half. . . as having been spent in a state of

[27] Hyde, *I Believed*, p. 298.

indecision. . . . Almost two thirds of the respondents had doubts about remaining in the party for more than a year before the final break.[28]

These are impressive figures, but they are not surprising. Membership, after all, serves psychological needs. The typical member faces problems for which his social movement has become a solution; he has tied up feelings and aspirations with the aims of his movement; he has roots planted and interests vested in the life of the group. More subtle effects have also taken hold, such as the changes in thinking and outlook we have discussed in Chapter 7. The member has come to perceive the world from the vantage point of his movement, and has accustomed himself to appraise events within the movement's frame of reference and to relate them to each other with the movement's logic. Thus, ten years after his defection, an American Communist admitted to one of Almond's interviewers that "I still occasionally think along lines taught by the Communist Party whenever I read a particularly virulent case of injustice in the newspapers."

We have also seen that every social movement is to some extent *protective*. It tends to create a congenial microcosm which members come to regard as familiar, dependable, and secure. Their situation is somewhat analogous, in this respect, to that of a certain group of Italian prisoners who committed petty crimes in order to be readmitted to their cells after an amnesty. "The world outside," their spokesman explained, "was cold and hostile." A member of the Mankind United Sect in California expresses similar sentiments slightly differently:

> When I walk along the streets of San Jose, it's like being in a foreign land among strangers. It's hard to explain. Perhaps it's caused by the evil vibrations of their thoughts. I feel lost and I want to get home to the laundry group. That's one of the important things that the project does. . . it brings "like-minded" people together. "Heaven is simply Harmony." We have harmony here. . . .[29]

In addition to safety and protection, membership also offers *predictability and structure*. The defecting member not only faces a cold world, but also an uncertain, ambiguous, and indeterminate one. The dramatist Gerhart Hauptmann captured this dilemma of defection in one of the prayers of Francesco, his renegade priest:

[28] Reprinted from *The Appeals of Communism* by Gabriel Almond by permission of Princeton University Press, Copyright 1954 by the Princeton University Press, pp. 336–337.

[29] H. T. Dohrman, *California Cult* (Boston: Beacon, 1958), p. 109.

"I was a carefully planted little garden, dedicated to your name," said
Francesco to God. "Now it is drowned in a deluge. . . . Formerly I knew my
path exactly. It was the one the holy Church traces for its servants. Now it
is more a matter of being pushed as knowing the goal and being sure of the
way.

"Give me," Francesco pleaded, "my former narrowness and my surety
and command the evil spirits to cease aiming their dangerous propositions
at your defenseless servant. . . . Please help me to find my way back to the
clearly delimited circle of my holy duties."[30]

Defection can also entail a serious loss of *social support*, with no com-
pensating gain. Almond quotes a former French Communist official, who
described defection as bringing "terrific isolation." According to this official,
membership in the Party conveys a "right to community." The former member not only loses this right—comprising ideological reinforcement, and intimate associations with fellow members—but also knows that he can expect
active rejection. Persons who disassociate themselves from a social movement are generally viewed with contempt by their former comrades. The
defector symbolizes yielding to temptations (see p.206). He is an objective
personification of the latent reservations carried by remaining members. The
defector also is often viewed as strengthening the hand of hostile external
forces.

For these and other reasons, the defector can become an object of fear
and hatred for his former coreligionists, a prospect that he usually has seen
exemplified in his predecessors. Some social movements even explicitly
serve notice, for the benefit of prospective defectors, of the negative esteem
in which they would be held. The apostle Peter, for instance, advised early
Christians (II Peter, 2:21–22):

For it had been better for them not to have known the way of righteousness,
than, after they have known *it*, to turn from the holy commandment delivered unto them.

But it is happened unto them according to the true proverb, The dog
is turned to his own vomit again; and the sow that was washed to her wal-
lowing in the mire.

This view makes the defector look to persons outside the movement
for support. *Here, however, he frequently encounters further contempt and
suspicion.* A former member of the Communist Party in an Almond interview, pointed out that

[30] G. Hauptmann, *Der Ketzer von Soana* (Berlin: Fischer, 1922), pp. 103–104.

. . . you're thrown out to people who have been your enemies for years. They despise you and say "even your own people have thrown you out."

You always meet people who want to know what you did that was wrong, or people—strangers—who sneer at you as a renegade. Or people who think you are still a concealed Communist.

The prospective defector must anticipate a protracted period in which he may have to justify his new status—both to himself and to other people. He must separate himself from his old identity, and yet must convey and retain a feeling of continuity. This creates a variety of reactions. Probably the most dramatic (though infrequent) is that of the professional ex-member, who advertises his hatred for the movement from which he defected—implicitly, a form of self-hatred. This pattern is nicely exemplified in the following comic-strip sequence:

DEACON: Ah, there! The Dove Brothers.

COWBIRD: 1:   It's nice to be recognized in a spirit of Bonafidism, friend Deacon! Most of the Pseudo-intellectuaries here think of us as Cowbirds.

COWBIRD 2:   Ugh.

COWBIRD 1:   We're reformed! Cast aside are the infantilisms of Entrenched Youth—The charlatanistic demagoguery spawned by the Machiavellian machines of masochistic manipulators are Indeed.

COWBIRD 2:   Yes! . . . An' anybody know what scurvy Scum We used to be![31]

The search for new identity

Individual resolutions of the paradox of ex-membership may range from complete loss of interest to the careful elaboration of new ideological positions; they may vary from nostalgia to dialectic swings, and they may cover the spectrum from advertised amnesia to full utilization of membership experiences. Whatever the outcome of the process, the search for new identity tends to be a long, laborious process, in which psychological destruction, doubt, and reconstruction uncomfortably follow each other, or painfully intermingle. "I had the lonely job of re-reading and examining all the classics," said one ex-Communist in an Almond interview, "and it took years." Another former Party member reported that "it took approximately a year and a half to break from the party and an additional two years to break from Marxism and all the trimmings."

In the course of this "working through" process, the ex-member is

[31] Walt Kelly, *Pogo* (Post Hall Syndicate, March 17, 1953).

exposed to a variety of pressures which make his task more difficult. Frequently, for instance, he is blackmailed into prudence or tempted to classify himself into some inapplicable category or group. Whatever his new attitudes, they will be viewed with skepticism by some, and reinterpreted by others.

Partly because of the myth, reinforced by popular accounts and unrepresentative publicity, which equates membership in one social movement with the susceptibility to join social movements in general, the ex-member may be pressed to commit himself to another cause. Since most ex-members wish to rejoin society in some fashion, the stereotype of the "true believer" can constitute an impediment for them. One example may suffice to make this point. In 1953, *The New York Times* revisited Mrs. Oksana Kasenkina, who five years before had jumped from a third-floor ledge of a Russian consulate, and who had been granted asylum in the United States. Mrs. Kasenkina's main problem, it turned out, was the tendency of people to "push her around":

> Persons pleading special causes "trouble" her, she said in halting English, especially Russian emigrés who demand that she side either with Monarchist or Social Democratic parties.
>
> "Nobody is interested in helping me to do something," she asserted, "but so many people are interested in pushing me into a political party. I do not understand such things; I have never been a member of a party."[32]

The problems of ex-membership do not end with difficulties in leaving the movement. Subsequently, and sometimes more acutely, the ex-member encounters two further (and related) problems: the first is the problem of his identity, and the second is his relationship to the world he has rejoined. In both these areas the ex-member is certain to encounter a variety of reactions which complicate an already difficult enterprise.

The road to defection

How does a well-intentioned member arrive at the point where he faces the predicament of reconstructing his identity? What can prompt a person to renew the search for meaning after once having claimed to have found meaning? It stands to reason that continued membership is a more natural course of action. Disaffection would seem to presuppose the presence of special motives or forces.

---

[32] *The New York Times* (August 12, 1953).

This consideration, of course, would not hold for persons standing at the threshold of a social movement, with hat in hand, as much "in" as they are "out." Where there is no commitment, there can be no disaffection. There is also no problem in understanding the occasional true believer, for whom the unique features of a social movement are only tangentially relevant.

The more typical member, however, does seem to cut a very sad figure as he withdraws his psychological investment at the cashier's cage, and heads for the exit. These steps are never lightly taken, even when compressed chronology disguises the cumulation of determinants which prompt them.

We are able to distinguish four stages in the development of disaffection, each increasing the probability of the one that follows. The first of these steps is one of *qualified joining*. Without being aware of it, a person may perceive his social movement in a very personal way, may make special demands in return for loyalty, hold unrealistic expectations, or circumscribe areas of belief or behavior in which he intends to operate as a separate agent.[33]

A succession of personal difficulties usually follows qualified joining, and can be thought of as a period of *symptomatic manifestation* of latent reservations. Such manifestations can run the gamut from obvious to furtive. In some instances, a member may reveal himself as a deviant so directly that his movement (if it is authoritarian) will promptly expel him, thus precipitating the last stages of disaffection. In other cases, only a very skilled observer—usually in retrospect—can differentiate symptoms of disaffection from minor variations which one expects among any group of persons. And it is characteristic of this stage that the member himself is not aware of the significance of his idiosyncrasies. He typically takes the objectivity of his viewpoint for granted. What does differentiate him from other members is that the reservations he holds are reinforced (rather than weakened) over time. He remains in a "susceptible" state which sets the stage for a *crisis situation*.

[33] That a member's perceptions of his movement differ from those of the leaders of the group, of course, does not prove that one of these is the correct view. It merely implies that there is a discrepancy that—given the fact that leaders are in a better position to shape reality to conform to their view of it—invalidates the perception of the member. Similarly, it is possible that the demands made by a member are legitimate, although the movement's unwillingness to "deliver" makes them potential sources of disaffection. The definition of latent qualifications is also somewhat circular: it rests on the discrepancy between demands and offerings, and frequently this discrepancy can be deduced only from an existential encounter.

Crisis situations result when susceptible persons encounter precipitating events. An effective precipitating event is a psychological catalyst which makes latent predispositions manifest. It owes its catalytic potency to the fact that it ties into latent predispositions, or (more usually) creates conditions under which these can come to the fore. The simplest type of crisis situation is one in which the reinforcing mechanisms of membership are suspended. More complex types of crisis include traumatic events, which "shake up" the motives that sustain membership. It is characteristic of crisis situations that the person externalizes the changes he experiences. Rather than recognizing the subjective origin of latent material that reaches awareness, he perceives emerging transmutations in the movement. Such disillusionments tend to appear gradually, showing that latent material is progressively sifted, and is selectively permitted to emerge. If precipitating events have created an emergency, however, so as to make continued membership intolerable, this process may be accelerated in the form of a "deconversion."

Finally, the disaffected member undergoes a period of *cognitive reorganization*, during which he tries to arrive at alternative solutions to his problems, independent of the social movement. For some members, this represents a return to a past commitment that has subsisted ready-made throughout membership. Most disaffected members, however, have to tackle this problem by stages, slowly discarding beliefs and attitudes as new ones become available. Not infrequently, the first stages of this process make it appear as if the movement had won out, although time fast dispels this illusion.

The act of defection, which generally occurs sometime after the psychological break from the movement, does not mark the end of the period of cognitive reorganization. It is merely a symbolic act (analogous to the taking out of a membership card) which certifies that the process has become irreversible. It is an important act, however, because of its consequences. Having discarded the label of membership, a person must arrive at some definition of ex-membership. He must establish his *future* identity, incorporating, somehow, his *past identity as a member*. He faces the injunction "to thine own self be true," and this need for consistency presents him with a bitter paradox, which can easily haunt him for the rest of his life.

three

Determinants and motives

WE have shown in previous chapters that membership in social movements springs ultimately from institutional deficits. We have demonstrated that there is a meaningful relationship between the type of problems that face a person and the kind of movements that attract him. We have also endeavored to describe typical sequences leading from problem situations to membership. We have, thus, indirectly traced the emergence of the member's motivation to join.

Since motivation is often viewed as the fundamental problem of psychology, it merits separate consideration. In this chapter we shall deal directly with the problem of motives. We shall inquire whether it is possible to provide a straight answer to the question, "What impelled him to join?" The main point we shall try to make is that one can obtain a meaningful answer to this question only by first letting the object of the inquiry speak for himself. We shall try to examine the advantages and limitations of this method.

Attributed motives

In a posthumously published letter, President Theodore Roosevelt indicated that one of America's top needs was "that every molly-coddle, professional pacifist, and man who is 'too proud to fight' when the nation's quarrel is just, would be exiled to those out of the way parts of China where the spirit of manliness has not yet penetrated."[1]

Opponents of pacifism have postulated innumerable motives for membership in peace movements. They have claimed that pacifists are afraid, impotent, and atheistic, and that their love of peace shows hatred for their country. Another favorite assumption has it that pacifism is a manifestation of mental instability. The spirit of this contention is reflected in the Mauldin cartoon in which a man intercepts a female peace picket and asks her, "What are you—some kind of nut or something?" This type of question is purely rhetorical; it is not intended to be answered, because it serves notice that answers will be ignored.

The cabalist in Chayefsky's play *The Tenth Man* relates:

> A deaf man passed by a house in which a wedding party was going on. He looked in the window and saw all the people dancing and cavorting, leaping about and laughing. However, since the man was deaf and could not hear the music of the fiddlers, he said to himself: "Ah, this must be a madhouse." Young man, because you are deaf, must it follow that we are lunatics?[2]

The point of this parable holds for any prejudgment of motivation. Whenever we attribute motives to a person we place ourselves outside his frame of reference. We erect a partition between ourselves and our subject, through which we can view his protestation of innocence with coldness and skepticism.

Self-characterization of motives

A congressional committee recently initiated an investigation into Women Strike for Peace, a female pacifist group organized in 1961. The investigation was announced with the statement:

> It was with reluctance that the committee deems it necessary to conduct hearings which touch upon alleged peace activities in this country.
>
> Unfortunately, the Communist conspiracy, through treachery and deceit has established a long record of converting man's greatest dream into tools for bringing about man's most tragic losses of dignity and freedom.[3]

As the hearings opened, an official of the women's peace group told committee members, "I don't know why I'm here. But I know why you're here—because you don't understand the nature of the movement."

[1] *The New York Times* (July 18, 1962).

[2] From *The Tenth Man* by Paddy Chayefsky, p. 104. © Copyright 1960 by SPD Productions, Inc. Reprinted by permission of Random House, Inc.

[3] *The New York Times* (December 7, 1962).

She then proceeded to characterize the motives that prompted women to join her group:

> It is motivated by the concern and love of mothers for their children.
>
> At breakfast time they see not only cereal and milk, but Strontium 90—and they fear for the health and safety of their children.
>
> You should be grateful for the Women Strike for Peace. Every nuclear test makes malformations, stillbirths, leukemia, cancer and the possibility of a nuclear holocaust.[4]

Eleanor Garst, another official of Women Strike for Peace, wrote that membership in the movement follows almost directly from a general concern for the future welfare of children:

> You just have to feel, when you look at children—regardless of their color or conditioning—the hope that they'll go on forever and ever, venturing into space and under the seas, exploring this world and its environs with the same compelling curiosity that has stirred you and me. Feeling so, you shout NO! to annihilation for the species. *Presto*, you're a Woman for Peace.

Experiments with spontaneous activity, Mrs. Garst pointed out, gave "Women for Peace" a feeling of accomplishment, and induced them to try repeat performances:

> The frustration felt by women when both sides in the Cold War stepped up the arms race demanded a new kind of expression. Public demonstrations and walks, with which the movement began, provided at least a measure of instant relief. Having found that they *could* stand up and proclaim their beliefs on the side of humanity, the women were not to be silenced.

Mrs. Garst also pointed out that Women Strike for Peace is a social movement which does not have much formal organization, and therefore it is relatively easy for members to translate their motives into actions:

> The second answer as to the "why" of it lies in the very fact that the women's peace movement *is* a movement and not merely another organization. Many women are beginning to feel that organizations had somehow become too unwieldy to respond at once to immediate crises. They wished to escape preoccupation with structure, hierarchy and self-perpetuation, which seems, in some organizations to have obscured their original goals.
>
> No one must wait for orders from headquarters—there aren't any headquarters. No one's ideas must wait for clearance though the national

[4] Lansing (Michigan) *State Journal* (December 12, 1962).

board—there isn't any national board. No one waits for the president or director to tell her what to do—there is no president or director to tell her what to do—there is no president or director.[5]

In addition to its lack of organizational structure, Women Strike for Peace—according to Mrs. Garst—has no dogma to which members must subscribe. As a result, any woman who shares the "belief that mankind deserves a future" can join, and can help to implement this belief.

Such is the portrait of the women's peace movement and its motives which congressional investigators would have obtained if they had been interested in a self-evaluation of the movement, rather than in investigating the hypothesis of Communist infiltration. Which of these approaches is more likely to yield a true picture of motivation?

Although it is difficult to answer this question in general terms, one or two comments are possible. First, it is obvious that any approach that seeks to confirm a hypothesis carries the risk of the hypothesis being wrong. Barking up wrong trees is a sterile occupation. On the other hand, inquiry into a person's own version of his motives is useful even when it results in questionable information.

A person's ability to tell us about his motives may be limited by the complexity or inaccessibility of his needs, by the crudeness of his language, and by his desire to make an impression. In extreme instances—for example, when people belong to social movements for blatantly selfish reasons or to satisfy primitive desires—self-characterizations of motives can be transparently unrealistic. Even here, however, there is information to be gained. The purity and rigidity of the authoritarian's self-image, for example, reveals his need to idealize himself. The direction that rationalizations take can permit us to understand the pressures under which motives operate. At least, we learn about the standard a person uses in assessing the worthwhileness of his own aims.

The evaluation of self-characterizations

We can question the validity of self-characterizations whenever we find discrepancies between stated goals and actual behavior, or internal contradictions. For instance, if member X tells us that he joined his movement to achieve objective A, but shows interest mainly in activity B, C, or D, we can begin to look for other aims he might have. If Mr. Pure joined

[5] E. Garst, "Women: Middle Class Masses," *Fellowship* (November 1, 1962), pp. 11–12.

the Movement Against Obscenity to "protect children against filth," but displays inordinate fondness for erotic material, insists on curtailing the reading of adults, or injects religious or political themes into his concerns, we can assume that child protection may not be his real motive for joining.

In general, self-characterizations would be rejected whenever they failed to supply a coherent, plausible account which can be reconciled with objective information about the member, his movement, and its social context. The person himself may supply us with the grounds for suspecting his testimony. If he tells us, for example, that he belongs to an anti-Semitic movement because there is evidence of a Jewish conspiracy, we can determine whether this information became available to him before or after his conversion to anti-Semitism. If the latter occurred (as in the case of Hitler), the question of motives remains open.

Women Strike for Peace represents the credible end of the continuum, because the self-characterization of motives easily accounts for available facts. The dangers of war which concern members are prominently detailed on the front pages of every newspaper. A desire for the well-being of children is routine among young mothers, and it is obvious that the possibility of a high Strontium 90 count in milk might appear disturbing in this context. The spontaneity and lack of organization of the movement is compatible with the fact that it serves as a vehicle for feelings of protest by housewives, who would tend to be unconcerned with sophisticated political action. In terms of what we know about the concerns of women, about the problems that face them, and about the opportunities presented to them by the peace movement, we have no reason to question their self-characterizations of motive.

The analysis of self-characterizations

When members of a social movement can validly tell us about their own motives, the problem of analysis is reduced to collating ready-made explanations. If members provide untrustworthy information, however, we must resort to supplementary research.

Unreliable informants usually furnish us with clues which permit us to construct alternative views of their motives. The approach required for such an analysis is to accept the person's own version of his motivation as a *partial* statement, which we can complete on his behalf.

Under no circumstances may self-characterizations be neglected in favor of independently elaborated hypotheses. First, there is obvious risk in "looking at the other fellow from our point of view."[6] Second, a prejudging outside observer is necessarily at a disadvantage in assessing the impact of events and the attractions of movements. At best, he can emerge with a cold and unsympathetic portrait—at worst, he may find himself explaining away reality in favor of logic and circumstantial evidence. He may find himself in the extreme position of the scholar who recently delivered a lecture proving the nonexistence of witchcraft, to an audience comprising students, professors—and several people who identified themselves as witches.[7]

Even though our analysis of motives may carry us far beyond the insights available to our subjects, we must *begin* with their own version of their aims. It is this first step in our analysis which tells us whether we must proceed further, and shows us the way.

In the novel *To Kill a Mockingbird* the father (Atticus) explains to his small daughter (Scout) the secret of coping with a difficult teacher:

> "First of all," he said, "if you can learn a simple trick, Scout, you'll get along a lot better with all kinds of folks. You never really understand a person until you consider things from his point of view—"
> "Sir?"
> "—until you climb into his skin and walk around in it."[8]

The intended point of this approach is not merely the obvious one of increasing tolerance, but rather the premise that *especially in instances where other people's views are different from our own, we must overcome this gap before we can try to arrive at explanations.*

Early in 1963, a group of pacifists set out to picket the Miami offices of a Cuban refugee organization which had sponsored one invasion of Cuba, and was in the process of planning another. The pickets carried signs including such messages as "Thou Shalt Not Kill," "Peace Corps, Not Marine Corps, To Save Latin America," and "Man Will End War, or War Will End Man." They were protected by police, since an influential Spanish language radio announcer had called for 10,000 Cubans to meet them, and "pick up the pieces." However,

---

[6] H. Cantril, *The Politics of Despair* (New York: Basic Books, 1958), p. x. The preface to Cantril's study of Communist voters contains a discussion of research methods that circumvent this error.

[7] *New York Herald Tribune* (February 26, 1964). The claim of self-styled contemporary witches is that they belong to an ancient sect, that has been persecuted unjustly because they practice white—as opposed to black—witchcraft.

[8] H. Lee, *To Kill a Mockingbird* (New York: Popular Library, 1962) p. 34.

. . . the crowd refused to disperse at police urging, and when we came into sight began shouting and throwing eggs (at the cops) and bottles and rocks (at us). As some Cubans explained later, they felt we were Communists, "because, even though they call themselves pacifists, they are against invading Cuba."[9]

The negative opinion of the pickets which was held by Cubans was to some extent reciprocated. One pacifist, for instance, referred to Cuban exiles as the "slimiest people on earth." By contrast, another member of the group concluded that most of the exiles were "sincere and impassioned at the conditions of Cuba." He reported the following effort to understand the motives of an elderly Cuban:

After pickets had distributed literature, one exile rushed out of his house, angrily waving a leaflet which had been left on his doorstep:

> Although he was 54 and just recovered from a heart attack, he wanted to be in the invasion forces, if only peeling potatoes. Why was this man so violently anti-Castro? Was he against the revolution? "No, I have always believed in social justice. What we had under Batista couldn't go on. The poor have rights. I suppose I am even a socialist."[10]

The picket, a member of the Catholic Worker movement, embarked on a conversation with the Cuban during which it developed that

> . . . he prayed for help to my favorite saint, St. Martin de Porres. In fact, he had even visited the saint's tomb in Peru, although (like all Cubans since the revolution) he was just an "ordinary worker." "Cuba is not like your country," he said. "We have never been against the Negro. St. Martin is a mulatto. I was even nursed by a Negro. No, this revolution shouldn't have gone on like this. The envious ones, the ones who never amounted to anything, have taken over."[11]

To illustrate the personal nature of his grievance, the Cuban complained that "the housing reform moved 17 people into the bottom half of our house."

This information had been obtained through sympathetic discussion and uncritical questioning, in an effort to determine the person's own version of his motives. *Once this had been accomplished, it became possible to review this "first person" picture, and to correct it where necessary.*[12] It

9 J. Lehman, "CNVA Cuba Project," *The Catholic Worker* (April 1963), p. 8.
10 *Ibid.*
11 *Ibid.*
12 The phrase "first person viewpoint" has been coined and used by Cantril to contrast the *phenomenological* approach to research that does not consider the vantage point of its subjects. See H. Cantril, *The "Why" of Man's Experience* (New York: Macmillan, 1950).

thus became apparent that the Cuban saw himself as a "worker," but was in fact a substantial citizen who had the means to travel abroad and owned a house whose bottom half could accommodate 17 people. Here also was an individual whose expressed desire for social justice disguised contempt for the underprivileged ("the ones who never amounted to anything") and possibly also ethnic prejudice ("I was even nursed by a Negro").

The person's own views of his motives could thus be supplemented with the hypothesis that his anti-Castro efforts might be due to his stake in the old order and that his belief in revolution and justice in part, at least, represented abstractions. *These alternate hypotheses, however, could be legitimately advanced only on the basis of the person's self-characterization.* As mere inferences from his economic status, they would have been inadequately based.

The contemporary view of motives

In addition to the fact that self-characterizations permit us to *locate* motives, they also enable us to *spell them out.* Cantril has shown, for example, that if a person is permitted to elaborate on an expressed desire for "an improved standard of living," widely different objectives can emerge:

> To an upper-middle class American, allowed to tell the story in his own words, an improved standard of living meant "enough money to own a boat and send my four children to private school"; to the wife of a worker in Havana, it meant "to have enough food and clothes so we don't have to beg for things." To a 57-year old farmer in the Dominican Republic, it meant "since I am poor, I need a house and some money, because I am suffering terrible hunger. There are days when we don't even eat at all for lack of ways to get money."[13]

Self-characterizations thus give us a way to preserve the *unique* characteristics of motivation. These are especially important in the study of social movements because individual concerns can be easily overlooked in any analysis of communal ventures.

Another reason why we must heavily rely on the person to supply us with information about his own motives is that motives *change.* Henri Bergson tells us in his classic *Creative Evolution* that

[13] H. Cantril and L. A. Free, "Hopes and Fears for Self and Country," *Amer. Behavioral Scientist*, Supplement (October 1962), p. 8.

The same reason may dictate to different persons, or to the same person at different moments, acts profoundly different, although equally reasonable. The truth is that they are not quite the same reasons, since they are not those of the same person, nor of the same moment. This is why we cannot deal with them in the abstract, from outside, as in geometry, nor solve for another the problems by which he is faced in life. Each must solve them from within, on his own account.[14]

We have seen in our examination of conversion that a person may be propelled to membership by a succession of experiences, each of which leaves its mark. We have seen that the dissatisfaction which may be latent at one stage may blossom into open indignation one or two disillusionments later. In tracing the effects of membership we have seen that an individual's motives are unique to his stage of membership in the movement. The mature member cannot be viewed merely as an ex-convert. As Gordon Allport puts it, "origins [cannot] characterize the mature belief as it now exists, nor explain its part in the present economy of life."[15]

Allport coined the term *"functional autonomy"* to denote the fact that human motives can become independent of the needs from which they spring, and can acquire a life of their own:

The pursuit of literature, the development of good taste in clothes, the use of cosmetics, the acquiring of an automobile, strolls in the public park, or a winter in Miami—all may first serve, let us say, the interest of sex. But every one of these instrumental activities may become an interest in itself, held for a life time, long after the erotic motive has been laid away in lavender. People often find that they have lost allegiance to their original aims because of their deliberate preference for the many ways of achieving them.[16]

This is of practical importance, because the average person can more easily describe his current motives than he can trace their origin. The automobile owner in Allport's example may be ready to catalogue the benefits he now derives from his car, but he might be reluctant or unable to tell us that his first automobile served as a substitute boudoir. To the extent to which motives have changed, however, such historical data do not help our

[14] H. Bergson, *Creative Evolution* (New York: Holt, 1911), p. 7.

[15] G. W. Allport, *The Individual and His Religion* (New York: Macmillan, 1950), p. 109.

[16] G. W. Allport, "The Functional Autonomy of Motives," *Amer. J. Psychol.*, 50 (November 1937), 146.

understanding.[17] If we are concerned with car purchases or driving habits, it is usually irrelevant to inquire into the early love life of the man behind the wheel.

By the same token, even if particular individuals happen to be pre-disposed to social movements by subconscious needs derived from childhood experiences, this fact may be of only passing interest. It may be of no con-sequence that a prominent member of a political movement was estranged from his family at an early age, could not tolerate his younger brother, or had a speech defect—even if these circumstances might have contributed to the beginnings of his political activity.[18]

Moreover, the relevance of functional autonomy increases with depth of commitment: the more dedicated and sophisticated a member becomes, the less important is it to consider motives of remote origins. At one extreme, we observe the person who joins a social movement to obtain security or social support or material rewards or other fringe benefits, and who remains a member on this basis. As we have seen in Chapter 8, he usually does not remain a member very long. His membership is precarious because his con-ception of ideology is self-centered and specialized, and because his loyalty to the movement is conditional. He is an *instrumental* believer, in the sense that he belongs because his personal needs are being satisfied, and retains his interest only while this is the case.

Contrasting with the instrumental believer is the fully committed and dedicated member whom we have described in Chapter 7. The motives of this member are *belief-centered*. He belongs to the movement primarily because he agrees with what it stands for.[19] Whatever extraneous needs may have entered—or may enter—into membership fade away as commitment

[17] To the extent to which motives have remained the same, this point obviously does not hold. For example, the father of Malcolm X, former intellectual spokesman for the anti-white Black Muslim movement, had been violently killed, possibly at the hands of a lynching mob. His house had been burned to the ground by the Ku Klux Klan when X was six years old. According to X, "The firemen came. . . and just sat there without any effort to put one drop of water on the fire. *The same fire that burned my father's home still burns in my soul.*" L. E. Lomax, *When the Word Is Given* (New York: New American Library, 1964), p. 49 (italics added).

[18] For examples of the kind of analysis characterized here, see H. Lasswell, *The Psychopathology of Politics* (Chicago: Univ. of Chicago Press, 1930).

[19] This distinction is the same as that drawn by G. W. Allport and his collaborators between "extrinsic" and "intrinsic" religious believers, and similar to Almond's classifica-tion of Communist Party members into "esoteric" and "exoteric" members. See G. W. Allport, in Academy of Religion and Mental Health, ed., *Religion in the Developing Personality* (New York: New York Univ. Press, 1960); G. Almond, *The Appeals of Communism* (Princeton N. J.: Princeton Univ. Press, 1954).

deepens. The belief-centered person may even reach the stage where he carefully avoids all ulterior motives. A traveler to Russia relates that "Once when I was looking up at ikons on the ceiling of a church in Kiev, a young man behind me tapped me on the shoulder and said "You are disturbing the worship; this is not a museum!"[20]

The needs of an individual can merge completely with the objectives of his group, and the characterization of one may substitute for the definition of the other.

Motives and ideology

In every social movement, the motives of members are to some degree preclassified in the official ideology. To the extent to which the movement specifies its objectives, each member can determine whether his individual aims correspond to the purposes of the movement. He is able to decide how closely the movement is designed to respond to his needs. If he then joins, we can assume that he feels he can effectively operate through the movement.

A pacifist movement that might illustrate this point (because it has a fairly explicit ideology) is the Fellowship of Reconciliation. F.O.R. describes itself as

> . . . a religious organization based on the belief that love, such as that seen pre-eminently in Jesus, must serve as the true guide of personal conduct under all circumstances. Members of the F.O.R. seek to demonstrate this love as the effective force for overcoming evil and transforming society into a creative fellowship. Although members do not bind themselves to an exact form of words,
>
> They refuse to participate in any war or to sanction military preparations; they work to abolish war and to foster good will among nations, races, and classes;
>
> They strive to build a social order which will suffer no individual or group to be exploited for the profit or pleasure of another, and which will assure to all the means for realizing the best possibilities of life;
>
> They advocate such ways of dealing with offenders against society as shall transform the wrongdoer rather than inflict retributive punishment;
>
> They endeavor to show reverence for personality—in the home, in the education of children, in the association with persons of other classes, nationalities, and races;

[20] H. J. Berman, "The Russian Orthodox Church," *Harvard Alumni Bulletin* (November 24, 1962).

They seek to avoid bitterness and contention, and to maintain the spirit of selfgiving love while engaged in the struggle to achieve these purposes.[21]

Persons are invited to become members of F.O.R. if they "conscientiously support this affirmation of purpose." The sequence of arriving at membership is described as follows:

> [Members] do not become pacifists because the Fellowship persuades them to; they join the Fellowship because their consciences have led them to take what, for want of a better word, we call the pacifist position. They do not join in order to receive directions as to their daily activities, but to become members of a fellowship of people who believe in the unity of the worldwide human family and wish to explore the possibilities of love for discovering truth, dispelling antagonisms and reconciling people, despite all differences, in a friendly society.[22]

An illustration of the application of this description is offered by a letter from a new member:

> Dear Editors:
> I have taken some time to come around to a full acceptance of the credo of F.O.R.—this in spite of a Quaker background. But the course of my thinking forces me now to accept, with some sense of relief at being able to clean the air, your principles. Qualms about the practicality of pacifism in this day and age tend to dissolve upon a full consideration of the potentialities of the *positive* side of the rejection of violence. If this world is to have a better future—perhaps *any* future—it is, I believe, to be achieved only on the basis of compassion, an understanding, that recognizes the oneness of man—a concept I see best reflected in the work of the Friends and F.O.R.[23]

This letter implies a process which can be divided into the following stages: (1) socialization into Quaker beliefs; (2) a growing concern with the problem of war; (3) an interest in pacifism, accompanied by doubts about its practicality; (4) increasing concern with the problem of war; (5) the extension of Quaker beliefs to a view of pacifism as a positive, religious stance; (6) the recognition that this same orientation underlies the ideology of F.O.R.; (7) self-identification as a pacifist of the F.O.R. variety; and (8) membership in the movement.

[21] Statement entitled "That Men May Live. . . in Peace Together," repeatedly reproduced in F.O.R. literature.
[22] Fellowship of Reconciliation, . . . *Only by Lawful Means* . . .(Nyack, N. Y.: Fellowship, 1963, leaflet), pp. 4–5.
[23] "Letters" column in *Fellowship* (November 1, 1962).

Other illustrations of the relationship between F.O.R. ideology and the motivation of F.O.R. members are provided in the following autobiographical excerpts from a statement drafted by church leaders active in the Fellowship:

> I like the Fellowship because it is a quiet, steadfast, resolute group of men and women, who refuse longer to make compromise with sin. It finds war between nations to be the greatest of all evils, and acts accordingly.
>
> So, as members of the F.O.R. we have to say "No" to war—each in terms of his own integrity. But the no is incidental. What is ultimate is the positive, reconciling power of God that would go to the cross rather than give up loving "enemies." This alternative to the threat of retaliation is what the F.O.R. emphasizes.
>
> I joined the Fellowship of Reconciliation when I was a sophomore in college in 1922. . . . I was trying to find a way to live in the social climate of Georgia without giving myself over to the hostility and the evil of my environment. . . . During all the years since, I have maintained my sense of belonging to the Fellowship because of the strength which it has given to a lifelong conviction that meaningful experiences of unity and fellowship between people are more compelling than the concepts, the ideologies, the fears or the prejudices that may separate them.
>
> When World War II came, I had already been a pacifist for several years. . . . When the war broke, I felt the need of the undergirding of others who shared the same convictions. So I joined the Fellowship of Reconciliation.[24]

Here one member reports that F.O.R. views war as the supreme sin, while the next member sees the rejection of war as incidental to the doctrine of love; one person tells us that he was attracted to the Fellowship because it helped him relate to people around him, while another shows exclusive concern with his own pacifism, and reports that he joined to gain communal support for his convictions.

For each member, the Credo may be the closest he can come to support of his convictions, although his convictions may be different from other persons who have the same feeling. Conversely, people with diverse motives *can* join the same movement—but *only* if each can relate his motives to the ideology of the movement.

[24] Excerpted from *Why We Belong to the Fellowship of Reconciliation*, as reproduced in *Congressional Record*, Proceedings and Debates, 88th Congress, First Session, Vol. 109, No. 70 (May 13, 1963).

Hypothetical and real members

Although we cannot deduce the motives of individual members from ideology, we can use ideology to construct an image of the *ideal* member— a hypothetical person who would feel uniquely at home in the movement. By examining the F.O.R. Credo, for example, we can infer that F.O.R. might appeal to a person who viewed premises such as those of the Sermon on the Mount as concrete and imperative guides to human conduct. Such an individual might refuse to contribute to war and might work to promote peace, for example, because he could not envisage conflict as an acceptable means to any end whatever. Simultaneously, such a person would wish to eliminate all kinds of social injustice—but would want to do so by peaceful means, through the promotion of love and understanding.

A detailed examination of ideology could spell out this ideal picture further, and information about the social context of the movement could complete the model. For example, if we know that F.O.R. exists during a tense cold-war situation, we can assume that pacifism might overshadow other concerns of members; the existence of civil rights problems would enable us to spell out the role of the ideal member in this struggle. We may even be able to infer the existence of *types* of ideal members—some, for instance, primarily concerned with war; others involved in nonviolent civil rights action; and a third group whose activities might encompass a variety of causes.

But such types are hypothetical characterizations, inferred from beliefs to which people nominally subscribe, and from the problems that face them. As such, they are in the realm of theory, until they are verified. Verification must consist of studies of *individual* members, which can show that the hypothetical motives (or others) were involved in bringing people to the movement. Such direct evidence can also tell us about the relative prevalence of various types of motives, and can concretely depict the process whereby particular motives come into being.

The problem situation as an incentive

Just as ideologies can preclassify needs by defining their objectives, problem situations can type motives in relation to the conditions that mobilize them.

The complexity of this relationship may be illustrated by considering the impact of the arrest of Rosa Parks on December 1, 1955. Mrs. Parks, it will be recalled, was arrested on a bus in Montgomery, Alabama, because she refused to yield her seat to a white man:

Shortly after Mrs. Parks sat down (in the Negro section of the bus) the white bus driver ordered her, along with three other Negroes, to move back and let white standees have their seats.This meant that Mrs. Parks, sore bunions and all, would have to stand while a white man sat in her seat. The other three Negroes moved when told to do so; Rosa Parks refused.

For this crime against the long established order and peace, Mrs. Parks was arrested. There was no disturbance on the bus as the police led Rosa Parks away. Some white people were heard to murmur about "uppity niggers" and a few Negroes giggled. The entire episode was over in a matter of five minutes.[25]

Mrs. Parks was only one of many persons arrested under parallel circumstances over the years. Each arrest had stimulated discussion, but by 1955 tempers had worn thin. During the days following the arrest of Mrs. Parks, groups of indignant citizens began to consider possible retaliatory measures. Ultimately the Rev. Martin Luther King was commissioned to distribute leaflets calling for a bus boycott. White newspapers publicized the prospective event, and the Montgomery Walk to Freedom came into being. On December 5, 1955, 99 per cent of Negro commuters walked to work, or used car pools.[26]

Most students of the Montgomery movement agree that its impetus was a cumulation of degrading experiences analogous to the treatment of Rosa Parks. The Rev. King wrote, for instance, that

> The present situation here in Montgomery on the part of the Negro citizens grows out of many experiences—experiences that have often been humiliating, and have led to deep resentment. The Negro citizens of Montgomery compose about 75 per cent of the bus riders. In riding buses, they have confronted conditions which have made for a great deal of embarrassment, such as having to stand over empty seats, having to pay fare at the front door and going out to the back to get on, and then the very humiliating experience of being arrested for refusing to get up and give a seat to a person of another race.[27]

Louis Lomax tells us that the Freedom Walkers "struck back for cursings, slappings and jailing that had been their daily fare for more years than they had the courage to remember.... They only wanted decent treatment."[28]

[25] L. E. Lomax, *The Negro Revolt* (New York: New American Library, 1963), p. 17.

[26] *Ibid.*, pp. 92 ff.; also in Fellowship of Reconciliation, *Martin Luther King and the Montgomery Story* (Nyack, N. Y.: Fellowship, comic book, undated).

[27] M. L. King, "Walk for Freedom," *Fellowship* (May 1956), p. 5.

[28] Lomax, *The Negro Revolt*, p. 94.

The Montgomery movement started with limited objectives—there was a demand for Negro bus drivers, a request for courteous treatment, and a proposal that passengers be seated on a first-come, first-served basis. These aims reflected the urgency of immediate grievances. If change could be instituted, the first impulse was to insure a future free from the most painful and humiliating embarrassment of the past. Later—as external pressure and internal enthusiasm increased—leaders of the movement were able to expand their aims to include the desegregation of buses.

From its inception, the Montgomery bus boycott was a movement of nonviolence. The Freedom Walkers returned smiles for abuse, accepted unwarranted traffic tickets, restrained their reactions when their homes were bombed, and permitted themselves to be jailed. When they returned to ride the buses, they did so under instructions such as:

> If cursed, do not curse back. If pushed, do not push back. If struck, do not strike back, but evidence love and goodwill at all times. . . .
>
> If another person is being molested, do not rise to go to his defense, but pray for the oppressor and use moral and spiritual force to carry on the struggle for justice.[29]

Nonviolence is obviously not the first, impulsive reaction when people are faced with provocations. Unless other motives intervene, one expects frustrating situations to induce acts of aggression.[30] The absence of this development, in the case of the Freedom Walkers, can be attributed to several reasons.

First, many of the participants in the movement (both leaders and rank and file) were profoundly religious, and were convinced of the moral principle of nonviolence. Second, many held the conviction (based on past experience), that "violence never solves problems. It only creates new and more complicated ones."[31] Third, there were practical considerations, since the movement's opponents had absolute power. As Rev. King put the matter, "we did not have access to the instruments of violence."[32] Fourth, passive defiance could (for some people) serve as an expression of aggression. Fifth, nonviolence involved action, and many people seemed prepared to do almost

[29] The Montgomery Improvement Association, *Integrated Bus Suggestion* (Montgomery, Ala.: 1956, leaflet).

[30] This relationship has been stated as a psychological law (the Frustration Aggression Principle) by a group of psychologists at Yale University.

[31] M. L. King, "Facing the Challenge of a New Age," *Fellowship* (February 1957), p. 7.

[32] King, "Walk for Freedom," p. 6.

anything, as long as it helped to express protest or promised to promote change.

In the Montgomery movement—as in all social movements—different people held different conceptions of the ends to be attained. Varying patterns of these conceptions became predominant at successive stages of the movement. At first, aims seemed relatively directly tied to the precipitating situation and its broader context. The object was to eliminate the most hurtful features of the system—while retaining the system. Persons who saw this perspective as too limited (such as NAACP members) were unenthusiastic bystanders of the first Freedom Steps. Soon, however, needs grew functionally autonomous of precipitating grievances. Ultimately, the sequence that started with a protest against physical inconvenience and embarrassment grew into a civil rights movement of national proportions.

In the course of time, the original problem situation multiplied its connotations, became part of a cluster of grievances, and eventually merged as one contributing drop in a wellspring that flooded the nation, comprehended every sphere of human activity, and ranged back in history to the first indignities of slavery. The Freedom Walk had been transmuted into the Negro Revolt.[33] And as the movement expanded, *the problem that inspired it had kept pace.*

The relationship between problem and motive can be a reciprocal one. Problem situations originate discontent and liberate needs, which in turn draw attention to problems. Precipitating conditions as such are of course constant—persons are slapped, segregated, or arrested, whether they object or not. But to the extent to which they rebel, a precedent is set which can open the way to further discovery. Questions can lead to unsatisfactory answers; institutional reactions can point to broader areas of disagreement and the exploration of problems can reveal their ramifications.

In this fashion, the objective of today can spotlight the problem of tomorrow. As the social movement moves, incentives and aims expand, each in relation to the other.

A definition of motive

Our discussion has drawn attention to the fact that motivation in social movements must be defined in relation to several sets of factors.

First, the definition of motivation must make provision for the individual member's perception of his aims, and must be able to relate this to

[33] Lomax, *The Negro Revolt.*

his past experiences and his conduct. Second, the definition must account for the person's relationship to his movement, including the nature and degree of his commitment. Third, it must relate the individual's aims to the objectives of the movement, and must characterize the way in which membership can be a means to the achievement of the member's objectives. Last, the definition of motives must point to specific situations in which the person finds incentive to action.

Taking into account all these factors, a characterization of a person's motive would be a *statement of the situational improvements he wishes to obtain through the process of membership*. This statement must overlap with the defined motives of fellow-members, because incentives and solutions are partly shared. It must also, however, be unique. Every member's motives must comprise an admixture of feelings, aspirations, attitudes, and needs which creates a highly personal and yet sharable conception of intolerable reality and a singular but shared perspective of desirable change.

SOCIETY not only gives rise to social movements, but also helps to determine their subsequent fate. The relationship of social movements to the world at large may promote, deflect, or retard their growth or decline. In this chapter, we shall examine some of these relationships between social movements and conventional society.

Models

The first point in the development of a social movement where the outside world can play a decisive role is in helping to resolve whether problems lead to susceptibilities. By presenting underprivileged people with proof that their condition is not inevitable, for instance, society can help to create discontent. Colonies surrounded by new nations, poverty in the shadow of wealth, hunger bordering on satiety provide contrasting perceptual stimuli that often drive home the realization that a better world is concretely attainable.

A recent letter in *The Progressive*, signed "Theophrastus Such" and addressed to a wealthy woman in Palm Beach, Florida, provides an illustration of this point. The letter started out as follows:

I have just read the recent article about Palm Beach in *Look* magazine. The description of your home—"the ultimate in Palm Beach luxury"— enchants me. A house with 129 rooms, 36,000 Spanish and Portuguese tiles, a nine-hole golf course, and a tunnel to the Bath and Tennis Club! What grandeur! What *ultimacy!* And I on my part shall be frank to say that if I pretended not to envy you, I should be a hypocrite.

Not that I am *too* badly off. I have a pleasant little place of my own, with a spare room, a tile stove (with nine Swiss tiles) a set of rosewood chess men, and a wife I can beat at chess.

The letter then went on to quote from a communication to the Los Angeles *Times* by an American service man in Korea who described conditions in a Korean orphanage:

"We just found out that the children of this orphanage didn't get any food today. When we got to the orphanage, we found the little children cold and hungry and crying. This had happened many times before and will happen again unless something is done. The director of the orphanage (Mr. Kim Woon) is supporting it alone from his meager funds. . . ."

Mr. Such comments,

Some of these orphans—not all of them, of course—will live to grow up *and grow up to be Communists.* Agitators will tell them about your 36,000 tiles and my nine and about your 129 rooms and my spare room. And sure as shooting—[1]

Awareness of contrasts in wealth and well-being can drive under-privileged persons into social movements—not only to close the gap between their actuality and their expectations, but also to express feelings of protest against persons who appear unfairly advantaged.

It is not surprising, for instance, that anti-American sentiments can be made more intense by exposing people to reconstructed State Department appeals containing information such as

We now have the highest standard of living in the world.

With our national wealth being more and more widely distributed, the average family has purchasing power enough to enjoy the products of our farms, our factories, and our technological advances. For example, there are now more privately owned automobiles in the United States than there are families. As most people know, the American housewife has an efficient and well-equipped kitchen with a mechanical refrigerator, an electric or gas stove, hot running water. Millions of workers have television in their homes. . . . .[2]

[1] *The Progressive* (May 1962), p. 9.
[2] H. Cantril, *The Politics of Despair* (New York: Basic Books, 1948), p. 244.

This type of information may stress the limits of one's own horizons, and thus create frustration, bitterness, and resentment. It may also give focus to these feelings, since it is a short step from seeing property accumulation to perceiving unfair advantage.

Of course, success stories of a slightly different kind can have the opposite effect. If they involve underprivileged persons, they can show that the "job can be done." They can provide incipient social movements with *models of successful collective achievement*. Fidel Castro, for instance, has said of the Cuban revolution, "We are a source of ideas, a source of light for the workers and the peasants of Latin America, for the oppressed Indians of Latin America."[3]

The "March of Latin America," a Cuban anthem which has been quoted by Castro, proclaims,

> Cuba, beacon of the Americas,
> Proudly and haughtily awaits you
> When the arms of liberty
> Angrily you raise.

This "beacon" theme presupposes the possibility of other Latin Americans adopting the Cuban solution because they can identify with the Cuban problem. It assumes that a Central American plantation worker or a South American miner could come to see a Castro-style social movement as a means to his ends, because he feels his condition to be comparable with that of the prerevolutionary Cuban. Fidel Castro has even stated that

> In many countries of Latin America pre-revolutionary conditions are incomparably superior to those which existed in our country. There are Latin American countries, sacked and exploited by monopolies and oligarchies, where hungry and desperate masses wait for an opening, so as to erupt into history.[4]

A state analogous to the Latin American one exists in Africa, where disaffected people in colonial areas are in a position to pattern nationalist movements after those in neighboring newly independent nations. When Jomo Kenyatta, former suspected leader of the Mau Mau movement (and later prime minister of Kenya), was asked in 1961 when his country should be afforded her independence, he answered "today," and added, "Look at Sudan, look at Tanganyika, look at Somalia, just next door. I don't think

[3] "Fidel Castro en un aniversario glorioso," *Obra Revolucionaria*, No. 20 (1963), p. 20.
[4] *Ibid.*, p. 12.

that these countries are any more advanced than Kenya, yet they have achieved their independence!"[5]

Parallel statements have been made by participants in every recent African nationalist movement. A young private in the Angola Liberation Army, speaking in a jungle enclave in the North of Portuguese Angola, illustrates the impact of models on the rank-and-file member: " 'I've seen freedom in the Congo,' he said. 'My boy is never going to have to do what I had to do.' "[6]

The impact of temptations

Models of achievement not only affect entire social movements, but can have a special impact on particularly susceptible members. They can sometimes act as temptations, attracting some people away from movements, or reducing their adherence to ideology. A Communist, for example, may be led to defect from his Party by evidence of attractive conditions in the non-Communist world; a militant labor leader may be bought off by industry through promotion or other rewards.

To minimize the impact of temptations, social movements may stress their uniqueness, and may discourage interactions with outsiders. Members of the early Christian movement, for instance, were enjoined: "Be ye not unequally yoked together with unbelievers: for what fellowship hath righteousness with unrighteousness? And what communion hath light with darkness? . . . Wherefore come out from among them, and be ye separate . . ." (II Cor. 6:14, 17).

Christians were repeatedly warned not to view secular society with a sympathetic eye. "Being of this world" was a phrase expressing contempt, and "wisdom of the world" was explicitly equated with "foolishness with God" (I Cor. 3:19).

Protecting their members from conventional society is especially important for social movements that offer a Spartan existence, make heavy ideological demands, or maintain rigid restraints on the freedom of members. Such movements may have to go to great lengths to protect their younger affiliates from contact with material advantage and conventionality. Parents in Old Order Amish communities, for instance, have had to defy court orders and serve jail sentences to try to prevent their children from attending public school beyond the eighth grade. Even more dramatic is the defiance of the Sons of Freedom sect of Russian Doukhobors, who live

---

[5] *The New York Times* (April 12, 1961).
[6] *The New York Times* (December 16, 1963).

in parts of Canada. Rather than permit their children to become exposed to the secular influences of the educational system (including history lessons discussing wars, physical education classes in which children wear shorts, and homework that interferes with Bible study) Doukhobor parents have staged unclothed demonstrations in deep snow, set fire to schools, and dynamited the Canadian Pacific Railway.

Differences in susceptibility to temptation within any given movement come about in several ways. The most obvious, which applies particularly to children, derives from the fact that (as we saw in Chapter 7) some members are involved in their movements to a greater degree than others. A fully indoctrinated, heavily committed member is less likely to be seduced than a person whose induction is incomplete or who is only lightly toying with membership.

We have dealt with other causes of differential susceptibility in our chapter on disaffection (Chapter 8). Some of these relate to the motives sustaining membership. People who have strings tied to their loyalty can transfer such strings with relative ease. If the social movement satisfies a need for status, for example, a person may leave the movement once he becomes convinced that more status may be secured elsewhere with less effort. Similarly, career seekers make poor members when the going gets rough, and a materialistic orientation (such as that displayed by some American servicemen in Korean POW camps) invites bribery.

Another factor related to differential susceptibility is the relative presence or absence of conflicting interests. A person who has some problems that predispose him toward membership, but others which direct his attention elsewhere, makes a risky member. He is a perpetually unstable focus of pressures, and may move toward one of several appeals, depending on the problem most salient for him at the moment.

An apt illustration is the worker-priest movement in the Catholic Church. This experiment consisted of members of the clergy working on assembly lines in industrial plants, in an effort to cement ties between Catholicism and the working class. The Church discovered, however, that more dramatic changes occurred among the priests involved in the movement than among workers. In September 1954 a letter was sent in the name of Pope Pius XII to various labor organizations, in which the Vatican warned:

> May the clergy, deeply interested in these [social] problems, and impatient to see them solved, not surrender to the blandishments of theories upheld by adversaries of the Church as though these alone were valid or as though

they furnished a more fruitful doctrinal contribution of greater vigor of action.[7]

Four days later, the worker-priest movement began to be abolished. The Sacred Congregation of Seminaries in Rome ordered all Catholic seminaries in France to forbid their students to work in factories. The reason for this action, according to *The New York Times*, was that "some of the priests have become so immersed in their work that they have come very close to supporting the Communist Party line."[8]

The genesis of internal conflict

There are various reasons, then, why some groups within a social movement may be more susceptible to pressure or seduction than others. For any such reason, social movements may yield *unevenly* to the impact of pressures and temptations, and warring traditionalist and modernist factions may be created.

The Swedish Lutheran state church was recently divided in this fashion when a law embodying the recognition of female rights caused women to be ordained as priests. A large segment of the church, relying on the Biblical injunction "Let your women keep silent in the churches" (I Cor. 14:34), threatened to boycott the newly appointed female clerics. Another faction, equally vehement, ceremoniously welcomed the ladies. Attempts to bridge the gap between the two camps were completely unsuccessful.[9]

Such stalemates are not uncommon. A parallel situation developed, for instance, in the Congregation Beth Tefilas Moses, a Jewish synagogue in Michigan. Formerly Orthodox, this temple had restricted the main portion of its services to men. Women had been seated in the balcony, in accordance with immemorial tradition. However, the twentieth century asserted itself in the form of an ever-increasing reform faction, which eventually reached majority status and voted to desegregate the sexes. As a last resort, the Orthodox minority requested remedy from the courts, who refused to intervene.[10]

Another illustration of uneven adaptation is provided by the Black Muslim movement, a group which is militantly anti-white and anti-assimilation. The movement, however, faces pressures to soften this militancy, in order to secure respectability. Thus, when President Kennedy died the Muslim leader Elijah Muhammad issued a statement in which he declared that

[7] *The New York Times* (September 13, 1954).
[8] *The New York Times* (September 17, 1954).
[9] Lansing (Michigan) *State Journal* (April 20, 1960).
[10] Lansing (Michigan) *State Journal* (January 10, 1959).

"We, with the world, are very shocked at the assassination of our President." At the same time Malcolm X, addressing a Muslim rally at Manhattan Center, commented on the President's demise by quipping: "Being an old farm boy myself, chickens coming home to roost never did make me sad; they've always made me glad." Elijah Muhammad promptly suspended Malcolm X from all official functions, after pointing out that his second-in-command had not spoken for the movement.[11]

Progressive factions need not necessarily emerge victorious when some members respond to social events and others do not. A very common outcome of internal conflict is a conservative victory, as may be illustrated by considering the 1963 Congress of the National Society of Daughters of the American Revolution.

Over the years, some chapters of the D.A.R. have become aware of the realities of American involvement in world affairs. Several of these groups had announced reservations to the D.A.R.'s anti-United Nations stand. The Cumberland Chapter of Pennsylvania, for instance, had objected to

> ... anything which in any way weakens our country's position in the world through criticism of the United Nations, which is at present the best agency for promoting peaceful international cooperation; and to any attempt to thwart the compassionate projects of UNICEF.

Similarly, the Louisiana Purchase Chapter of DeSoto, Missouri, drafted a resolution asking the Society to rescind its demand for U.S. withdrawal from the United Nations. Instead, the Louisiana Purchase Chapter argued, the D.A.R. should press for "improvement" of the U.N.[12]

The passage of the anti-United Nations resolution at the 1963 Congress in the face of this kind of opposition has been concisely described as follows:

> Eleanor McDowell of Glens Falls, N. Y. said that the Daughters must reaffirm their faith in the U.N. as "an imperfect but valid instrument of peace." A lady from Fargo, N. D. supported her; but then up stood a lady from Florida to say that the U.N. had already seized 21 counties in South Carolina. Ann Gilbert of the District of Columbia closed the ranks: "Every day we delay this resolution we are giving the Communists a chance to go deeper into our national security."
>
> They delayed no more. Perhaps 100 dissenters (out of some 2,000 delegates) were observed on the standing vote. There was no disturbance on succeeding resolutions, beyond the faintest rustling of no's.[13]

[11] New York *Herald Tribune* (December 5, 1963).
[12] *The New York Times* (April 11, 1963).
[13] *The Progressive* (May 4, 1963).

The progressive minority was thus defeatea, and the D.A.R.—a blatantly isolationist movement—continued to resist the "temptation" of international involvement.

Of course, not all conflicts within social movements are the result of selective adaptation. Divergent views may merely be *attributed* to outside pressures, so as to impugn the motives of their exponents. In a dispute within a religious movement, for instance, each faction may accuse the other of secular tendencies, while warring Communists may perceive each other as bourgeois stooges, despite the fact that such charges are unwarranted in both instances.

Another complication is that members of a social movement who are dissatisfied for any reason can draw on the world outside for symbols to give expression to their dissatisfaction. The mechanism is illustrated by the prevalent tendency for rebellious teen-agers all over the world to sport American habits as a way of manifesting their feelings. Thus, for instance, one may encounter a gang leader named Coca Cola, in Bangkok, Thailand.[14]

Soviet officials have expressed the view that chewing gum, listening to jazz, wearing zoot suits, fancying painted neckties, and similar manifestations of bad taste represented a desire to become alien. The same types of reactions have issued from other Eastern European and Asian Communist countries. Thus, a Rumanian spokesman described Boogie Woogie and Jitterbug as "features of the ethics of American imperialism designed to destroy the creative intelligence of our youth." A Polish newspaper attacked what it called "Bikiniism" as "an expression of foreign and hostile ideology smuggled into Poland by imperialist agents."[15] The intensity of such reactions reflects an awareness of the fact that adoptions from abroad are frequently symbolic expressions of resentments at home.

Inflexibility

Although members of a social movement may *individually* react to the pressures and enticements of society, each social movement must also *collectively* resolve the problem of its identity. To what extent should members of the movement function as members of the outside community? How much cooperative effort with outside agencies is possible without prejudicing the aims of the movement? How much should the concerns of the movement

[14] *The New York Times* (April 27, 1963).
[15] *The New York Times* (April 18, 1954).

branch out? What kinds of "compromises" in beliefs are legitimate? An excessively conservative answer to these questions can easily convert a social movement into an anachronism that invites extinction.

A striking illustration is provided by the Poujadist movement in France, which achieved phenomenal popularity within one year of its inception, but disappeared equally rapidly a year or two later. The movement began in 1955, under the leadership of Pierre Poujade, the owner of a small stationery and book store in the village of St. Cere. In the election of January 1956, Poujade and his "Union for the Defense of Commerce and Artisanry" (U.D.C.A.) received 2,600,000 votes—over 12 per cent of the ballots cast. As a result, 53 Poujadist Deputies obtained seats in the French National Assembly. Within one year, most of these legislators had become the laughing-stock of France. Many of them had resigned. Poujade's chief lieutenant had joined the Army. Pierre Poujade himself ran for office in a "safe" district in Paris in 1957, and went down to crushing defeat with six per cent of the total vote. In 1962, Poujade was observed in southwestern France, the area of his erstwhile popularity, making speeches to audiences consisting of his "campaign manager, . . . a foreign newspaper man, a taxi driver, and the candidate's wolfhound."[16] What accounted for these paradoxical developments? How did Poujade achieve such dramatic success and then experience such dismal failure?

The Poujadist movement had been a protest movement of the middle class. The shopkeepers of St. Cere under Poujade's leadership had successfully revolted against the government of France. They had refused to pay taxes, and merchants in other towns had decided that if a "one-horse town like St. Cere can get away with it, we can do the same thing here."[17] Poujade began to travel from town to town, organizing anti-taxation resistance, and making speeches about the plight of the French bourgeoisie:

> We are the mules of the nation. They (the government) are not simply killing us. They are beating us to death. We must rise and we must act, and not in the traditional manner. They have their laws, but their laws are illegal.[18]

> Despite all their adversities and calamities, the middle classes have refused to permit themselves to be covered by the tombstone the inhuman regime tries to erect on them. By means of hard work, sacrifices patiently ac-

[16] *The New York Times* (November 15, 1962).
[17] B. Ehrlich, "France: The beefsteak revolt of Pierre Poujade et Cie," *Reporter* (March 10, 1955), p. 31.
[18] *Time* (January 3, 1955), p. 21.

cepted, strict economy, and a thorough devotion to duty and probity, the middle classes are being reborn.[19]

Poujade never minced words in referring to the enemy. "They closed all the brothels in France," he said of the French National Assembly, "but they left the biggest one open:"[20] He characterized government officials and legislators as "old garbage and young prostitutes," "pimps of the system," "old horses," "defeated toads," and worse.[21]

Although Poujade's only concrete proposal, in his early speeches, was that of a tax boycott, he made continuous references to the need for a general revolt against the regime:

> Our ancestors took the bastille; a king, a real one paid for not having made the reforms that were necessary. No less than two centuries later, will their sons accept a tyranny which is in no way different except in its mediocrity and anonymity?
>
> We should like to be patient and nice, but it would be better if one doesn't provoke us further. It is not prudent to smoke next to a powder keg.[22]

The Poujadist Program, as published in July 1955, consisted basically of proposals for abolishing or curtailing government agencies.

A vote for Poujade in 1956 thus represented pure defiance and protest, and the electorate contained large enough numbers of disaffected storekeepers over whom the twentieth century had ridden roughshod. The result was a Poujadist landslide. This election victory, however, placed the Poujadist movement into the midst of their enemy's camp. How could Poujade react in this situation?

Neither Poujade's victory speech in the Velodrome d'Hiver (the Madison Square Garden of Paris) nor his press conferences following the elections revealed any change in his orientation toward the government. Although he now controlled 51 legislators, he still asserted that "the Assembly controls nothing. Worse yet, it has been degraded by pirates who have destroyed our institutions, discredited our country abroad, and led it down the path to oblivion."[23]

A new version of his platform, published January 18, still concentrated on the need for fiscal reform, and contained proposals to limit the authority

[19] S. Hoffmann, *Le Mouvement Poujade* (Paris: Armand Colin, 1956), p. 210.
[20] *Time* (January 3, 1955), p. 21.
[21] Hoffmann, *Mouvement Poujade*, pp. 215, 216.
[22] Ehrlich, "Poujade et Cie," pp. 33–34.
[23] *France Observateur* (January 12, 1956).

of Parliament or to circumvent it by means of Estates General—a stratified popular assembly.

The Poujadist Deputies, once elected, announced their intention to obstruct the work of the legislature:

> We are now studying the rules of procedure of the National Assembly to discover all the methods available for blocking its labors.
>
> We will abstain during debates on political questions.... It will be as if we did not exist. We will vote, on the other hand, for economic and fiscal laws which would lighten the burden of trade.[24]

The first part of this program was carried through admirably. Day after hectic day the Assembly had to be adjourned amid Poujadist singing, shouting, desk-banging, and filibusters. When the Assembly ousted several Poujadists for election irregularity, "... within seconds the well of the house was a heaving mass of bodies, with tail-coated Assembly attendants struggling to separate the opposing forces in an uproar of confused shouts and banging desk tops."[25]

By the end of April, *Le Monde* was able to report:

> It is a fact that in three months no member of the [Poujadist] group ever went to the rostrum to make a speech worthy of attention on any important subject. It is also a fact that no noteworthy bill was ever presented by any of them.

In a discussion of this fact, *Le Monde* observed:

> Having achieved electoral success without any program—priding themselves almost in not having one—the Poujadist representatives and leaders seem to be becoming aware of this dangerous deficiency as they are confronted by daily political realities.[26]

As a result of this awareness, the Poujadist movement was splitting at the seams. Some members called for positive programs, while others demanded a return to the days of the "Siege of St. Cere." Poujade himself declared that his group would remain an "economic and social movement" and would resist "transformations."[27] He decided on a continued legislative boycott: "We must have ... a royal disdain for these circus games. Our deputies will no longer take part in these games."[28] Poujade also threatened to storm Paris with a mass demonstration.

[24] *France Observateur* (January 5, 1956).
[25] *The New York Times* (February 16, 1956).
[26] *Le Monde* (April 29–30, 1956).
[27] *Le Monde* (May 3, 1956).
[28] *Le Monde* (May 4, 1956).

In the interim, five Poujadist deputies defied their leader's orders and supported the Mollet government on the Suez question. Simultaneously, the antipolitical wing of the movement formed a dissident group that accused Poujade of "[drowning] our movement in the 'bath'" of politics.[29] Many of the original supporters of the U.D.C.A. shared this view. One of Poujade's erstwhile backers, who failed to vote for him in 1957, put the matter as follows: "Things are no longer the same. Ah, the politicians got him, our Pierrot! He's become a puppet, just like the others."[30]

A late effort to concentrate attention on the Algerian question, and one or two attempts at parliamentary coalitions, failed to stave off political defeat. A run-off election in November 1958 marked the end of the Poujade movement as a factor in French politics.

The Poujade movement had, by and large, "stuck to its guns" despite a change in its status in 1956. It continued to behave as a protest movement opposed to a social system of which it had become a part. It could no longer serve its original functions in its new role, but it refused to change its ideology and its approach to serve new needs. This inflexibility converted the movement's original appeals into inscriptions for its political gravestone, and turned its victory into the beginnings of defeat.

This illustration demonstrates that social movements must evolve in a changing world. The inability to respond to new and different situations can destroy a movement's appeal.

Institutionalization

To survive in a changing world, social movements must undergo adaptive transformations that are designed to enhance their attractiveness in competition with the outside.

These kinds of changes, when they occur in a successful social movement, tend to convert it into an institution. When adaptive changes continue beyond this point, institutions tend to lose their identity, and merge into society at large.[31] A radical socialist movement, for instance, may become less militant and eventually transmute into a socialist party, which can

---

[29] *The New York Times* (April 1, 1956).

[30] *L'Express* (January 25, 1957).

[31] This definition of "institutionalization" differs somewhat from current sociological definitions, which stress other aspects of the process, such as bureaucratization and the formalization of norms. Our own definition is intended to stress adaptive psychological reactions, rather than to facilitate classification of groups or to describe their changes.

gradually become indistinguishable from other political groupings, as in the following illustrations:

The (German) Social Democratic Party, seeking votes in West Germany's important middle class, turned its back this weekend on "economic planning."

A declaration of faith in private enterprise was proclaimed by Socialist leaders at an economic conference held by the party in Essen.

Dr. Heinrich Deist, the party's economic theorist, in another repudiation of a traditional socialist tenet, said strikes "belong to the past" as a way of accomplishing labor's demands.

The Essen conference, which shifted Socialist economic policy to a position hardly distinguishable from that of West Germany's Christian Democratic Government, represented another long step in the evolution of German social democracy from a "class" to a "people's" party.

Socialist leaders began the evolution five years ago by scrapping the party's Marxist manifest.[32]

The Marxist trappings of the Italian Socialist Party are still in evidence, but they received what amounts to a *coup de grace* at the 35th [party] congress that ended Tuesday.

The obvious result of the congress was an agreement to try and form a government with other center-left parties. Behind this agreement lies the real meaning of the congress—the repudiation of 70 years of militant revolutionary Marxism. . . .

As Paolo Vittorelli, chief of the party's foreign policy commission, explained: "We were sick with Hegelian dialectic and Marxism. Now, after all these years, we have realized that the opposition is not the place to be. Our goals can best be achieved through sharing in the power of government. . . .

"The conditions do not exist for a revolution. We are moving away from the soft-thinking and murky mystique of the working class struggle toward a new pragmatism."[33]

Institutionalization as a process is characterized by the tendency to relegate ideology more and more to a position of a means to ends. Whenever a belief becomes an impediment to public acceptance, it is modified or abandoned. Changes in belief may even represent anticipations of future inconvenience for the adapting movement.

The recent Vatican Council was convoked, for instance, to "streamline"

[32] *The New York Times* (October 8, 1963).
[33] New York *Herald Tribune* (November 2, 3, 1963).

the Catholic Church; earlier, the Council of Trent initiated theological reforms under the impact of the Protestant Reformation. The Mormons abandoned Celestial Marriage under the guns of the U. S. Army, but considered admitting Negroes to the priesthood "in the light of racial relationships elsewhere."[34]

Conventional religious denominations in the United States are products of institutionalization that illustrate the process in its extreme form, because American religion has derived considerable prosperity from ideological compromise and formalization.[35] Any surface examination shows high religiosity among Americans. Some 50,000,000 adults (approximately half the population) have gone to church weekly in the last six years.[36] One out of every four Americans engages in some form of missionary activity on behalf of his church.[37] Almost all Americans express agreement with a variety of conventional religious beliefs: 90 per cent of a recent nationwide sample believe that Jesus Christ was the Son of God, 74 per cent feel that there is a life after death, and 61 per cent profess belief in the devil.[38] One American in five claims to have at some time experienced a religious event of a sudden dramatic nature, usually consisting of an other-worldly feeling unrelated to any specific faith or doctrine.[39]

On the other side of the ledger, there emerges a discrepancy between professed faith and more concrete evidence of beliefs and practices. For instance, although fully 91 per cent of a 1948 survey sample reported that they faithfully followed the injunction, "Thou shalt love thy neighbor as thyself," two-thirds of the group declared themselves unwilling to love enemies of their country, and the same number felt that they could not love a member of a political party which they considered dangerous. The *Ladies' Home Journal*, which conducted the 1948 study, concluded that

> . . . it is evident . . . that a profound gulf lies between America's avowed ethical standards and the observable realities of national life. What may be even more alarming is the gap between what Americans think they do and what they *do* do.[40]

[34] *The New York Times* (June 7, 1963).

[35] Among the sociologists who have studied change in American religion from the sect to the secularized church, probably the most important is Max Weber, who dealt explicitly with this problem in his essay "The Protestant Sects and the Spirit of Capitalism."

[36] *Public Opinion News Service* (December 30, 1962).

[37] *Ibid.* (December 25, 1957).

[38] *Ibid.* (April 19, 1957).

[39] *Ibid.* (April 15, 1962).

[40] L. Barnett, "God and the American People," *Ladies' Home Journal* (November 1948), p. 236.

Other investigations show that active church members are not involved in theological concerns. The Presbyterian Church, for instance, examined their church families and found that

> . . . for many, if not most, the Christian faith was either coincidental with moralism, or else about the same as communion with nature.
>
> Many equated Christianity with "the American way of life." And there was a prevalent view that it is important to have faith, but that it doesn't matter much in what or in whom.

Most religious families viewed the church as "a building with an employed staff and a scheduled program" which is engaged largely in "character building." Membership, they felt, provides "a sense of belonging" and an opportunity for children to participate in wholesome activity. In general, a church was perceived as "a good thing for a community to have—like substantial banks, swim clubs and a city dump."[41]

Even the clergy fails to personify traditional doctrinal concerns. Thus, a substantial number of Methodist ministers smoke and drink,[42] and one out of every eight Episcopalian priests admits that he does not believe in the virgin birth of Jesus, which is an Episcopalian dogma.[43] These kinds of laxities would lead one to expect that religious denominations are no longer doctrinally very distinct, a fact that may be confirmed by a closer look at almost any congregation.[44]

The appeals of churches also reflect decreasing distinctiveness. Commercials enjoin the public to "attend the church or synagogue of your choice," with the clear implication that whatever arguments one can use to promote religiosity are universally applicable. Appeals increasingly emphasize what Herberg has characterized as the promise of "prosperity, success and advancement in business."[45] Religious faith is recommended for its psychological benefits. Advertising proclaims that "peace of mind and rest

---

[41] Excerpts quoted by L. Cassels, in "Many Persons Vague about Faith, Survey Shows," Lansing (Michigan) *State Journal* (May 10, 1961). The full survey is reported in *Families in the Church; A Protestant Survey* (New York: Association Press, 1960).

[42] *The New York Times* (August 9, 1959).

[43] *The New York Times* (July 10, 1963).

[44] H. Toch, and R. Anderson, "Religious Belief and Denominational Affiliation," *Religious Education* (May–June 1960), pp. 193–200.

[45] W. Herberg, *Protestant, Catholic and Jew* (New York: Doubleday, 1960). See also M. E. Marty, *The New Shape of American Religion* (New York: Harper & Brothers, 1959), and L. Schneider and S. M. Dornbusch, *Popular Religion: Inspirational Books in America* (Chicago: Univ. of Chicago Press, 1958).

come . . . through power found in trusting God," and points out that beliefs are "resources" for "the tempo of life today."[46]

There is obvious sacrifice of ideology in this emphasis on believing, since the content of belief is assigned a secondary role. And even less ideological is the trend toward church-sponsored nonreligious activities, ranging from card parties and sewing circles through dances and hay rides. These secular functions are explicitly designed to attract a maximum number of persons, who can then be induced to attend services. Religious beliefs and practices alone are no longer viewed as sufficiently appealing, and it is assumed that they must be attractively packaged and sold in disguise. It is also assumed that persons who are not interested in religious beliefs and practices still constitute desirable members.

Krech, Crutchfield, and Ballachey point out that the new element here is not the concern with nonreligious activities, but the fact that churches concern themselves with "nonreligious functions in a nonreligious manner."[47] To illustrate this, Krech *et al.* quote Andrew Mackerel of *The Mackerel Plaza*, pastor of "the People's Liberal Church of Avalon, Connecticut," which is "designed to meet the needs of today, and to serve the whole man." Pastor Mackerel's description of his fictitious church corresponds closely to the type of "community church" that has become prevalent in middle-class American suburbs:

> Our church is, I believe, the first split-level church in America. It has five rooms and two baths downstairs—dining area, kitchen and three parlors for committee and group meetings. . . . Upstairs is one huge all-purpose interior, divisible into different size components by means of sliding walls and convertible into an auditorium for putting on plays, a gymnasium for athletics, and a ballroom for dances. There is a small worship area at one end. . . .[48]

Community churches, however, are only the extreme form of a trend to seduce people into religious activity. Chayefsky's play, *The Tenth Man*, contains a telephone conversation between an experienced rabbi and a young man facing his first congregation. The old rabbi's advice includes the following:

[46] "Attend the church of your faith regularly each week," advertisements, Lansing (Michigan) *State Journal* (February 9, 1963; May 4, 1963).

[47] D. Krech, R. S. Crutchfield, and E. G. Ballachey, *Individual in Society* (New York: McGraw Hill, 1962), p. 399.

[48] P. De Vries, *The Mackerel Plaza* (Boston: Little, Brown, 1958), as quoted in Krech *et al.*, p. 399.

You've got to be a go-getter, Harry, unfortunately. The synagogue I am in now is in an unbelievable state of neglect and I expect to see us in prouder premises within a year. But I've got things moving now. I've started a Youth Group, a Young Married People's Club, a Theatre Club which is putting on its first production next month, *The Man Who Came to Dinner*, I'd like you to come, Harry, bring the wife, I'm sure you'll have an entertaining evening. And let me recommend that you organize a little-league baseball team. It's a marvelous gimmick. I have sixteen boys in my Sunday School now. . . . Harry, listen, what do I know about baseball? . . . Harry, let me interrupt you. How in heaven's name are you going to convey an awe of God to boys who will race out of your Hebrew classes to fly rocket ships five hundred feet in the air exploding in three stages? To my boys, God is a retired mechanic. . . . Well, I'm organizing a bazaar right now. When I hang up on you, I have to rush to the printer to get some raffles printed, and from there I go to the Town Hall for a permit to conduct bingo games. In fact, I was so busy this morning, I almost forgot to come to the synagogue. . . . (*He says gently*) Harry, with my first congregation, I also thought I was bringing the word of God. I stood up in my pulpit every Sabbath and carped at them for violating the rituals of their own religion. My congregations dwindled, and one synagogue given to my charge disappeared into a morass of mortgages. Harry, I'm afraid there are times when I don't care if they believe in God as long as they come to the synagogue.[49]

"Coming to the synagogue," "joining the union," or "getting votes for the party" are objectives that require no justification once institutionalization has made them ends in themselves. Beliefs still receive attention, but this may be cursory, formalized, or embued with a readiness to compromise, water down, or sacrifice whatever may detract from organizational objectives.

Institutionalization and social change

Institutionalization is thus both a negative and a positive process. The *positive* feature of institutionalization is its concern for self-perpetuation or expansion—with existence for its own sake. Institutionalization pursues "Three P's": Prosperity, Power, and Popularity. The *negative* aspect of the process is its lack of concern for all ideology, except for beliefs that have immediate survival value (see footnote 31, p. 214).

These changes can both insure the life of a group and bring about its

[49] P. Chayefsky, *The Tenth Man* (New York: Random House, 1960), pp. 81–82.

demise. Institutionalizing groups decline because they become increasingly oriented toward people who have no real needs,[50] and because they come to aggravate rather than facilitate the problems of the underprivileged.

They do so in three ways. First, they cater to members who can help them in their accumulation of the "Three P's," and as a result unsuccessful persons must be passed over. The institutionalized labor union seeks skilled workers who can pay dues and who represent bargaining power, rather than unemployable persons who would constitute a liability for it. Political parties evidence more concern for powerful pressure groups than for needy minorities.

Second, the person who searches for ideology in an institutionalizing group is viewed as an unrealistic, muddleheaded troublemaker whose insistence on irrelevant criteria is an embarrassment to his respectable coreligionaries. No serious politician, for instance, would be able to tolerate the demand for a return to the fundamentals espoused by the founder of his party. In the same spirit, Dostoevski's Grand Inquisitor felt forced to burn Christ at the stake.

Last, institutionalization is geared to whatever social institutions are current, and therefore has a strong vested interest in them. An institutionalizing group may lobby for minor adjustments in the system to improve its own status, but it cannot question the system, or operate with unconventional premises. For these and other reasons, the underprivileged, in turn, cannot operate through institutions. They find them cold and unresponsive, hollow and formalistic. They reject them as irrelevant or worse. In the case of religion, they flock to the fringe sects, dismissing conventional churches "as obstacles to the close relationship between man and God."[51] Jehovah's Witnesses, for instance, proclaim that "today's popular religion is without power to save anyone to everlasting life in God's new world."[52] Niebuhr writes that

> . . . whenever Christianity has become the religion of the fortunate and cultured and has grown philosophical, abstract and formal and ethically harmless in the process, the lower strata of society find themselves religiously expatriated by a faith which neither meets their psychological needs nor sets

[50] This change in orientation has been described by Weber and by other sociologists concerned with the evolution of sects. For instance, Liston Pope points out that a church (as opposed to a sect) is more often composed of property owners, is interested in wealth, affirms prevailing culture, cooperates with other institutions, tries to extend its membership, is characterized by a "psychology of dominance," defines its ideology in conventional terms, becomes passive, formalistic, and remote—and undergoes other related changes. (L. Pope, *Millhands and Preachers* [New Haven: Yale Univ. Press, 1942].)

[51] "The Third Force in Christendom," *Life*, p. 113.

[52] "The Popular Worship of Faith," *The Watchtower* (January 15, 1959), p. 55.

forth an appealing ethical ideal. In such a situation the right leader finds little difficulty in launching a new (religious or secular) movement.[53]

Only reversing the trend of institutionalization can convert the potential clients of social movements to members of conventional groups. But institutionalization becomes reversible only when discontent has become overwhelming, so that power and privilege comes to be obtained at the hands of the underprivileged. At these junctures, however, new social movements have usually pushed past efforts to suppress them, and institutional reforms and reformations are too late.

After the recent advent of a nationalist rebellion in Angola, Portugal decreed full citizenship for Angolans, embarked on a crash educational program, raised wages, and enacted a variety of other reforms.

According to a reporter on the scene, the Angolans reacted as follows:

Yes, they say, it is perhaps true that the Portuguese have built new homes for them and given seeds and free plots to every family. And yes, they have heard that the Portuguese are now seeing to it that African farmers get the same price for their coffee as the Portuguese plantation owners, thus eliminating an old abuse.

Yet they cannot quite accept that life might be better now under the Portuguese than it was before the revolution.

"Whatever the Portuguese do, it is too late," said Joao Esteves, an aging man permanently stooped with rheumatism.

His bitterness, and the bitterness of many of the refugees in the mountains, seemed to stem from years of grievances.

A leader of the Angolan government in exile was quoted as describing the same dilemma with the question, "How does one dismount from a tiger?"[54]

Conventional society is rarely restored through the salvaging operations and rear-guard actions of dying institutions. It rather tends to be reborn through the first stages of institutionalization, which turn the victorious social movements into new institutions.

The suppression of social movements

Inflexibility and institutionalization are both forms of natural death for social movements operating in a changing world. A third form of natural demise occurs in movements that outlive their original demands. The fol-

---

[53] R. Niebuhr, *The Social Sources of Denominationalism* (New York: Holt, 1929), pp. 32–33.

[54] *The New York Times* (December 16, 1963).

lowing item in a 1945 issue of the *Nation* magazine illustrates this state of affairs:

> Due to the extreme age of [our] few remaining members, the famous Mt. Lebanon Shaker property is now offered for sale. 250 acres, 3 acre lake, ski run, woods, unsurpassed Berkshire view . . . several dormitories; 3 smaller houses; barn. Ideal for summer theater.[55]

But many social movements do not die of natural causes. Instead, they are deliberately and violently suppressed by conventional society.

A case in point is provided by an incident that occurred in 1953 in a remote Arizona valley near the Utah border that was occupied by a group calling itself the "United Effort Church." United Effort was a cooperative colony founded by individuals who had become disaffected with the Mormon Church. The colony consisted of 122 adults and 263 children, all engaged in farming and handicrafts.

The State of Arizona disapproved of United Effort because the colony practiced polygamy. Governor Pyle described the group as a "lawless and commercial undertaking" dominated by "greedy and licentious men" who promoted "white slavery" and produced children "to become chattels of this totally lawless enterprise."

One hundred and twenty peace officers participated in a raid on the community, which was described as follows by *The New York Times*:

> Despite elaborate secrecy precautions during protracted preparations for the raid, word of the plans had reached the community.
>
> The raiding party, which had half expected resistance or flight by the inhabitants, found most of the community assembled at 4 A.M. Pacific daylight time on the grassy school yard, where they had raised the American flag in the middle of the night and waited for the raiders.
>
> In the faint light of a moon approaching a total eclipse, the cultists joined in singing "America" as the raiding convoy of more than fifty cars rolled in over the dusty one-lane dirt road leading to U. S. Highway 89, forty miles to the East.

The victory, over two years in preparation, marked the end of the United Effort cult. Children were allocated to foster homes. Adults were held for trial. According to Governor Pyle, the jailed cultists were to be charged with "bigamy, adultery, open and notorious cohabitation, statutory rape, con-

[55] "Notes by the Way," *Nation* (August 4, 1945), p. 110.

tributing to the delinquency of minors, income tax evasion, misuse of school funds and facilities, and falsification of public records."[56]

In many instances, authorities may use *force* in an effort to prevent a social movement from getting under way. Most revolutionary movements, for instance, tend to be physically suppressed in their initial stages. Totalitarian regimes seeking to maintain anachronistic social arrangements may suppress even mild and indirect expressions of discontent. In Franco Spain, for instance, labor unrest is punished as "subversion."[57] South Africa has resorted to a wide variety of measures to prevent the formation of social movements among oppressed Negroes. These measures have included massacres, curfews, evictions, antisubversive laws, prohibitions against collective bargaining, pass laws, antidemonstration laws, ad hoc taxation, and the establishment of tribal puppet administrators in native ghettoes. Every form of sanction, from shooting and prison to starvation and physical isolation, are used in an effort to wipe handwritings from the wall.

Laws may be employed to prevent the formation of social movements or to eliminate unwanted movements. This expedient may take a fairly direct form, as in countries outlawing opposition groups, or it may consist of legal harassments which make life in a social movement sufficiently unpleasant for people to think twice before joining it. In the United States, for instance, membership in the Communist Party has carried a variety of penalties. Another American illustration is a law in South Dakota that prevented Hutterite colonies from acquiring land in the state, and thus forced them to relocate.

Informal means of suppression frequently make legislation unnecessary. In Iran, for instance, it has been the practice for a group of wrestlers headed by a gentleman nicknamed "The Brainless One" to administer terrible beatings to opposition sympathizers during the elections. Suspected Communists have had their heads shaved, and according to one report, "the admiring police, who get in a few kicks and punches themselves, promptly arrested (the) astonished shorn or unconscious victims." [58] Similar collusions between private pressure and law enforcers have suppressed the Negro voting registration movement in several Southern states.

Many social movements have been wiped out by one or another com-

---

[56] *The New York Times* (July 27, 1953).
[57] *The New York Times* (November 29, 1963).
[58] *The New York Times* (March 3, 1954).

bination of sanctions. Other social movements have had to migrate in search of safety—sometimes over impossible distances—while still others have had to go underground for extended periods of time.

The conspiracy argument

What motives prompt the suppression of social movements? Why do powerful societies expend disproportionate resources on efforts to exterminate small groups? Officials argue that society must defend itself against the depredations of persons intent on the destruction of law and order. "These social movements," proclaim spokesmen for witch-hunting tribunals and antisubversion squads, "would harm every one of us if they were not destroyed. It goes without saying that we are in favor of people thinking as they please. It is the conspiracy to impose dangerous ideas on other people which must be curbed." Sidney Hook, in a volume apparently designed to justify the persecution of American Communists, puts the matter as follows:

> The failure to recognize the distinction between heresy and conspiracy is fatal to a liberal civilization, for the inescapable consequence of their identification is either self-destruction, when heresies are punished as conspiracies, or destruction at the hands of their enemies, when conspiracies are tolerated as heresies.[59]

Mr. Hook defines "heresy" as "a set of unpopular ideas or opinions," and "conspiracy" as "a secret and underground movement" ready to play "outside the rules of the game." There are several implicit problems in these definitions. The most obvious problem is that the persecutors are the ones who generally define the "rules of the game," and that they habitually do so after the fact. King Hassan II of Morocco, for instance, was questioned during a recent visit to New York about the impending execution in his country of three leaders of the Bahai sect, a social movement which preaches brotherhood and rationality. His Majesty responded that "Islam was the state religion of Morocco but that there was freedom to all, to Christianity, Judaism, and Islam. '*Bahai is not a religion, rather something that attacks public order.*' "[60]

A similar line of argument has been followed in an infinite variety of settings. In the 1938 anti-Trotskyite trials in the U.S.S.R., for instance, the

---

[59] S. Hook, *Heresy, Yes—Conspiracy, No* (New York: John Day, 1954), p. 21.
[60] *The New York Times* (April 2, 1963, italics added).

charge was not ideological dissent, but "treason to the country, espionage, committing acts of diversion, terrorism, wrecking, undermining the military power of the U.S.S.R., and . . . provoking a military attack of foreign states upon the U.S.S.R."[61] A contemporary historian of the Antinomian Controversy in colonial Massachusetts wrote that the dissenters

> . . . all went on in their former course, not only to disturb the Churches, but miserably interrupt the civil Peace, and that they threw contempt both upon Courts, and Churches, and began now to raise sedition amongst us, to the indangering of the Common-wealth; Hereupon for these grounds named, (and not for their opinions, as themselves falsely reported, and as our godly Magistrates have been much traduced here in England) for these reasons (I say) being civil disturbances, the Magistrate convents them . . . and censures them; some were disfranchised, others fined, the incurable amongst them banished.[62]

A real difficulty in the distinction between disagreement and conspiracy lies in the fact that it is the *stated* ideas and *expressed* opinions that are the bones of contention. The unspoken content of the mind does not lie in the public domain. Before a person can be identified as a dissident, he must state his views. But *once he has stated his views, he has taken political action.* A statement of views, whether in the form of a list of theses posted on a church door or a letter to a friend, may exert influence, and therefore can be categorized as conspiratorial. "As soon as a man talks with another man," writes Mao Tse-tung, "he is engaged in propaganda."[63] "For by thy words thou shalt be justified," proclaims Christ, "and by thy words thou shalt be condemned." (Matthew 12:37.) Once a social movement states its beliefs, it becomes a conspiracy when public officials classify these beliefs as harmful.

What is true of aims also holds with regard to means. The distinction between "legitimate" and "underground" activity is largely a product of outside pressure. In a completely open society, underground ventures are pointless. It is only when public avenues of action are closed that social movements generally find it necessary to resort to byways and dark alleys.

---

[61] People's Commissariat of Justice, U.S.S.R., *Report of the Court Proceedings of the Anti-Soviet "Bloc of Rights and Trotskyites"* (Moscow: 1938).

[62] C. F. Adams, ed., *Antinomianism in the Colony of Massachusetts Bay*, Vol. 21 (Massachusetts: Prince Society Publications, 1894), p. 87.

[63] Mao Tse-tung "In Opposition to Party Formalism," in B. Compton, ed., *Mao's China: Party Reform Documents 1942–1944* (Seattle: Univ. of Washington Press, 1952), p. 44.

The seduction premise

Why, then, are social movements *really* persecuted? What makes some groups such sources of bitter irritation to the societies in which they operate? Tyson, in *The Lady's Not for Burning*, advances the following argument:

> We must burn her, before she destroys our reason. Damnable glitter.
> Tappercoom, we mustn't become bewildered
> At our time of life. . . .
>   . . . Must be burnt
> Immediately, burnt, burnt, Tappercoom,
> Immediately.[64]

Peter Austeri, the leader of the Albigensian revolt, who was roasted alive in the presence of a vast multitude on April 9, 1311, stepped into the flames with the words, "If I had been allowed to preach to you, you would all have embraced my faith."[65]

Social movements are frequently assumed to hold a powerful attraction for the unaffiliated. In this context, suppression is viewed as removing the source of temptation—sometimes at the point where large masses of dupes are about to succumb to it. Cardinal Newman, in defending the persecution of heretics by the Catholic Church, defined the victims as "tempters" who endangered the souls of thousands.[66] The verdict of the Protestant Council of Geneva, which condemned Servetus to the stake, began with the words, "You have tried to make schism and trouble in the Church of God by which many thousands have been ruined and lost, a thing horrible, shocking, scandalous and infectious."[67] In somewhat less emotional and more secular language, Webster's dictionary defines "heresy" as "an opinion held in opposition to commonly received doctrine and tending to promote division and dissension."

All social movements are potentially tempting because they arise from deficits in conventional society. If people become aware of these deficits, and if they respond to this discovery by joining a social movement, other people may follow. From the viewpoint of the social order, this danger can be

---

[64] C. Fry, *The Lady's Not for Burning*, (London: Oxford Univ. Press, 1949), p. 72.

[65] H. J. Warner, *The Albigensian Heresy*, Vol. II (New York: Macmillan, 1928), p. 209.

[66] *Ibid.*, p. 218.

[67] R. H. Bainton, *The Travail of Religious Liberty* (Philadelphia: Westminster Press, 1951), p. 93.

counteracted in one of two ways. The first is to deal with the problem situations that give rise to social movements, so as to eliminate temptability. The second is to destroy the social movements. In most instances, the second alternative is far less expensive. In South Africa, for instance, repressive measures are a strain on the defense budget, but to give up apartheid would mean the loss of quasi-slave labor on which the white economy completely depends.

But susceptibility springs out of problem situations, and *any attempt to by-pass this consideration is not only doomed, but self-defeating.* This is the case because suppressions compound problems. They produce new ramifications to suffering and new occasions for discontent. Moreover, real social movements (as opposed to institutions) are not discouraged by practical difficulties, since they don't feed on success. The logic of suppression thus purchases an illusion of safety with counterfeit currency. At best, it produces short-run stability by increasing the probability of drastic change in the future. At worst, it results in senseless discomfort and embittered conflict.

The life cycle of social movements

We have illustrated the fact that from first to last, the life cycle of a social movement shows the ever-present impact of the outside world. This impact is complex and frequently self-contradicting: pushes and pulls oppose each other, and pressures toward assimilation or oblivion are exercised by the same agencies. Institutions furnish problems, and refuse to admit solutions. They accentuate inequities, while rejecting expressions of protest. Once discontent is manifest, the measures taken to suppress it may only serve to add fuel to the conflagration.

Typically, the emerging social movement encounters difficult times in its transition to adulthood. Problems of identity may trouble it in its battle with opposition and temptation. If the self-definition resulting from this play of forces is inadequate, and fails to meet the requirements of potential members, the young movement may go the way of most experiments. To survive, a social movement must be compounded of whatever proportions of conventionality and uniqueness the world demands at the time. It must maintain identity through self-segregation, but it cannot do so to the point of making the world within more frustrating than the world without. It must serve as an instrument for persons alienated from the world but still usually part of it.

In its efforts to pass these tests, a social movement can usually depend on continuing inspiration from without. Society rarely reacts to symptoms by attacking the disease. Instead, the gulf between institutions and their alienated members tend to deepen. Generally it is only when voices in the wilderness are compounded into a chorus that belated reforms are enacted. However, institutional reform is rarely effective when it is no longer optional, and when social movements have acquired a momentum of their own.

If and when a social movement becomes dominant in a society, its victory makes it vulnerable to two forms of self-destruction. If the movement persists in playing a protest role, the inappropriateness of this stance invites loss of membership. If, as is more usual, the movement proceeds to consolidate its new power, it risks becoming absorbed in the effort. The life cycle we have described may thus be renewed. The movement may lose its original identity and become blind to developing needs. In due time, it may have to suppress the manifestations of discontent of new underprivileged groups.

11 ▷ THE PSYCHOLOGICAL EVALUATION
OF SOCIAL MOVEMENTS

IF we decided to call our times the "Age of Social Movements," our predecessors might justifiably dispute the label. Almost every historical period could point to its own brand of social ferment, and could claim that more people were more concerned about more issues than had been the case within memory. Even the relatively quiescent Middle Ages would be in a competitive position, given the magnitude and intensity of their heresies, inquisitions, crusades, dancing manias, and secular revolts.

If we can stake a claim to pre-eminence, it is not because our social movements are more widespread or bloodier or more enthusiastic than the collective efforts which preceded them, but because *they are of more universal concern.* Today—more than ever before—there is no place for the unconcerned bystander, viewing his more committed fellow-citizens with tolerant amusement, and likening the ebb and flow of spontaneous collective action to the evanescent foam covering the more meaningful currents of the societal mainstream. Ours is a shrinking world, increasingly tied by communication networks and economic interrelationships into the kind of mutual dependence that causes repercussions for every one of us from events in remote corners of the globe.

It becomes increasingly difficult to retain the illusion of permanence and stability when institutions are eroded away under our feet. The aware-

ness of unsettling change has occasioned among many a spontaneous appre-
hensiveness of social movements. The Rev. Martin Luther King notes that

> ... there are those who would contend that we live in the most ghastly
> period of human history. They would argue that the rhythmic beat of the
> deep rumblings of discontent from Asia, the uprisings in Africa, the na-
> tionalistic longing of Egypt, the roaring cannons from Hungary, and the
> racial tensions of America are all indicative of the deep and tragic midnight
> which encompasses our civilization.[1]

Others view social movements as the equivalents of surgical operations
—painful, ugly, and unsettling, but ultimately beneficial and regenerative.
Eric Hoffer, for instance, tells us that "in receiving this malady of the soul
the world also receives a miraculous instrument for raising societies and
nations from the dead—an instrument of resurrection."[2]

The majority of interested spectators take a more positive position. As
they watch various collective efforts pass before their grandstand, they often
find themselves moved by sympathy, admiration, fascination, and envy. They
indulge in these feelings selectively, of course. They may applaud revolutionary ventures and admire participants in civil rights actions, but may view
fascists with trepidation and religious sectarians with contempt. They may
cheer "progressive" movements and deplore "retrogressive" ones. They
may admire the dedicated member, but suspect "fanatics," "radicals,"
"zealots," or "bigots." And even when they pity and defend persons on
the "wrong" side, they may add the provision that "they know not what
they do."

Social scientists as private individuals cannot avoid sharing such feelings. As scientists, however, they are presumed to be dispassionate. It is
assumed that each scientist will try to deposit his own individual prejudices
outside his laboratory doors. But this does not mean that his work is free
of evaluations. New values are born inside the laboratory; new biases derive
from the kinds of questions the scientist must ask. Some are related
to scientific inquiry in general; others spring from specific approaches
to particular problems. In this final chapter we shall try to illustrate
the values which are implicit in the viewpoint we have outlined in this
book.

[1] M. L. King, "Facing the Challenge of a New Age," *Fellowship* (February 1957),
p. 3.

[2] E. Hoffer, *The True Believer* (New York: Harper & Brothers, 1951), p. 166.

Antisocial movements: a layman's view

Several years ago, when the Black Muslim movement first gained prominence, a news magazine published a detailed account of a Muslim rally in New York. The story began:

The Black Supremacists
"Every white man knows his time is up," snapped the frail-looking Negro in the embroidered pillbox to 5,500 Negroes packed into Manhattan's St. Nicholas Arena last week.

The account continued with a sobering description of the Muslim leader and his message. It described the speaker as "scowling" and "incendiary," and his speech as "pouring out scorn." According to the story, a "purveyor" of "cold black hatred" was "calmly feeding" the "rankling frustrations of urban Negroes" with "virulent anti-Americanism and anti-Semitism." This "doctrine of total hate" had been publicized by "some Negro newspapers" to "exploit Negro hopes and fears." It was even noted that the movement "trained muscle" to "protect its racist chief."[3]

This type of characterization reflects the reaction of some laymen to an extreme movement, and provides a standard against which we can gauge the social scientist's position. The evaluations implicit in the language of the magazine report are:

1. the movement (Black Muslims) is dangerous;
2. the movement is directed against civilized society;
3. the legitimate concerns of members are being transformed into illegitimate feelings;
4. these illegitimate and destructive feelings are successfully engineered;
5. the instigators of the process are deliberately malevolent individuals.

The recommendation implicit in these premises would be to try to curb the Muslims' leadership. Since the movement is viewed as springing from the *exploitation* of hopes and fears, major reforms would not be a necessary condition for the suppression of the movement.

The social scientist's perspective

In contrast to this view, we might cite several excerpts from an evaluation of the same movement by a social scientist (C. Eric Lincoln):

[3] *Time* (August 10, 1959), pp. 24–25.

The [Black Muslim] Movement provides outlets, short of physical violence, for the aggressive feelings roused in its members by the callous and hostile white society. Muslims tend to be Negroes for whom the pressures of racial prejudice and discrimination were intolerable, whose increasing resentment and hatred of the white man demanded release . . . :

In several important ways, the Muslims tend to strengthen the dignity and self-reliance of the Negro community. . . .

The very existence of the Muslims—their extreme black nationalism and their astonishing growth and vitality—is functional to the extent that it forces the larger, Christian community to face the realities of racial tensions, to acknowledge its own malfeasance, and to begin a spiritual and moral reform. . . .

Lincoln also sees *liabilities* to the movement. Like the lay observer, he deplores "the Black Muslims' virulent attacks on the white man." He notes that these may increase existing tensions. He also sees dangers in Black Muslim attempts "to break all contact between the Negro and white man in America."

Despite problems of this kind, however, the social scientist opposes arguments favoring suppression. He would assume that

. . . in shattering the movement we shall not eliminate the tension and the need which created and catapulted it to its present momentum. Out of the ashes of the Black Muslins, another "black" specter will inevitably rise to challenge us, for we can destroy the Muslim organization but not the Negro's will to freedom. The essence of the Black Muslim Movement will endure—an extreme expression of the American Negro's rising dissatisfaction with the way things are, and his deepening conviction that this is not the way things have to be.

The meaning for America is clear. We must attack the disease, not its symptoms. We must confront the issue of racism and discrimination. When we have done so with the determination and moral conviction so brutal a problem deserves, there will be no Black Muslims. There will be no need for them. And America will be a better place for us all.[4]

The evaluation of the social scientist is premised on several assumptions. First—unlike the layman—he views human behavior as *inspired, caused,* or *impelled* in some way. This orientation makes the social scientist less prone to assign credit or blame, because he must divide responsibility among a multitude of conditions that lead up to every human act. His viewpoint produces statements such as "Switchknife Blacky and Bicycle-Chain Harry are

[4] C. E. Lincoln, *The Black Muslims in America* (Boston: Beacon, 1961), pp. 249–255. Reprinted by permission of the Beacon Press, Copyright © 1961.

products of broken homes and slum conditions"—which the average lay-man may perceive as blatant white-washing efforts.

For the social scientist, antisocial behavior is a reaction to pressures to which a person is subjected. This kind of assumption produces two conse-quences: (a) it places the social scientist on the ideological left—in the sense that it makes him assign blame to the powerful for the undesirable actions of the underprivileged—and (b) it produces proposals for remedial action which the average layman regards as remote, unrealistic, a trifle sub-versive, and out of proportion with the desired result. It may strike the lay-man, for instance, that the recommendation "curb the Black Muslims by eliminating every vestige of segregation" sounds somewhat like "make it rain so I can take a shower" or "plant apple trees to make a pie."

A second premise of the social scientist reinforces this view. Whereas the layman tends to focus his reactions on obvious and irritating symptoms, the social scientist tends to be concerned about more subtle processes and conditions, which can only be *inferred*. To the layman a revolutionary move-ment is real, but the frustrated expectations that underlie it are difficult to perceive. As James Reston pointed out, the lay journalist is

> . . . very good at reporting change when it is violent. When the bull-dozers start to change property-values at home or the guns produce change in Cuba or Vietnam, we are there. But we were not very good about reporting the economic and social conditions in Cuba that produced Castro, and we're remarkably indifferent to the unemployed in Pittsburgh and the social and economic conditions in Harlan County, Kentucky, and the Appalachian South.[5]

Different assessments of what is "real" are reflected in different esti-mates of what is important and produce divergent appraisals of what should be changed. To the person who sees guerrillas in Southeast Asia as a problem (rather than the result of a problem), it makes no sense to attack Com-munism by distributing land, or by increasing the political participation of coolies.

A third difference lies in the fact that the social scientist is a *student of social conflict* but the lay observer remains a *partisan*. The layman evaluates social movements in terms of their implication for his interests. If a move-ment attacks something the lay observer regards as sacred, he classifies it as an evil. The white American thus comes to resent the Black Muslims when

[5] J. Reston, "The Biggest Story in the World," *The Progressive* (May 4, 1963), p. 15.

he hears himself described as a "blue-eyed devil," or when he learns that Muslims disclaim loyalty to the United States.

The social scientist's view—as we have seen in Chapter 10—encompasses the sentiments of both social movements and their antagonists. The social scientist perceives the impact of one on the other, and studies the dialectic process that occasions changes in both. His evaluations reflect this comprehensive view. He thus rejoices when a social movement inspires society to review practices that have produced unhappiness and inequities, and he regrets spirals of hate that produce no noticeable benefit.

The social scientist's role as an observer also makes him sensitive to the *internal* merits of every position, irrespective of his view of its significance to others. He may deplore the social effect of Black Muslim hatred, but he will be sensitive to its basis; he may listen to Black Muslim bitterness apprehensively, but will also do so with the awareness that—in the words of Muhammad—

> If you listen well, you can hear the screams of a Negro co-ed in Tallahassee as she vainly begs her four white abductors to leave her virtue intact; if you listen a little longer you can hear the pleas of a Milwaukee black mother as she begs police to free her six and seven year old daughters from a white abductor who held them captive and took carnal liberties with them for over an hour.[6]

The social scientist is more likely to listen than the partisan white observer—who may prefer to view his enemy as unjustly motivated. The social scientist must assume that human reactions make sense at some level. In uncovering the inner logic and subjective justification of acts, he tends to destroy caricatures and stereotypes (which are comparatively easy to hate) and to substitute real people who can evoke sympathy and fellow-feeling. The partisan, obviously, cannot afford to put himself into his enemy's shoes; the social scientist who tries to do so—by the same token—cannot afford to be partisan.

The social scientist's willingness to listen is not based on naïveté, but rather (as we have tried to show in Chapter 9) on his desire to secure all relevant data before submitting them to evaluation. His scientific role forces him to listen with the same care to the twisted logic and callous insensitivity of the concentration-camp commander as he would to the gentle convictions of a saint. He knows that truth lies in the completest possible picture, which can only be secured through unreserved exposure to data.

[6] E. Muhammad, "Justice for My People," *The Islamic News* (July 6, 1959), p. 7.

He also knows that preselection of what is important may distort one's view of the people one tries to understand. The Black Muslims, for instance, may be a "hate" movement, but not exclusively so. The scientific observer—unlike the magazine editor—bases his evaluation on *all* aspects of the movement. He listens to the Black Supremacy doctrines of the group, but he also takes note of its less newsworthy premises. He may thus record Muhammad's contention that

> We are they who want to be treated like human beings; we are they who want freedom, justice and equality; we are they who want a moral reformation of our people as well as a spiritual reformation; we are they who love unity among the so-called Negroes; we are they who want to do for ourselves; we are they who want a home on this earth that we can call our own, we are they who want deliverance out from the midst of our 400-year enemies, who keep us subjected to the status of servants, and subjected to every brutality and murder known to civilized man. . . .[7]

These self-characterizations—if and when confirmed—make evaluation of the movement an extremely complex task. Evaluation of *which* movement? There is the movement that preaches hate and wistfully predicts an imminent battle between black and white; and there is the movement that promotes the material advance of its members and instills self-respect, group solidarity, concern for social justice, and puritan ethics. These different components of a movement have different consequences—some obviously constructive, others self-defeating, and some contingent or uncertain. In certain ways a movement may seem to help its members; in other ways it may magnify their problems. In some respects it may stimulate progress in society, while in other ways it may erect barriers to remedial efforts. These diverse effects of diverse aspects of a movement must enter into the social scientist's evaluation.

The evaluation of relative gain

For the psychologist, the main criterion for evaluating social movements must be their relationship to individual members. What benefit does the movement provide? What adverse impact does it have? These are the commodities to be assessed and compared.

This type of evaluation is not easily made. How can one, for instance, weigh the security provided by faith against the blindness and poverty of

[7] E. Muhammad "What is Un-American?" *Muhammad Speaks* (December 1961), p. 4.

the closed mind? How is one to assess the benefit of hope, versus the cost of living a lie? How can self-respect be gauged against the consequences of hate?

Further, what constitutes a solution to a problem, and how can one assess the relative benefits of alternative solutions? How can one even separate a given solution from the context that facilitates and nurtures it?

"Correct" and "incorrect" solutions

Toward the end of the nineteenth century, Booker T. Washington, the spokesman for the Southern Negro of his day, told a white audience that

> As we have proved our loyalty to you in the past, in nursing your children, watching by the sick-bed of your mothers and fathers, and often following them with tear-dimmed eyes to their graves, so in the future, in our humble way, we shall stand by you with a devotion that no foreigner can approach, ready to lay down our lives if need be, in defense of yours, interlacing our industrial, commercial, and religious life with yours in a way that shall make the interests of both races one. In all things that are purely social we can be as separate as the fingers, yet one as the hand in all things essential to mutual progress.

Washington assured his listeners that "the wisest among my race understand that the agitation of questions of social equality is an extreme folly."[8]

In opposition to Washington's position, there emerged in the first decade of the twentieth century a completely different solution—that of fighting for equality. This approach was eloquently argued by the Niagara movement, whose spokesman was W. E. B. DuBois, who later became a founding father of the NAACP. DuBois proclaimed:

> We shall not be satisfied to take one jot or tittle less than our full manhood rights. We claim for ourselves every right that belongs to a free-born American: political, civil, and social; and until we get these rights, we shall never cease to protest and assail the ears of America.[9]

DuBois advocated an end to discrimination and segregation. He led early efforts to secure full civil rights for Negroes in all spheres of life.

In these aims, DuBois was opposed not only by Washington and

---

[8] B. T. Washington, *Up From Slavery*, as quoted in O. C. Cox, "Leadership among Negroes in the United States," in A. W. Gouldner, ed., *Studies in Leadership* (New York: Harper & Brothers, 1950), pp. 238–239. By permission of the editor.

[9] W. E. B. DuBois, *Dusk of Dawn*, as quoted in Cox, "Leadership," p. 242.

other "moderates," but also by early exponents of Negro nationalism—foremost among whom was Marcus Garvey. Garvey advised his followers:

> Negroes, teach your children that they are direct descendants of the greatest and proudest race who ever peopled the earth; . . . it is because of the fear of our return to power, in a civilization of our own, that may outshine others, [that] we are hated and kept down by a jealous and prejudiced contemporary world.[10]

Garvey espoused a program very similar to that of the Black Muslims. He called the attention of American Negroes to their rich African heritage, and urged them to have pride in their identity. He exhorted them to frugality and to self-improvement. He favored segregation, and suggested to whites that they could benefit by facilitating the development of a separate Negro community. However, unlike the Black Muslims, Garvey advocated migration to Africa as a means of achieving separation.

Most evaluators of Negro social movements praise the predecessors of today's integrationists. Washington is customarily viewed as weak, or as a self-serving Uncle Tom. It is pointed out that Washington's main concern was "that of developing means of approach to the rich for obtaining funds to operate and develop the school. In the process he evolved a philosophy of race relations and gradually became a conservative leader among Negroes."[11]

According to Oliver Cox, the program advocated by Washington was designed to solve the problems of Southern whites. His leadership among Negroes was therefore probably a consequence of white sponsorship:

> The ruling class, having divested the Negroes of power and excluded them from the means of demanding public services and civil preferment by right, is now able to endow its conservative leader with power capable of inspiring reverential fear and admiration in his people, and this, at a cost incomparably smaller than that which would have been involved had the full rights of citizens been available to them.[12]

Marcus Garvey in turn is condemned largely because of the unrealistic nature of his "solution." (It is usually conceded, however, that Garvey must be credited with impact on subsequent social movements, including those advocating constructive reforms.)

[10] A. J. Garvey, *Philosophy and Opinions of Marcus Garvey* or *Africa for the Africans,* as quoted in Cox, *ibid.,* p. 262.

[11] Cox, *ibid.,* p. 246. The school referred to is the Tuskegee Institute, of which Washington was founder and president.

[12] *Ibid.,* p. 256.

The functional equivalence of solutions

Retrospective evaluations of unsuccessful social movements tend to make little allowance for the frame of reference of the times. Booker T. Washington was influential among economically destitute persons living in the fear-inspiring atmosphere of the post-Reconstruction South. His advocacy of vocational training (which seems designed to retain the educated Negro in servile occupations) often represented a way of achieving a livelihood where no alternative means of advancement were available. For Washington's followers, his program also became acceptable *by virtue of the fact that it tied in with their past experiences.* The title of Washington's book—*Up from Slavery*—was not arrived at by chance. Washington addressed himself to ex-slaves. He urged them to escape from the extreme bottom of a socioeconomic hierarchy to which many of them were reconciled. Ironically enough, once Washington's prescription had been followed, the door was open to vistas which would have seemed too glaring before. Moreover, Washington arranged for this first step to be taken under the noses of apprehensive ex-slavemasters, who were unable to foresee its consequences.

In this connection, we must remember that the reactions of persons in the outside world are not an indication of the motives of members. We have pointed out in Chapter 5 that movements which are *approved* are not necessarily *manipulated.* In the case of the post-Reconstruction South, whites and Negroes *did* have overlapping interests. Thus, both Negroes and whites shared the need to keep the declining Southern economy alive. Washington may have failed adequately to recognize *controversial* needs of his followers, but much of his program did serve *some* of their needs. The young men and women who worked their way through the shops and classrooms of the Tuskegee Institute did wish to improve their standard of living. If they had gained the tacit approval of persons interested in not having them progress too far, this fact does not convert them into dupes, nor does it qualify the reality of their ambitions.

To the extent to which Booker T. Washington was guided by financial and power considerations *but did not appeal* to Negro followers, his operation formed part of the institution of the Southern status quo. However, *to the extent to which Washington did evoke a response among the Negro masses, he formed part of a meaningful social movement, giving expression to Negro desires for advancement.*

To be sure, in the context of the broad contemporary drive for Negro civil rights, the group that assembled at Niagara Falls in 1905 may occupy a more central role than Washington's efforts at limited gain. This kind of evaluation, however, is not for the psychologist to make. What psychology can determine is that among post-Reconstruction social movements some movements responded to more time-bound and localized needs than others. Whereas the Black Star Fleet of Marcus Garvey served as an avenue of escape for persons who had completely lost hope in the American Dream, and Washington responded to stirrings of limited hope among the enslaved, the protest leaders gave voice to those who demanded social justice. The solutions being offered differed—but so did the clientele. Garvey's followers (like the members of other movements advocating improbable escapes, such as those described in Chapter 2) were persons who found themselves in corners and blind alleys of American society; Washington appealed to the intimidated second-class citizens of the South. The first efforts of the civil rights movement, on the other hand, took place among individuals with rising aspirations and limited opportunities—a group that today encompasses the majority of American Negroes.

Within its own context, each of these movements was a legitimate response to the susceptibilities of its members. To any observer who evaluates groups for their effectiveness in responding to needs rather than for their relationship to objective conditions, the social movements of Washington, Garvey, DuBois, and others like them, are *equivalent—for their day*. If some failed at the expense of others, this must be viewed as a product of changing needs, rather than as a function of intrinsic worthlessness.

The evaluation of psychological consequences

Does our position imply that membership is self-validating? We have pointed out (in Chapter 1) that social movements often compete for the loyalty of the same potential members. A revivalist preacher may draw his congregation from the ranks of prospective revolutionaries; leftist and rightist leaders may address their appeals to the same rallies. Solutions such as escape and social action, fear and hope, despair and protest may offer themselves as responses to similar problems.

Within social movements various ideologies, strategies, and tactics may actively compete with each other. Among news pertaining to the civil rights movement, for instance, we find items such as these:

> The Congress of Racial Equality last night threatened to stage a "sleep-in" at the [Arizona] state senate building in support of demands for anti-segregation legislation.

In recent days the state capitol grounds have been picketed by members of the local branch of the NAACP. *The NAACP, however, has declined to support the sleep-in.*[13]

There was a question, however, as to how long the [Atlanta] coalition could be held together. At a meeting last week it was all the more conservative leaders could do to keep the youth groups from breaking off and taking direct action against segregation.

Atlanta has five Negro colleges that supply participants to demonstrations, sit-ins and boycotts. *This group believes that little will be accomplished in continued negotiations.*[14]

Does the adoption of one alternative solution signify that it provides the *best* means to the desired ends? Is a group which prevails in an ideological dispute necessarily to be adjudged the most meritorious?

Clearly, the answer to such questions must be *no*. Hitler's victory in Germany was not the best solution to problems posed by the Versailles Treaty and the depression; incipient strikes in totalitarian settings, which result in starvation, death, and the imprisonment of strike leaders with no material gains, are clearly not the best means of coping with the workers' dilemma.

We must be concerned not only with the extent to which movements satisfy the needs of their members, but also with their psychological *consequences*—with their effects on the lives of persons on whom they impinge. And although we may assume that as a general rule (except where force is used) a winning movement is one which has had appeal, it is not true that a movement's ascendance necessarily brings psychological benefit.

The Nazi movement gained the unquestionable support of the majority of Germans. It restored their pride and gave them a feeling of national identity; it explained the past and unfolded a hopeful future; it solved economic difficulties—creating prosperity and full employment; and it even satisfied deeper needs, ranging from the thrill of parades and the reassurance of dependable leadership to the satisfaction of demonstrated superiority in war. It is doubtful whether the more pedestrian solutions of social democracy could have matched the multidimensional range of this fulfillment.

But what of the cost? Apart from military defeat (which was not a necessary consequence of the movement), there are two areas in which the typical Nazi clearly suffered as a result of his enthusiasm. First, he was impelled to develop or to accentuate his authoritarian outlook and per-

[13] *The New York Times* (March 27, 1964, italics added).
[14] *The New York Times* (November 23, 1963, italics added).

sonality structure. National pride became chauvinism, suspicion of non-Germans turned into consuming hatred, and faith in leadership became blind dependency. Second, the appeals of the movement revealed themselves as deceptive offerings. Economic prosperity, for instance, hinged on warfare, and the worker in search of employment found himself in uniform. Except for a few industrialists, professional soldiers and others, persons who joined the Nazi movement had more problems created for them than they had solved.

This kind of consequence can lead us to negatively evaluate a social movement. Instruments that become tyrants, tools that pose new tasks, and solutions that create unhappiness in place of fulfillment are ventures which must be viewed as at least partial failures.

The impact of social movements on nonmembers

The Nazi movement—like other social movements—came into being in order to solve the problems of its members. The movement also presupposed, however, that its goals required damage to nonmembers. The purity of the race, for instance, necessitated the "Solution of the Jewish Question"; territorial readjustment had to occur at the expense of neighbors, and centralization of the economy required the elimination of trade unions.

The prescriptions of social movements frequently imply harm to outsiders. Only rarely does this include genocide, as in the case of Nazi Germany and Stalinist Russia. In such instances, the benefits that a movement provides may be clearly overshadowed by the misery it creates for its victims. In other situations, it is not as easy to assess the relative weights of profit and damage. In the case of a successful Latin American revolution, for instance, how many patrons of the old order should the new government be allowed to execute to balance a decline in infant mortality rates, a higher level of literacy, and a more adequate diet? A social scientist cannot make this judgment.[15] All he can do is carefully to catalogue the full impact of social movements, in order to neutralize the one-sided assessments of partisans.

If an evaluation of the destructive impact of social movements *in general* were to be made, two considerations would favor a calm assessment. For one, when social movements harm nonmembers, they generally do so in an

---

[15] One social philosopher who made the attempt, by evolving a system of "hedonic calculus," is Jeremy Bentham. See J. Bentham, *An Introduction to the Principles of Morals and Legislation* (Oxford: Clarendon Press, 1907).

effort to undermine vested interests. It is thus possible to deflect the destructive impact of movements by relinquishing or modifying the use of power. Colonial regimes that grant independence to their colonies, for instance, can mitigate the negative consequences of anticolonial movements: plantation owners may then receive compensation for redistributed land, loss of life may be avoided and residues of hatred may be reduced to a gradually decreasing minimum.

Moreover, "harm" is a relative term. Persons who are damaged in the short run may be ultimately benefited. The prejudiced American, for instance, may suffer at the hands of the civil rights movement when he is impelled to send his children to an integrated school, or when he must eat in a desegregated restaurant. Certainly, some of his feelings are violated and his sense of identity may be impaired. In the long run, however, the principal values that the "damaged" person holds sacred may in fact be preserved. This is the case because social movements may attack deficits in institutions, the elimination of which may ensure the survival of the institution as a whole. In the case of the civil rights movement,

> The drive of the Movement is clearly *into* our changing System and its present benefits and endless possibilities for human safety, freedom and growth. The immense and high-minded demonstration of the March (on Washington) presented every Negro leader and the masses present in complete agreement and with faith in the potentialities of our System to which they demand entry.[16]

The *interaction* among social movements can also help to minimize or control possible damages to nonmembers. For instance, any potential danger of the Black Muslim movement could be forestalled by yielding to the less damaging efforts of integrationist groups. Within the civil rights movement, effectiveness can be maximized through the energizing influence of young radicals on conservative Negro groups who might be tempted to compromise or to temporize. Thus the competition of movements and of groups within movements can help to define a rate of change which brings a maximum of benefits with a minimum of cost.

Relevant and irrelevant criteria

Clearly, the evaluation of a social movement is a complex task. Among the information that the evaluator must keep in mind are (1) the urgency of the problem that the movement solves, (2) the nature and extent of

[16] M. Long, "The Unity of the Rifting Negro Movement," *The Progressive* (February 1964), p. 14.

benefits provided by the movement's solution, (3) the new problems which the movement creates for its members, (4) the damage caused to nonmembers, and (5) the long-term impact of the movement on society at large.

These criteria can be effectively applied only if one is not distracted by the temptation to pre-categorize movements in a fashion that implicitly prejudges them. For example, it is not helpful to classify a social movement as a "crackpot" movement because its ideology seems to contain traces of psychological abnormality. The decision as to what is abnormal represents a value judgment. Mental illness is not a concrete, observable condition like measles, cavities, flat feet, or broken ribs. A person usually has to be *adjudged* normal or abnormal, and this occurs on the basis of the extent to which he conforms (or adjusts) to some norms.[17] The label "abnormal" denotes that something is unpleasantly unusual. In the case of social movements, the term thus tends to be reserved for movements whose interpretations of reality deviate considerably from those of the typical observer.

One social movement fitting into this category—which was extremely successful during the nineteen thirties and forties—is the Kingdom of Father Divine, otherwise known as the Peace Mission Movement.[18] The leader of this movement is the Rev. M. J. Divine, who claims to have been "combusted" (born) in Harlem, around 1900. Father Divine also claims to be the incarnation of God.

Father Divine's claim to divinity is viewed with skepticism by the outside observer, but members of the movement all believe that he is God. They believe it to the extent of abandoning their families, sacrificing their possessions, and leading a monastic existence in Father's "heavens."

At one time, Father Divine's "children" numbered many thousands. When Father proclaimed "stay your Hands!" during the 1936 presidential election, Harlem polls "were virtually deserted on election day."[19] Few Negroes living in the slums of New York or Philadelphia failed to profit from Father's banquets at the height of the Great Depression. Father's Peace Missions even today may be found in Australia, Europe, and Africa,

[17] T. S. Szasz, *The Myth of Mental Illness: Foundations of a Theory of Personal Conduct* (New York: Hoeber-Harper, 1961).

[18] Among the sources that best cover Father Divine are: R. A. Parker, *The Incredible Messiah* (Boston: Little, Brown, 1937); J. Hosher, *God in a Rolls Royce* (New York: Hillman-Curl, 1936); and S. Harris, *Father Divine: Holy Husband* (New York: Doubleday, 1953). A classic psychological study of this movement is H. Cantril and M. Sherif, "The Kingdom of Father Divine," *J. Abnorm. Soc. Psychol.*, 33 (April 1938), pp. 147–167. This study is reprinted in H. Cantril, *The Psychology of Social Movements* (New York: Wiley, 1941).

[19] Cantril and Sherif, "Father Divine," p. 158.

as well as in various locations in the Eastern portion of the United States, although membership in the movement has substantially dwindled.

From the vantage point of an outside observer, Father's "heavens" were strange places. Individuals claiming names such as "Quiet Devotion," "Glorious Illumination," "Celestial Virgin," "Fineness Fidelity," "Flying Angel," or "Rolling Stone" might have looked out of touch with reality. Endless banquets punctuated with songs, testimonials, and choruses of "Thank You, Father!" might have appeared somewhat irrational. And Father's sermon (in the event of his attendance) could easily give the impression of extreme obscurantism:

> It is a privilege to realize GOD as INFINITE, EVERPRESENT and OMNIPOTENT, and yet INCARNATABLE and REPRODUCIBLE and RE-PERSONIFIABLE, as HE has been PERSONIFIED. GOD would not be OMNIPOTENT, the same today, yesterday and forever, if HE were not REINCARNATABLE. GOD would not be the same today, yesterday and forever, if HE were not RE-PERSONIFIABLE. Now isn't that wonderful?[20]

But the observer's impressions would be irrelevant to a meaningful evaluation of the Kingdom of Father Divine. More germane are the problems that faced Father's followers as the Great Depression aggravated their already marginal status, and particularly relevant is the effectiveness of Father's solution to these problems. Cantril points out that the Harlem of 1931, in which Father Divine opened his hospitable doors, was "famous for its congestion, poverty, high rents and general squalor."[21] Hosher describes the setting as follows:

> In many tenements basic sanitary facilities are unknown. Open fireplaces are used to heat congested railroad flats. In 1931 the death rate from tuberculosis was three times as high in Harlem as in New York City as a whole. The infant mortality rate in central Harlem was highest for any district in Manhattan. Other diseases were disproportionately high. The National Urban League reported in 1932 that in a single block in Harlem 70 per cent of the tenants were jobless, 18 per cent were ill, 33 per cent were receiving either public or private aid, and 60 per cent were behind in their rent. There were practically no recreation facilities for children. . . . [22]

All the satisfactions that the hostile, prejudiced, and painful white world failed to provide were available in Father's Kingdom. There, food was

[20] *Ibid.*, p. 152.
[21] *Ibid.*, p. 162.
[22] *Ibid.*, p. 162.

ample and excellent, and lodging was clean and comfortable; there, love and peace replaced hatred and conflict; there, every individual was equal, and skin color was meaningless; there, all enjoyed the protection of omnipotence, and the status of closeness to God. There, externality became unreal, and wounds could begin to heal. It became possible to truthfully and joyfully proclaim:

> I have found Heaven, Heaven at last.
> I leave behind me all of my past.
> I come to rest on his sacred breast.
> I thank you Father.[23]

As for the requirement of accepting Father's divinity, what was farfetched about it? In the words of one follower, "Now, all in all, I ask you, what more of a God do you want, than one who'll give you shelter, food to eat, clothes to wear and freedom from sickness, worry and fear? Isn't that wonderful?"[24]

Father himself pointed out that "we are talking about a God here and now, a God that has been Personified and Materialized, a God that will free you from the oppressions of oppressors and the segregations of segregators."[25]

To be sure, the social scientist evaluating this movement could find liabilities that he could set against its assets. The requirement of celibacy, for instance, posed obvious problems for Father's followers—particularly for separated married couples in the movement. The injunction to retain Father in one's awareness at all times presented difficulties to some. There was much fear attached to Father's publicized powers of retribution. And there were probably many who found the atmosphere of heaven to be excessively confining.

Liabilities such as these, however, could not outweigh the extreme benefits of membership. Given the indescribably painful alternatives of life in Harlem, only a radical solution could offer assistance. "Hell" demanded a "heaven." And in the face of this requirement, the ratio of benefit to cost in the Kingdom of Father Divine was surprisingly favorable.[26]

Social movements are creatures of crises. Given this fact, evaluations

---

[23] *Ibid.*, p. 161.
[24] *Ibid.*, p. 150.
[25] *Ibid.*, p. 162.
[26] This observation would no longer apply as soon as improvement of conditions eliminated the need for Father's enveloping protection. Father Divine's movement today might thus be negatively evaluated.

of their effectiveness cannot be guided by considerations of "rationality," "normality," "sanity," logic," and by similar categories evolved and applied by untroubled spectators.

Social movements and social change

In this last chapter, we have tried to face the problem of distinguishing between "good" and "bad" movements. We have suggested that the social psychologist can evaluate movements in terms of the benefits they bring to members, with allowances made for happy and unhappy side effects.

One final question we may ask is: to what extent must a social movement *really* solve the problems that bring it into existence? Are movements that eradicate problem situations—such as successful revolutionary ventures—of the same benefit as movements that improve the subjective well-being of their members, but which leave them physically no better off? Must a successful social movement be an effective agent of social change?

Sometimes a movement obviously cannot be gauged in such terms. There can be no merit in a group which invites its own destruction by blindly attacking insurmountable obstacles. Where material improvements are impossible, the amelioration of unhappiness must constitute a complete solution. To demand more would be analogous to requesting a physician to perform a hopeless surgical intervention when he can only relieve pain.

But what of instances in which an operation would cure? Supposing a social movement has the personnel and means to eradicate a problem situation—can it legitimately resort to half-way measures? Must we not distinguish between movements that make good on their promises and those that present quasi-solutions and pseudo-solutions to the problems of their members?

The social scientist hesitates before he responds affirmatively to this question. First, he is aware of the distinction between problem situations and problems. He knows that movements are responses to suffering and despair, and that feelings do not necessarily mirror reality. It follows that if the aim of movements is the amelioration of discomfort, their success must be gauged in terms of their *felt* benefits rather than in terms of the *objective* changes they bring about.

Second, the solutions of social movements must be those that are congenial to their members. Correct but unpopular solutions do not make social movements. Here as elsewhere, the detached observer's viewpoint cannot be substituted for one that considers the experiences and feelings, values and preferences, attitudes and beliefs of persons who are faced with the necessity and opportunity of choice. By contrast, solutions produced through hindsight and logic frequently combine neatness and inapplicability, comparable to battle lines drawn in a sand box. They also tend to constitute unrealistic standards of conduct.[27]

Finally, we must recall that problem situations are usually posed by imperfections in the social matrix. The task of remedying such imperfections cannot be assigned to those who suffer their effects. It is true that social movements ultimately may abrogate to themselves the prerogative of social change. But they do so only after first enabling society to help itself—if it cares to. Through their existence, social movements alert us to unsatisfied or frustrated needs. They draw our attention to areas in which we can exercise the option of alleviating suffering and furnishing hope to our fellows.

Social movements, in their capacity as gadflies, are indirect agents of change. They do their part by coming into being, and by pinpointing problems through their efforts to cope with them. Sympathetic observers (such as social scientists) must decipher these efforts and must deduce their implications for action. Society has to do the rest.

[27] The unfair character of abstract evaluations is illustrated in analyses of Nazi concentration camps in which inmates are taken to task for their lack of resistance.

INDEX

Abdul, S., 6*n*.
abnormality, mental, in movements, 243–246
absolutes, 116–118
Acheson, Dean, 47, 60–61, 62
Adams, C. F., 225*n*
Addison, John M., 90
adolescents, 116, 210
Adorno, T. W., 58*n*., 59*n*., 60*n*.
Adventism; *see* Millerites, Seventh Day Adventists
advertising, 15–16, 95, 103–105
Africa, 205–206; *see also* South Africa
aggression, outlets for, 232
aging, health food fads and, 101–107
Albigensian heresy, 226
Alcoholics Anonymous, 80–83, 84
aliens, as perceived threat, 22, 23
Allport, F. H., 116*n*.
Allport, Gordon W., 151, 193, 194*n*.
Almond, Gabriel, 131, 157–159, 161, 163, 167–168, 174–178, 194*n*.
American Humanist Society, 19
American Mercury, 52–53
American Nazi Party, 24

American Sunbathing Society, 21–22, 162–163
Amish communities, 206
Anderson, R. T., 117*n*., 217*n*.
Angolan rebellion, 221
Anti-Defamation League, 47–48
Anti-Digit Dialing League, 16–17
Antinomian Controversy, 225
anti-Semitism; *see* Jews
antisocial movements, 231–235
appeals, 13–23
    commercial, 15
    of conspiracy, 50–55
    contrived, 87–88
    evaluation of, 241
    latent, 20–21, 90–91, 93
    of religious denominations, 217–219
    sequence in, 26–27
    susceptibility to, 13–17
Arieti, S., 56*n*.
Arnold, Paul, 163*n*.
Augier, R., 31*n*.
Austeri, Peter, 226
authoritarian personality, 57–60, 63, 70
    motivation of, 188

Date Due